CW00826095

VINCE EAGER'S
ROCK 'N' ROLL FILES

Foreword by Jack Good...

Whenever music and mischief have come together in the past 50 years, it seems that Vince Eager hasn't been far away. From his skiffle group roots in Grantham, Lincs, he became a pioneer of TV pop, before wowing the world in the title role of the West End hit musical, Elvis. Vince rubbed shoulders with the giants of the music world, and with his big heart and sense of fun, he left a trail of admiring friends wherever he roamed. From outwitting Robert Mugabe's security police, to ticking off the Rat Pack, he's been there, sung the song and come out smiling.

VINCE EAGER'S
ROCK 'N' ROLL FILES

Vince Eager's Rock 'n' Roll Files

by

Vince Eager

Magna Large Print Books
Long Preston, North Yorkshire,
BD23 4ND, England.

British Library Cataloguing in Publication Data.

Eager, Vince
    Vince Eager's rock 'n' roll files.

    A catalogue record of this book is
    available from the British Library

    ISBN   978-0-7505-2993-8

BIRMINGHAM LIBRARY SERVICES
LP3/10

First published in Great Britain 2007 by VIpro

Copyright © Vince Eager 2007

Cover illustration © Vince Eager

The right of Vince Eager to be identified as the author of this
work has been asserted by him in accordance with the
Copyright, Designs and Patents Act, 1988

Published in Large Print 2009 by arrangement with
Vince Eager

All Rights reserved. No part of this publication may be
reproduced, stored in a retrieval system, or transmitted in any
form or by any means, electronic, mechanical, photocopying,
recording or otherwise without the prior permission of the
Copyright owner.

Magna Large Print is an imprint of Library Magna Books Ltd.

Printed and bound in Great Britain by
T.J. (International) Ltd., Cornwall, PL28 8RW

Dedication

This book is dedicated to:
My sons Simon and Christie,
daughter-in-law Karen and
Chris, 'Fred', 'Albert' and Pete of
ROCKOLA

They help make a geriatric rocker
very happy!

(Thanks for the bus Sarah!x)

www.vinceeager.co.uk

Acknowledgements

Huge thanks go to Sue Atkinson,
Sue Barlow, Antoinette Hardy
John Pinchbeck, Brian Tansley and
Harry Whitehouse for their editorial,
publishing and proofing expertise.

Their professional support has been
invaluable.

Special thanks also go to my loving wife
Anette (yes it does only have one 'n') for
her support, encouragement, patience
and wonderful cooking!

Graham 'The Hit Man' Fowell and
Jill for being such good mates!

Carol Burns, Michael Cox,
Wee Willie Harris, The Grantham Journal
and The Daily Mirror.

Foreword by

Jack Good

Producer of TV Shows:
Six Five Special – Oh Boy –
Boy Meets Girl – Wham – Shindig
Producer of Musical Hits:
'Elvis' – 'Rock My Soul'
Jack is the Godfather of
British Rock n' Roll

I remember when rock was young,
Elton and Suzie had so much fun...
...or was it Bernie?

Anyway! I really do remember when rock was young, and I had to come up with 30 minutes of TV rock every Saturday.

The show was called Oh Boy and was in fact, not fiction but the very first TV show worldwide that was devoted to rock 'n' roll music.

It was not a lip-synch Top Twenty show, such as the pitiful Dick Clark's American Bandstand, where the climax would always be the Cashbox number one, even if that happened to be *Ebb Tide* or the *Dead Man In Saul.*

Oh Boy was live!

It went out even if the walls of the Hackney Empire were caving in with the noise of a frantic audience.

So I was always looking for talent who could survive the onslaught of immediacy.

There was no looking back. When you were on you were on, and the nations rock n' rollers were taking you in or spewing you out.

So it was with some anticipation – not entirely hopeful for the chances of finding a potential survivor – let alone a star – who were few and far between in those days – that I attended a Sunday Night Concert presented by Larry Parnes at the Romford Odeon.

It starred Joe Brown and Vince Eager.

Well, I knew those two. They were more than survivors, they were entertainers.

It became highly memorable when that dashing, daredevil Vince decided to jump off the stage, onto the forestage and into the audience.

Unfortunately he hadn't realised that the forestage had been lowered. He finished up in the bowels of the orchestra pit and then carried on singing in his characteristically penetrating vibrato as he clambered out of the pit.

Of course it helped that he was about six foot five and in good shape.

PJ Proby tried the same trick some ten years later at the Astoria, some would say he never quite emerged.

That was in my show 'ELVIS' the first of those beastly rock anthologies. At least I was first and the first shall be the last!

When 'ELVIS' went on tour Vince took over the role. Unfortunately I didn't see Vince in the role but I understand he was outstanding, although anyone less like Elvis I can't imagine.

But then, nor can I imagine Elvis losing his own personality if he had to perform in the role of Vince.

Elvis was a troubled genius.

Vince is your ultimate survivor – an entertainer who has seen it all, done most of it, knows the score and delivers.

I revered Elvis.

I trust Vince.

Jack Good
August 2nd 2007

Contents

Welcome to My Rock 'n' Roll Files

'What you and Billy Fury got up to with Mandy Rice Davies and Christine Keeler, being part of a cultural revolution, befriending and touring with the likes of Eddie Cochran, Gene Vincent, Joe Brown and Marty Wilde, your 5 years as the lead in "Elvis the Musical" and being shot at by Greeks and Turks! That's what people want to read about! Not how you won the cross-country or how you lost so much schooling due to your bad eyesight. You write like you talk! It's as long as *War and Peace* and you haven't left school yet!'

That was the response from my wife Anette after I had entrusted her to read the first chapter of my book in the hope that she would find it worthy of a Booker prize and shower heaps of praise on my, up until now, hidden literary talents.

'How about a coffee table style book so people can open it at any page and read as much or as little as they want at any time?' she went on to say.

Anette being quite complimentary of my

writing style, and my good mate and top caricaturist and cartoonist, Graham 'The Hit Man' Fowell, offering his amazing talents to illustrate many of the stories, plus my kids wanting to know what dad got up to when he was younger, encouraged me to continue.

From singing rock 'n' roll in a works canteen, to singing it on luxury cruise ships, rock 'n' roll has proved to be a great leveller and a lifelong friend.

It has travelled with me to over 100 countries, and we have witnessed people being transformed by this wonderful music that increases the beat of your heart and puts a spring in your step.

In choosing tales and anecdotes of varying emotions from my years as one of Britain's pioneering pop idols, relishing the lead role in the award winning West End Musical 'Elvis', through to my years as a Cruise Director on American Luxury Liners, I hope the selection I have chosen hits the spot and encourages you to return again and again to my Rock 'n' Roll files.

Happy reading!

The Yellow Bellies

The Iron Ladies

The choir mistress and organist at St John's Church in Grantham, Miss Dean, was a lady not to be fooled with. She was tougher than any of the men in her charge, and never took prisoners. She was cast from the same mould as fellow Granthamian, and ex British Prime Minister, Margaret Thatcher. Whoever decreed that church organists should have their backs to the choir when playing was definitely a kindred spirit of choristers, as it saved my skin on many occasions. Yes, she did have wing mirrors on the organ, which enabled her to keep an eye on her charges, but they had their blind spots.

The out of vision position I occupied as a chorister was one that came with seniority. I'd been turned over to Miss Dean as a junior chorister at the age of eight and initially I thought it had nothing to do with music and that it was purely a disciplinary manoeuvre and a sort of baby-sitting service. My sister and brother, eight and 10 years my seniors respectively, had both spent time under Miss Dean's watchful eye and appeared to have turned out to be uncomplicated, so I guess, there was hope for me.

Vocally I soon began to make inroads into Miss Dean's affections. Solos, a new cassock and surplice, a new hymnbook and her words of praise to my grandmother gave every indication of success.

It was during the Yuletide season of 1951 that I tarnished my image. Carol singing along the highways and byways of Grantham, Lincolnshire with the church choir was proving a lucrative venture collectively but not individually; the occasional mince pie and season's greeting being our only personal reward. Because my entrepreneurial spirit was calling me to achieve great things in the world of commerce, I went it alone. A rebel at the age of eleven!

Working another district of suburban Grantham, I discovered the wonderful echo effect I could get by singing in the passageways between the terraced houses of our neighbours in Stamford Street, Grantham. In my later teens they became the most effective place to let off Mighty Atom bangers on November 5th. At this stage though, it was one quick carol, usually a verse and chorus, a knock at the door, and bingo! 'That was lovely, please sing some more.' My first encore, and a licence to print money. A life in show business had to be on the cards! My decision not to forsake the choir's carol singing programme, but to alternate with it, helped me keep my moonlighting venture a secret. Why oh why couldn't Christmas be a twelve-month deal?

Possibly the only match for Miss Dean was my grandma, loving, and like most post-war grannies, also something of a magician. She managed to produce goodies that mums declared were either rationed or victims of the war and unavailable.

Custard pies, sweets and toffee, fruits with an intergalactic appearance such as pomegranates and bananas, and fizzy sweet tasting drinks were all available at my grandmother's. I discovered in later life that she wasn't really a magician but a member of the local Co-op board and she could scare employees into handing over the goods just by looking at them.

I spent much of my time with my grandmother, although it wasn't just the secret 'goodie mine' that was the attraction. No. She also had a record player. The biceps I developed in my right arm from the constant winding of the player would have stopped Charles Atlas in his tracks. It was never turned off. Sandy Powell was my pre-puberty rock 'n' roll. *Sandy The Postman*, *Sandy The Goalkeeper*, and *Can You Hear Me Mother* were just a few of the gems that grandma would always be telling me to turn down, a towel or duster in the sound horn acting as a volume control.

Imagine my delight when, 20 years later, I

introduced Sandy Powell onto the stage in a summer show at Teignmouth in Devon. I was in awe. Every night after the show we would retire to the pub opposite the theatre where we would drink behind closed doors until the early hours. Sandy may have been a vaudeville comedian, but he was a rock 'n' rolling partygoer.

He's Behind You!

It was my grandmother who instructed my grandfather to get me an audition with his works' social club theatrical company. They produced an annual pantomime, which enjoyed the reputation of a professional company and their productions ran for 10 days.

Pantomime was a medium that I associated with the annual January pilgrimage by my father's factory social club to Nottingham's Theatre Royal or Ice Stadium where Norman Evans and Laurel & Hardy were names that would grace the bills. With my brief insight into panto, as it is affectionately called, my successful audition piece of *Now Is The Hour,* paved the way to my being a regular member of the revered company.

The producer & director was Arthur Moreton, a man with the deportment and persona of a solicitor and the theatrical attributes of a Bernard Delfont. He was very business-like and had the time of day for all ranks; principal girl, dancers or scene-shifters, all were respected by Arthur.

With my first role being that of Simple Simon in Mother Goose, Arthur assured me that my lanky gangly appearance and not any mental shortcomings made me ideal for the role.

A popular movie at the time was 'Moulin Rouge', and the title song; *Where Is Your Heart* became Arthur's choice for my solo piece. Apparently he had been impressed with my rendition of *Now Is The Hour* at my audition and took the unprecedented step of giving me a solo in my first production.

There just weren't enough rehearsals in a week for me. I loved everything about it. What healthy young lad wouldn't? Lovely young ladies dancing in various stages of undress. Girls and music. It was Utopia!

As the rehearsals progressed so did my confidence and my ego. The senior members of the cast were very encouraging and full of compliments about my vocal performance.

On the opening night my rendition of *Where Is Your Heart* received an amazing reception with the audience shouting for more. This prompted the musical director to tell me to sing it again.

There was, however, one exception to the members of the company who offered me congratulations following my performance –

Ethel Richardson, a wonderful soprano and the company's vocal matriarch. Unfortunately it soon became apparent that Ethel was uncomfortable with my vocal presence. Having been the company's lead soprano for many years she was not yet ready to relinquish her title to a lanky skinny runt! She should not have worried as during the following year the inevitable happened. Nature took its course. They dropped! And my voice broke. For the following year's production, I was relegated to being a mere thespian with Ethel assuming her rightful role.

My vocal disaster however did not materialise into being the end of the world, as I fear it would. The enforced hiatus from singing gave me the opportunity to pursue other more interesting activities, such as table tennis, the harmonica, girls and SKIFFLE!

Uncle Harry's Kingdom

The YMCA was the place to be if you were interested in table tennis. It was here that I would ping away one or two nights a week with Roy Clark and Brian Locking, a couple of really nice guys who played harmonicas. I borrowed a harmonica, the duo became a trio and the Harmonica Vagabonds were born. Ping-pong became history as we spent more time honing our harmonica skills. Social clubs, village halls, and the local Granada Cinema on Sunday nights, became our arenas. The latter becoming the jewel in our itinerary crown.

Harry Sanders, the Granada manger, was affectionately known as Uncle Harry to the cinema patrons, his showmanship was legendary and his love for his cinema and its patrons unquestionable. He would hold court every Sunday evening when those of us who dared to miss church would queue to enter his kingdom. The back row seats had to be earned and it could take years of working your way backward to get prime snogging property for you and your date.

It didn't take us, The Harmonica Vaga-bonds, long to assert our presence on the hallowed back row. Being asked by Uncle Harry to perform on stage before the main movie clinched our VIP Sunday night status. We were celebrities!

Before the main movie, sing-a-longs, which consisted of a bouncing ball picking out the syllables of the song's lyrics on the screen, were popular events. The bouncing ball was generally predictable by its tempo. But one tune turned the bouncing ball into a blur. At the end I saw there with my mouth wide open. I had just heard the song that was to change my life forever.

I immediately sought out Uncle Harry,

who was in his usual position of ensuring that the back rows didn't indulge in too much hanky panky. I begged him to tell me who recorded the song. I hadn't seen the title or the artist. He told me to be in his office in 30 minutes and he would have the answer.

'It's *Rock Island Line* by Lonnie Donegan and his Skiffle Group, Roy,' said Uncle Harry. The recording was to shape the course of British popular music and its international dominance.

A Record for a Record

The journey home after purchasing *Rock Island Line* was fraught with anxiety as 78rpm records were notoriously fragile and should have carried a health warning of 'not to be transported on a bicycle by anyone of a nervous disposition.' When I arrived home I placed it lovingly on the turntable of my Dansette record player. I turned the play knob, waited for the initial crackling to die and felt the hairs on the back of my neck stand up as the first chord was strummed.

Thankfully my parents had quite a large house so I could indulge in Lonnie for as long and as loud as I wanted. Lifting the record player's retainer arm had the effect of achieving musical bliss, as the record would keep repeating as long as the arm was in the up position. Had the Guinness Book of Records existed, that Monday would surely have qualified as the most times a record had been played in one day.

On Tuesday night my musical pals Roy and Brian dropped by to hear my musical jewel. I played the record and watched their faces intently in the hope that their reaction to it would be the same as mine. It didn't take long. They were into it like the proverbial dose of salts. We were one. Before *Rock Island Line* had faded into the distance our plans to form a skiffle group were already taking shape. It would have helped of course if we had known what a skiffle group was, but that didn't concern us too much.

That Friday, the New Musical Express weekly music paper ran an article on Lonnie Donegan and his Skiffle Group in which they explained about the instruments that could be used to play skiffle. The banjo, guitar, washboard and T-chest bass appeared to be the most popular so we put our thinking caps on.

I had a banjo that had been given to me by my parents as a last night present when I appeared in pantomime, Roy said he could get a guitar and Brian said he would love to play the bass. At last I was able to take advantage of my high grades in woodwork and my chosen profession of joinery and I put my expertise to work on making Brian a tea chest bass. If not the first in Britain it was certainly one of them and it gave birth to The Vagabonds Skiffle Group.

On and Off the Buses

As the Harmonica Vagabonds, we failed to exploit our popularity by using it to greater effect for picking up girls, so when in the early days of our Sunday night Granada appearances, a lovely looking girl named Audrey approached me and said 'Would you like to walk me to my bus after the movie?' I was gob-smacked. I was under the impression courting etiquette decreed that it should be me asking her. Still, who was I to question the rules of courting? I accepted nervously. There was a proviso however. 'Meet me at the back of the cinema and don't tell anyone,' she instructed. Not wishing to kill the deal, I didn't ask any questions and agreed.

Up to this stage of my life, it has to be said, my sexual activity was zero. I really thought she meant 'Walk me to my bus.' When I arrived at the pre-arranged meeting place, she wasted no time in de-flowering me. I was putty in her hands; totally at her mercy. Following the encounter, I leant against the wall that had so kindly supported us throughout, and gazed into the starry night air.

'You won't tell anyone will you?' she asked.

'Like who?' I asked.

'Like nobody,' she replied.

'I've got to tell somebody I've just had my first shag,' I said.

'O.K. but please don't say it was me,' she pleaded.

I couldn't figure out if she was embarrassed at having been with me or if she had a boyfriend. It sure wasn't because it was her first time. She tidied herself up and said she would find her own way to the bus. Two days later I saw her in town and she invited me for a coffee. As well as a possible prelude to another intimate encounter, I was hoping she would also enlighten me as to the mystery surrounding our first liaison. She told me her mother didn't approve of her having a boyfriend and she would be in big trouble if she was caught. Her mother lived six miles from Grantham, which was a bonus as she wasn't in Grantham very often. I agreed not to tell a soul and our clandestine relationship took another step forward with a visit to a badly lit park. We then began to meet a couple of times a week, the Sunday night post-cinema session being the most regular. I kept my promise and didn't tell a soul about our relationship.

After approximately six weeks I noticed that Roy and Brian were never around after the Sunday movie. I asked Roy about it and he let me into a little secret that I wasn't to tell anyone. It transpired that he had a girlfriend he'd meet near the bus station where they would fulfil their desires before she boarded the bus home. Two weeks later Brian bared his soul by telling Roy and me that he also had a girlfriend. She'd get off her bus after three stops, spend 30 minutes with him and then catch the next bus home.

We all thought it would be great if we could get together with our girlfriends one night, and decided to arrange it. A couple of weeks later Audrey was in her usual seat at the Sunday night movie. Brian pointed her out discreetly and said, 'That's the girl I meet off the bus'. Roy retorted surprisingly: 'She's the girl I put on the bus' and my gob smacked contribution was, 'She's the girl I see before she goes to the bus.' We had all been perfect gentleman in keeping our secret, and she'd not told a soul she was shagging all three Harmonica Vagabonds!

'Licorice' is Born

It was a journey we made to fulfil an Easter weekend gig in Skegness that was to have a lasting influence on British popular music. Halfway between Grantham and Skeggy, was the rural town of Boston, a popular mid-point watering hole for anyone making the two-hour trip to Skegness from Grantham.

Boston gave us an added incentive to stop. A town centre café had a jukebox, which we were always happy to ply with penny coins. It also had a novelty shop next door, which sold beach and holiday items for your visit to the coast.

On this particular day the novelty shop was selling plastic trumpets, saxophones and clarinets. Brian, Roy and I purchased one each. A clarinet for Brian, a trumpet for Roy, and a sax for me. They all used tissue paper and were based on the kazoo, consequently they all sounded alike, and differing only in shape.

As the journey progressed we became more and more proficient on our instruments, to the extent that our driver would introduce us for our solo pieces. 'It's Roy on the saxophone', 'It's Roy on his golden trumpet' or 'It's Brian on his "Licorice" stick.' As we approached Skeggy our driver said, 'OK, instruments away, we're here.' Both Roy and I put down our new toys but Brian continued to play. 'Brian, put that "Licorice" stick away,' I said mimicking John the driver.

That evening I introduced Brian as 'Licorice' Locking and from that day on I have never called him Brian, only 'Licorice'. Even when he took over from Jet Harris in Cliff Richard's Shadows, he was, and still is, referred to as 'Licorice'.

Bassic Instincts

Surprisingly, we had the sense to realise that we shouldn't rest on our laurels but seek to improve the success we were enjoying. Our first decision was to incorporate a washboard player. John Holt was a good friend and partner in another passion of mine, my marionette puppet theatre. Thankfully for John, musical ability was not a prerequisite for filling the position. Enthusiasm, a friend with a van and living close by also helped. John fulfilled all the requirements and he soon added a refreshing new dimension to our sound.

Brian's tea chest bass was without doubt the most versatile instrument we had in our line up. The amount of items you could carry in the tea chest made it a sort of bottomless pit. In spite of the tea chest's amazing versatility, 'Licorice' wanted a double bass. We all agreed it would improve the sound, but would it spoil the novelty value of the act? The only way to find out was to purchase a double bass.

We read the musical instruments for sale section in the local paper to find 'Double Bass for sale. Excellent condition, a bargain at £20'. The down side was its location.

Lincoln – 24 miles from Grantham.

Following the three-of-us-in-a-telephone-box call to Lincoln, we decided to view the bass. Due to the nature of Roy and 'Licorice's' jobs, I was the one delegated to travel to Lincoln, to view, and if necessary purchase the bass.

The one hour twenty minute journey to Lincoln was a twisting affair, the road being more like a switchback. Upon my arrival in Lincoln, I soon located, and made the decision to buy, the bass. The fun then started. How do I get it back to Grantham? I didn't realise they were so big!

The Lincoln to Grantham bus was a double-decker and the thought of transporting the bass to Grantham became more daunting by the minute. The only way to find out if I would succeed would be to do it. The bus conductor didn't exude confidence as I took the bass onto the bus. 'You can't take it inside!' he said firmly. 'The platform is as far as you can go.'

Having paid the fare, no extra charge for the bass, I gripped the instrument with my right hand and held the chrome upright pole on the platform with my left, spreading my feet to give me maximum stability, I then prayed that the driver would not take the bends along the twisting road to Grantham too fast. No one was more surprised than I, when, upon arriving in Grantham, I was able to unfurl my fingers, fingers that I felt were sure to be a permanent fixture on the bass fingerboard, from their white knuckled grip of the previous one hour and twenty minutes.

It didn't take 'Licorice' long to master his new companion. We had recently seen Lonnie Donegan in concert at the De Montfort Hall in Leicester and Brian was soon emulating his hero, and Lonnie Donegan's bass player, Mickey Ashman.

'Licorice' caused great consternation amongst the local taxi firms, as they were often responsible for transporting the bass within Grantham's boundaries. A regular taxi bass drop off was my parents' house where we would rehearse every Monday evening. This led my father to be the least impressed of all with regard to Licorice's playing skills. It had nothing to do with his prowess as a budding bass player. It was the honeycomb effect he achieved on my father's brand new tiled kitchen floor with the support spike that protruded from the bottom of his bass.

When Bill Got the Measure of Me

In order to extend our skiffle play list, I took my beloved Dansette record player to work. I was an apprentice joiner for Fosters, a respected building firm in my hometown of

Grantham, Lincs. I placed the Dansette under my bench, and much to the consternation of my workmates, played Lonnie Donegan records all day.

The writing was on the wall with regard to my future, or lack of it, when I was given the job of working with a new and expensive material, Formica. The instruction was to cut 100 pieces of Formica at 2 feet 4 inches x 2 feet 6 inches. With my trusty Dansette blurting out a selection of Lonnie's best, I set about the task in hand.

After a few hours the job was completed. I place the 100 pieces of cut to size Formica in the appropriate place and clipped my job sheet on the 'job completed' board. The next morning, during a coffee break, I was summoned to the office of Bill Measures, the foreman.

Bill was a nice, gentle man; non-aggressive, non-confrontational and a man who would let you do your job without bringing pressure to bear as long as you did it right. Being summoned to his office held no fear, as he was a man who never raised his voice and never swore. He spoke in gentle tones. As I walked into his office all appeared to be normal. He gave me a pleasant welcoming smile and asked me to sit down. As I did so he handed me the Formica job sheet and asked me if it was my signature at the bottom. It was, and I told him so.

'You like your music don't you Roy?' he asked.

'Yes Bill,' I replied.

'Do you think it affects your work?' he enquired.

'No Bill,' I said. 'I think it helps me to concentrate.'

'Just measure this piece of Formica for me,' he asked calmly, handing me a ruler and the piece of Formica.

'What does it measure?' he asked.

'24 x 26 inches,' I replied.

'So why the fuck didn't you cut it to the size stipulated on the job sheet … 2 feet 4 inches by 2 feet 6 inches?' You and your fucking music, you and fucking Lonnie Donegan have just cost this company more than £100. I'm going to take your fucking record player and throw it in the River fucking Witham. Get out of my office and take Lonnie fucking Donegan with you!'

My opinion of Bill had changed. He could get upset. I thank God we had the meeting in his office. The workshop would have offered him too great a choice of objects to hit me with.

Needless to say, the Dansette went home with me that evening and I was transferred to the wastelands of the building sites, where there was no such thing as electricity for record players. My days of comfort were behind me. I had been banished to the great frosty outdoors, where I would have to arrive at work much earlier in order to catch a lorry to the building site of the day.

Nevertheless, before long we had all of Donegan's songs on our play-list. We were a hot item and could whip our audiences into a frenzy. Our popularity knew no bounds. From Skegness to Leicester we were in demand.

Aunt Mary

Spitalgate Airfield on the southeast borders of my hometown of Grantham had been a base for training pilots in the Oxford aircraft during the war, and the Luftwaffe had often paid them visits. But it was after the war that the base became a target for the testoster-one-driven young men of Grantham when it was converted into a WRAF Station, where young women recruits would get their first taste of life away from the scrutiny of their parents as they trained to become 'Snow-drops', or RAF Policewomen.

Grantham's nightlife took a definite turn for the better with the arrival of the girls in blue and Friday nights were never the same again.

Following their 'passing-out' ceremony, the girls escaped the base to celebrate. The reaction of the local lads could be compared to greyhounds being released from the starting gate. Once out, they were determined never to return until their prey had been worn down and their appetites satisfied.

John Fryer, a Grantham taxi proprietor and driving instructor, was also a good friend of mine. John told me to let him know within 24 hours of my wanting to take my driving test and he would arrange it by telling one of his pupils that they were not quite ready – then he would switch the test to me.

This went according to plan and I also had a pretty good idea that I would pass when the first question the driving examiner asked me was: 'When the test is over would you sign a photograph for my daughter and the girls in the office,' who were at the time blowing kisses from the office and waving. How could I say no?

John used his initiative to turn our friendship to a profitable advantage. Being the main supplier of taxis transferring the girls from RAF Spitalgate to Grantham town centre, Johnny had the idea that he could throw in a detour and charge sixpence extra, to go via my parents' house. A 'Vince Eager sleeps here,' type tour.

Fridays were usually busy days in London for me when I would be rehearsing for TV shows to be aired the following evening. I was not often in Grantham when the taxis full of WRAFs in civvies would pull up outside my parents' house. But if I was at home, Johnny would encourage me to say hello to the girls, sign autographs and pose for pictures.

It was during a meet and greet with some of the WRAFs outside my parents' house that I met a lovely young lady by the name of Kathy. Not only did she have a great personality, she also had a lovely Scottish accent and thankfully my road manager Noel picked up on the chemistry and arranged a date.

Additional journeys to Grantham to meet up with Kathy gave the game away as to my feelings for her. It was a relationship that I really thought would go somewhere, until I met Kathy's Aunt Mary.

It was during one of our regular visits to Scotland that I first met Mary, the whisky drinking, chain smoking, Bible bashing Auntie who lived with Kathy's family in South Edinburgh – and a lady not to be messed with.

Aunt Mary's immediate response to my arrival at the family home, 10 minutes from my Edinburgh digs, was to grill me about my religion. On discovering that most of my formative years had been spent in the pews as a Church of England chorister, her quest began to turn me towards Catholicism with statements such as, 'You and our Kathy would make a lovely couple, but you must become a Catholic first.'

As intense as she was about converting me, she was a fun lady who really enjoyed life and those living it. Her ability to drink and smoke with the best endeared her to my band. So much so that it was the band who, possibly under the influence, invited her to travel with us to a gig in Ardrossan, a sleepy coastal town on the west coast, and three hours drive from Edinburgh.

With my road manager Noel Wallis driving and Kathy and me as passengers in the front, we set off on the return leg from Ardrossan. The show had gone really well and everyone was in high spirits – Aunt Mary especially so.

When driving at night, Noel would always close the partition between the driver's area in the front and the passengers' area in the back. As well as keeping the driver's cab dark, it would also isolate the band and the mischief they got up to. Mischief, which, at times, was best kept to themselves. The noise from the back of the van following shows usually abated once the adrenaline levels had returned to normal and the post-show booze had kicked in.

As I sat with my arm around a sleeping Kathy, while listening to Radio Luxembourg, I was aware of some unusual sounds from the back of the bus. Trying not to disturb Kathy, I gently pulled back the corner of the partition to reveal the reason for the unusual sounds.

There, under the soft lighting of the passenger area, and wearing nothing but a smile and her underwear, was Aunt Mary, doing things with the band, all of whom were in various stages of undress, that I wouldn't be telling my mother about and certainly didn't want Kathy to see.

Slowly returning the partition to its original position and then mouthing to Noel to increase the radio volume, I held Kathy a little closer in the hope that she wouldn't wake before we reached Edinburgh.

As the lights of Edinburgh drew closer I gingerly turned back the partition to reveal all the occupants in the rear of the bus looking more comatose than asleep, but at least they appeared fully dressed.

As we opened the side door of the mini bus, Aunt Mary almost fell out but just managed to retrieve her footing before staggering up the garden path, never to be seen again.

Kathy was much more the lady. Thanking me and kissing me goodnight she walked gracefully up the garden path. I did see Kathy again, but as she was being posted to a WRAF station far away, together with the lingering images of Aunt Mary in the back of the bus and the theological ear-bashing she gave me, my pursuance of the lovely Scottish lassie became a little less eager.

George Mills' Overcoat

The camelhair overcoat was all the rage in London. 'I'll make it for the cost of the cloth if you agree to have a publicity photograph taken wearing the coat so we can display it in our shop window,' the manager of George Mills Menswear in Grantham told me when I asked him how much it would cost.

'How much will that be?' I asked.

'About twenty pounds,' he replied.

Twenty pounds was a lot of money for an overcoat, two weeks' wages for my father.

The owner of the shop, George Mills, was a pillar of the community and a magistrate. I had met him a few times at local functions where he came across as being more Elgar than Elvis and a somewhat dour man.

A week after being measured for my coat I was summoned to appear in Grantham Magistrates' Court on 24 May 1960

My road manager Noel had been involved in a minor traffic accident, which wasn't his fault, and when presenting the car's documents at the local constabulary, we discovered the insurance didn't cover him to drive the car.

'Allowing a vehicle to be driven without insurance your honour,' replied the constable when asked by the magistrate why I was before him. 'Young man, I am determined to put a stop to people such as yourself thinking they can continually flout the driving laws,' he grumbled. Continually flouting the law? It was the first time I had been up before any magistrate.

He continued... 'With the high profile position you enjoy in this community you should be setting an example. I fine you £20 and your licence will be endorsed.' £20 was way above the average fine for similar offences and considering it was my first offence I couldn't believe my ears.

A few days later I received a letter to say the coat was ready. On arriving at the shop, I tried the coat on and it fitted, felt and looked great. As I admired myself in the mirror, looking ultra-cool, I then did something that, as a follower of fashion, broke my heart.

'I don't like it,' I told the manager. 'It doesn't feel good and it doesn't fit. I'll give you £10 for it.'

'The coat looks fine and it's worth a lot more than £20,' he replied.

'I know,' I said cockily, 'but I can't afford £20 as I've just been conned out of £20 by George Mills the magistrate.'

Then, walking out of the shop I said sarcastically, 'Tell His Honour he'll have a hell of a job finding a 6ft 5in skinny guy in Grantham who's got £20 in his pocket and is looking for a camel-hair coat.'

My next appearance at Grantham's Magistrates Court was 42 years later after it had been converted into what is now one of my favourite theatres.

On my return to the UK from America, my original road manager, good friend and fellow yellow belly Noel Wallis, showed me the theatre and suggested I do a show there with the original Vagabonds Skiffle Group. I booked the theatre for two nights and there was a queue when the box office opened. The tickets sold out within 30 minutes and we added a third performance, which also sold out.

I don't think George was there this time.

Bolognese and Beluga

Pop Star Mecca

Following our success in winning the East Midlands heats of the World Skiffle Championship, we headed by train for London and our appearance in the final on BBC Television's Come Dancing show.

Our good pal Noel, who had commandeered a Jowett Javelin, met us at London Kings Cross railway station. After squeezing our instruments, baggage and ourselves into the van, Noel drove us to Streatham and the Lacarno Ballroom, the venue for the World Skiffle Championship later that day.

Following a nerve-racking day we eventually made our television debut that evening and were placed second to a six-piece group named the Lumberjacks. They were from a Jewish orphanage in North London and were a great bunch of guys, but didn't deserve to be in the final let alone win it. When their guitarist Dave became a member of my band a few years later he never let me forget that they had 'stuffed us'.

The £150 runners-up prize from the skiffle contest helped us to purchase a new Selmer amplifier, a personal recording session at the HMV sound studio on Oxford

Street and a night on the town in London.

Our night on the town proved to be a worthwhile investment, as another Mecca was beckoning. Far from the giant dance floor, plush bars and revolving stage of the Mecca Lacarno in Streatham, this Mecca consisted of a tiny sweaty cellar beneath a small room dispensing espresso coffee, Coca Cola and Blue Riband biscuits. It was the Mecca for all budding pop stars. The 2 i's Coffee Bar in Old Compton Street, London W1.

With Noel our roadie at the wheel, the Jowett Javelin van edged slowly down Old Compton Street from Cambridge Circus. As we approached the 2 i's, we came upon a caravan of cars and vans parked there, with guitars, basses, washboards and drums sticking out of open windows and boots, a good indication that we weren't the only ones in search of fame and fortune.

I was elected to go into the 2 i's and suss out the lay of the land. At the entrance a giant of a man dressed in an American-style baseball jacket greeted me.

'We're full!' he shouted.

'I'm in a group and we'd like to play here,' I said nervously.

'You had better talk to that man there, Tom Littlewood, he's the manager.' The giant called him over.

'What is it, Roy?' the man said. How did

he know my name? He didn't. Roy was the giant on the door.

'This lad wants to play here with his group,' said Roy.

'So do the lads in the other vehicles parked outside. Get to the back of the queue and wait your turn,' he said.

'But we were on TV last night in the World Skiffle Championship from the Streatham Lacarno and we came second,' I said excitedly.

'In that case you'd better bring your van to the front and fetch your stuff in!' he yelled.

As I walked out of the door, he shouted at me again. 'What's the name of your group?'

'The Vagabonds,' I replied.

With that, I rushed outside to tell the boys the good news. Eventually we managed to park the van and began to unload, as we entered the 2 i's we noticed there was a chalkboard at the end of the bar, which read: 'Appearing Tonight! Television Stars – The Vagabonds. Admission 1/- (One Shilling).'

Getting our equipment downstairs and onto the stage was like tackling an assault course. The coffee bar was so crowded that the only way was to get guitars and amplifiers passed over the heads of the audience to the distant stage.

Once we were set up we began to play and it wasn't too long before we had the audience with us, although the packed conditions only allowed for tapping feet or singing along. With no air conditioning other than a ceiling trap door and an emergency exit that led up onto Old Compton Street, we soon looked like overworked horses covered in sweat.

We'd been playing for an hour when word reached us that we should stop. Due to the heat we didn't mind, it was a welcome relief, so when the cellar was empty we went upstairs to the coffee bar area where Tom Littlewood was organising his forces. He noticed us standing at the top of the stairs.

'Give them a Coke each,' he grunted to someone serving behind the bar. 'Have a 15 minute break and we'll let the next lot in,' he said to us. Bemused by what was going on, we did as we were told.

It was now 11 pm and after performing for yet another hour, the same thing happened. Get them out and get them in. Here we go again.

During the next break, Tom asked us if we would be interested in playing at the 2 i's on a permanent basis. 'I'll pay you £20 a week if you'll do it.'

We didn't know what to say. We would have to ask our parents. I was only earning £2.10 per week as an apprentice joiner so £20 per week was a fortune. We had to return to Grantham and make some decisions.

On the same day as our return to Grantham, we were given a hero's welcome at our regular Wednesday night dance, which was packed to the rafters. The atmosphere was electric, with our home fans making it obvious that they thought we should have won the skiffle contest. We played the record, *Money Honey,* we had recorded at the HMV studio in Oxford Street and the orders came flooding in at four shillings and six pence a time.

The following day was the day we had to decide if we would take Tom Littlewood up on his offer. Our parents were very supportive. Roy was halfway through an apprenticeship with a local engineering firm and his leaving to live in London would have meant a big sacrifice. Mick and I were also tied down to apprenticeships but not at such crucial stages as Roy's. 'Licorice' was a salesman and was capable of picking up where he had left off should he choose to do so. So, the decision was made. We accepted Tom's offer, Roy and Mick would try it out for a few weeks, 'Licorice' resigned from his position at Weaver to Wearer and my bosses greeted the news of my leaving with a sigh of relief. We were on our way!

Caffeine Capers

When we arrived back in London in a state of extreme apprehension, our priority was to find somewhere to stay. We were told of a men's hostel in Eastbourne Park that would suit us so we caught a tube and paid it a visit. It was exactly how I imagined a workhouse to be. Ten beds to a dormitory, large communal showers and all that was missing from the dining room was Oliver Twist. The standard rate was £4 per week, which included breakfast and an evening meal. 'It won't be forever, so we'll give it a try,' was our unanimous opinion. We left our belongings at the side of our beds and set off to start our residency at the 2 i's.

Occasionally established names like Tommy Steele, Terry Dene and Wee Willie Harris would drop in for a coffee and a song, along with those who were yet to make it such as Hank Marvin & Bruce Welch, Tony Sheridan, Cliff Richard and Sammy Samuel, Wally Whyton, Adam Faith and The Most Brothers, who were Britain's peroxide Everly Bros.

In spite of the 2 i's position in the heart of the West End, it was actually a safe place to hang out. The biggest dangers were caffeine poisoning, from an excess of coffee or Coca Cola, deafness due to the volume we racked up in such a confined area, or an unsocial disease passed on by one of the young ladies who were always very obliging. Thankfully, our medical histories do not include the latter.

The 2 i's manager, Tom Littlewood, was a law until himself. He possessed Godfather-like qualities and operated the bar under strict rules and regulations, all of which favoured him and the owners. Our first confrontation with Tom was at the end of our first and very successful week when we were excited at the prospect of collecting our wages.

At the end of our final Saturday night set, I went to Tom's little backroom to get paid. 'You did good,' muttered Tom as he handed me £20. 'Thanks Tom,' said I, nervously fingering the four £5 notes. 'You can give me the money for the rest of the guys and I'll give it to them. I said excitedly. 'What other money?' he snapped. 'That's it!' 'I thought it was £20 each,' I said nervously.

I was gutted. How could we live on £5 a week when our board and lodging was £4? The rest of The Vagabonds were equally devastated. We had all been under the impression that it was £20 each.

As we sat in the now empty 2 i's cellar, wallowing in our misfortune and misery, Tom emerged from the stairwell that came from the upstairs coffee bar. 'I don't know where you lads got the impression you were on £20 each,' he said, and I detected a sympathetic tone to his voice. 'Anyway, I'm not the one who determines what people get paid, Paul and Ray do that.' He went on 'If you lads continue as you started you shouldn't have a problem getting Sunday night gigs.' 'What Sunday night gigs?' we asked. 'As you don't work here on Sundays you should get some offers of ballroom or theatre gigs,' said Tom. 'We get Sundays off then?' I asked. 'Of course you do, do you think I'm a bloody slave driver?' snapped Tom. 'Maybe Mr Lincoln will use you on some of his Sunday concerts,' he went on. 'You could earn £30 between you for one of those shows.' Suddenly, the future looked a little rosier than it had done minutes earlier.

We talked to more and more people about getting Sunday gigs and the advice we received left us more and more confused. Paul Lincoln, Larry Parnes and Hymie Zahl were names that kept cropping up with regard to both our short and long-term futures.

Paul Lincoln, co-owner of the 2 i's was also a wrestling promoter with interests including managing a few acts such as Terry Dene, Wee Willie Harris and The Les Hobeaux Skiffle Group. We were told that he had received very good reports about us and that he was interested in signing us up. He also worked in conjunction with Hymie Zahl, an agent with the mighty Fosters Theatrical Agency who dealt with Larry Parnes, Tommy Steele and Marty Wilde's manager.

Within a few weeks of taking up our 2 i's residency we found ourselves on a coach to our first Sunday night concert at the Gaumont Theatre, Coventry. The booking came from Hymie Zahl at the Foster's Agency and it was on a Larry Parnes promotion supporting Marty Wilde and his Wildcats.

A Very Pink Period

During the return journey to London from Coventry following the Marty Wilde show, Larry Parnes told me how much he had enjoyed my performance and that he would like to manage me. 'You can stay the night at my apartment and we will discuss your future tomorrow morning,' he then said.

The arrival of our coach back in London proved to be much more of an event than our departure 12 hours earlier with everyone in high spirits as they wished Larry goodnight.

As Larry said his goodnights to those going their separate ways, it just left Marty's guitarist, Kenny Packwood, and me to accompany Larry to his car, a pink and grey Vauxhall Cresta. This heralded the beginning of a very pink period in my life.

On our arrival in Gloucester Road, Knightsbridge, I was faced with surroundings straight out a 1930s Hollywood movie. The ground floor entrance, which led to the lift up to Larry's penthouse, adjoined an

Italian restaurant, and this restaurant was to come to my rescue in more ways than one in the months ahead.

As we arrived at the penthouse door, I noticed the doormat had the initials LMP (Lawrence Maurice Parnes) emblazoned across it. Once inside the penthouse I felt I had been transported from Cricklewood to Hollywood!

There were Roman columns, marble tables, crystal chandeliers, a record player that would do justice to any sci-fi movie and lots of doors, leading to who knew where.

The marble pillars in the lounge would not have been out of place on the set of a historical Italian classical movie and the ornate silk-covered chairs with gold inlays would have been more suited for Cleopatra to clutch her asp on, than the sailors and marines who would slouch into them clutching their beers whilst being chatted up by Larry.

As for the beautiful Italian marble top table, which occupied half the lounge, I'm sure the motor racing mad Italians would have thrilled at seeing how perfect it was for Scalextrix car racing when Messrs Fury and Eager took to the track.

It was a chilly March evening and Larry insisted on showing me the apartment, especially the balcony that had a wonderful view overlooking Gloucester Road as it meandered towards Hyde Park.

The balcony would be used by a certain Mr Fury for much more than viewing the idyllic surroundings. Kenny Packwood then said goodnight as he gave me a wry smile, and disappeared down the long corridor flanked by doors.

'It's been a long day and you must be tired. We'll get to bed, then we can discuss everything in the morning,' said Larry.

As he opened the bedroom door I fully expected to see Jayne Mansfield draped over the bed. Everything was pink, much of it edged in lace. The kidney shaped dressing table featured two ornately framed photographs. One I recognised as Johnnie Ray, the 'Cry Guy' crooner from America. The other was what appeared to be a family photo. Larry emptied his pockets, placing his car keys and his money next to the Johnnie Ray photo, another of Larry's actions that was to feature heavily in the life styles of Messrs Fury and Eager.

'You can sleep on this side of the bed,' said Larry in a very mothering tone. 'The bathroom is on the opposite side of the corridor.'

Using the bathroom as a time killer, I brushed my teeth long and hard in an effort to put off the inevitable. It seemed an eternity before I returned to Larry's boudoir, and when I eventually did, he pulled back the sheet and told me to get in.

As I climbed into his bed, I pulled down

the upper sheet so I would be sleeping between the top sheet and the eiderdown. Larry didn't notice this until his hand met a satin sheet barrier as he started to try to get lucky.

'What have you done? You're not in bed properly,' he muttered in frustration.

'I always sleep like this,' I replied nervously.

As Larry looked towards me, I wrapped my hand menacingly around the pink china lamp that adorned the bedside table. The look in his eye indicated that he had understood the message about my intentions if he was to get fresh again. With that, my long, shallow night of sleep began.

Tommy Steele and Marty Wilde were the first of Parnes' protégés. When Larry recruited new members to his stable of stars, he always preferred to give them new names. He worked on the principal of finding a dynamic, rock 'n' roll surname – such as Wilde and Steele – but a homely Christian name.

This helped to project an aura of excitement, with a promise of underlying cosy domesticity, suggesting that these exciting rock 'n' roll stars were there to be snared by the girl in the street.

As Larry's housekeeper, Janet, cooked us an omelette for breakfast I heard her say to Kenny Packwood, 'I wonder what Larry will call this one?' It was like being with a serial mother who was giving birth. We didn't have to wait long for Larry's choice of name however.

'He seems very eager to get on,' I heard Larry say to someone over the phone. 'Eager, yes, that describes him, yes, I'll call him Eager.'

With that, Larry put down the phone, looked at me and said:

'You're a very eager young man aren't you?'

'Am I?' I asked.

'Yes, you'll be Eager. What would you like for a first name,' enquired Larry.

'I don't know, Larry, I like Roy.'

'No, no,' replied Larry in a camp but firm manner. 'Don't you have a favourite singer?'

My liking for both Gene Vincent and Lonnie Donegan met with an unfavourable silence.

'Gene? Lonnie? Neither of those are suitable,' replied Larry.

'What about Vince? Short for Vincent.' I asked, 'My brother's middle name is also Vincent.'

A smile of approval greeted my suggestion. 'Yes, Vince Eager. That's good,' said Larry. 'That's very good.' And so Vince Eager was born.

I still had to seek my parents' approval. They were totally unaware of what was going on. I was the first artist signed by Larry not to come from London, and the fact that my parents were not on the telephone increased their sense of isolation. It was also to prove a major handicap in dealing with Larry and his clandestine lifestyle.

The first day was a whirlwind of events. There was a record deal with Decca, although I had not been heard or seen by the company; lunch with Larry's partner John Kennedy; meeting the lawyers; being kitted out with star-quality clothes; and moving into Larry's apartment.

While all this was going on Larry had avoided mentioning The Vagabonds, so I brought the subject up. He assured me the boys would be my backing group. Tommy had the Steelemen, Marty had the Wildcats, I would have The Vagabonds.

The next few days were spent being shown off to Larry's family, colleagues, his sexual conquests, the press and his enemies, but not necessarily in that order. I was now one of 'Larry's boys,' a description I came to loathe. The connotations were obvious. My living with Larry only fuelled the gossip and nothing could have been further from the truth.

My counter-attack to the gossip was to be seen with as many females as possible. Larry was furious with my womanising. He would go on and on about how upset my fans would be if they knew I had girlfriends. Unfortunately I didn't have the guts to tell him they would be even more upset if they thought I was a puff!

My luck then changed when Larry told me he was moving to Marble Arch as he had bought a property there, but I could stay where I was as he would be hanging onto his Knightsbridge property for a while. Oh what hay there was to be made.

Moët and Coca Cola

Due to Larry not getting work for The Vagabonds as my backing group, Roy and Mick decided to return to Grantham and resume their apprentices, and 'Licorice' took up an offer to join Terry Dene's Dene Aces.

It was a few months after The Vagabonds split up that the first occasion arose where I needed a backing group.

As we parked outside Churchill's Night Club in New Bond Street, Larry lectured me on how I should behave if I got the job at the club. 'The owner Harry Meadows is a very nice man,' ('very nice man' was almost a catch phrase with Larry – used generally to describe someone who was gay. Harry wasn't) 'and you must be very polite to him and be a good boy.' ('Be a good boy' being another of Larry's catch phrases).

I may not have been the greatest singer; in fact I may not have been a lot of things. But one thing that I was, was well mannered. The times my mother would clip me behind the ear for not walking on the outside of the footpath for a lady, or opening a door, or standing when a lady left or joined a table, or helping elders with their coats. Yes, I would pass any good manners test Mr Meadows could throw at me. But could I pass the entertaining test?

Mondays were quiet nights in the West End. The 2 i's had proved that. My new group put together for the audition was made up of Tony Meehan on drums, who later joined The Shadows, Tony Sheridan on guitar, who played and recorded with The Beatles in Hamburg and Tex Makins on bass, who played for Georgie Fame's Blue Flames. Following our 11.00pm performance, we still didn't know if we had been successful.

Larry told us that Mr Meadows enjoyed the show but he couldn't gauge the reaction of the customers, as there were not enough in, so he wanted us to do the breakfast show at 1 am.

Sitting in the rest room with our chins on our knees, young ladies came in, smiled, perhaps had a coffee or took a phone call, then disappeared. Had we died and gone to heaven? One girl smiled and asked me what we did. 'I'm a singer and these guys are my musicians,' I answered.

'What do you do?' I asked nervously. 'I'm a hostess,' she replied casually, and with that she was gone. What were hostesses and what did they do? It didn't seem right to ask. None of us knew. But I knew someone who would.

Chris Reynolds and Mike Ward were Larry's press guys. They were Fleet Street pals of Larry's business partner John Kennedy and were expected to get 'Larry's Boys' as much publicity as humanly possible. It mattered not how. Fair means or foul could be employed.

I found Chris in the club waiting for the second show. 'What's a hostess Chris?' I asked sheepishly. 'They're high-class hookers. They get paid for getting a guy to spend a fortune on drinks on the club then they may take them home or to a hotel to get lucky,' he replied. 'Why?' he asked. 'Well, we're surrounded by them in the rest room upstairs. They come in, sit down, perhaps have a coffee and a cigarette, take a phone call and disappear.'

Chris then told me how the Maître d' would phone them in the rest room when a gentleman was at the front desk looking for a companion for the evening. Sometimes they would have guys come in to see them on a regular basis. They called them sugar daddies. I couldn't believe my ears. 'Does that mean we're working in a brothel?' I asked. 'Not really,' replied Chris. 'If they do shag them it's not on the premises.'

Show time was nigh and it was time for me to return to the rest room. When I arrived the boys were sitting around the table talking to three girls I took to be hostesses. 'Are you hostesses?' I enquired. 'No we're fucking not,' came the curt reply from a gorgeous peroxide blonde. 'We're showgirls.' It became apparent from our ensuing conversation with the showgirls that they were of the opinion the hostesses were slags while they, the showgirls, were entertainers. It didn't take long for us to find the contrary.

Tony Meehan, Tony Sheridan, Tex Makins and me were all hyped for the show. Meeting the hostesses and dancers had given us an added impetus. Now we really wanted the gig. We went on stage for the breakfast show and did a storm. The cigar and brandy-laden atmosphere was a far cry from the cigarette, caffeine and chocolate-soaked 2 i's but the outcome was similar. The audience gave us a fantastic reception.

During the euphoria of the show I noticed the smiling faces of some of the hostesses we had seen in the rest room earlier. Most hostesses were sitting with affluent looking guys who were groping them with one hand

and clutching a cigar or champagne with the other.

We took a bow at the end of our show and ran off stage to be greeted by a bevy of breasts. It was the showgirls waiting to go on for the finale. Topless dancers, high-class hookers. Please let Harry Meadows like us! There can't be anywhere else to work with perks like this. The only place I'd seen more tits was on the cows at Grantham Cattle Market when I was a young farmer!

On reaching the rest room we were basking in the glory of the show, and patting each other on the back, when Larry walked in with Harry Meadows. 'Excellent boys, but I want you to do one more show tomorrow then I will make a decision. I'll see you then, OK.' With that he was gone and we were left with Larry. 'He wants you, I know he does.' Larry said excitedly, 'but he wants to bring his wife in to see you.' Larry then said goodnight to the boys and told me to meet him at his table.

After I had changed I relaxed in the rest room before going to meet Larry. It was then that a lovely looking girl came up from the club. As she collected her coat from the rest room she turned to me with a very assuring smile – a smile that I was to see much more of – and said: 'That was a great show, see you tomorrow,' and she left.

The following night confirmed that Harry

Meadows did indeed want us. He booked us for four weeks, including the week we had already started.

Larry was prompted into pursuing my appearance at Churchill's Night Club by the success of Tommy Steele having recently appeared at The Stork Club. The Stork Club was the place to be seen, and Tommy's four-week booking had proved a major publicity coup. The press had a field day with great photographs of the aristocracy and the jet setters in their cocktail-dresses and tuxedos dancing the night away to the rock 'n' roller from Bermondsey.

Harry Meadows' proposition to Larry regarding my appearance at Churchill's came at an opportune time. He had only recently bought it from the previous owner, Bruce Brace, who had experienced financial difficulties and was forced to sell. Bruce was bitter at having to sell to Harry and vowed to return.

Following my official opening night we received great reviews and Larry soon had anybody and everybody coming to see me. One of the first was Russell Turner, the new producer of the top Saturday prime time pop show 'Six Five Special.' I joined them at Larry's table after the first show and Larry introduced me. 'Well done,' said Russell. 'You worked very hard.' I had been referred to in one national newspaper review as Mr

68

Perpetual Motion, mainly because I didn't stand still for long. Nobody could deny I worked hard, but was it a cop-out to avoid people saying they weren't keen on my singing? Russell and Larry then locked in heavy conversation ignoring me completely.

Larry's publicist, Chris Reynolds, was a regular at the club. He loved a drink, and this was a great way for him to get lagged for nothing. His prime reason for being there was to take care of my PR. When Larry was in the club, Chris would usually sit at his table immediately after every show.

Thankfully Chris was at the table as Larry and Russell locked into their verbal wrestling. It was the first opportunity for me to digest the surroundings and savour the atmosphere. I saw most of the girls who were in the rest room earlier and many of them were draped over their companions like a shawl, clutching a glass of champagne and looking the worse for wear.

'How can they keep drinking champagne like this every night,' I asked Chris. 'They don't drink much, they pour most of it on the carpet,' he said with great authority. 'Look at the girl on the table over there,' pointing discreetly to a blonde sat with one arm around an American looking guy and the other arm resting on the edge of the table, with her hand caressing a champagne glass. 'Watch her champagne glass,' said Chris.

Within a few minutes, while kissing her beau on the cheek to occupy his attention, she held the lip of the champagne glass against the white tablecloth edge, a tablecloth that almost touched the rich red carpet, and poured her drink onto the tablecloth edge so it trickled down to the carpet. Very soon her glass was empty and she was waving it in front of her companion letting him know she was ready for a refill. With that, the waiter approached the table, took the champagne out of the ice bucket and replenished her glass. She then held her glass up as if to toast her companion and took a sip. 'What the heck was that about?' I asked Chris in disbelief. He then explained. 'The girls work on commission. They get 40 percent of all the champagne they order. If they were to drink all they ordered they would be in a drunken stupor, so they pour it away and act drunk. They can make serious money.'

I couldn't believe it. I had told my parents I was working in a very posh West End nightclub and my parents wanted to come and see the show. If they knew what was going on I would be on the first train north.

Chris then continued his West End education of the naïve northern boy, by pointing out the soft toys, perfume, nylon stockings and cigarettes being sold by a foxy looking girl carrying a tray who was dressed like a playgirl bunny without the tail. He explained how the hostesses would ask their companion to buy something for them as a present. The club would then buy it back at 30 percent of the price.

All this seedy information Chris had fed me was against the backdrop of Larry and Russell's intense conversation, which appeared to become more heated when Tommy Steele's name was mentioned. When I returned backstage to get ready for the second show they were still locked in verbal combat.

It transpired that a deal was eventually struck where Russell would get Tommy for one Six-Five Special appearance in exchange for me doing six.

My Sugar Mummy

As the nights passed our popularity and credibility at Churchill's went from strength to strength and my new-found celebrity status put me in demand to join guests at their tables after the show. From lords and ladies to influential business people to Hollywood film stars. I certainly did my bit to swell Harry's coffers, but sadly I wasn't on commission like the girls.

My 2 i's Coffee Bar habit of Coca Cola would remain with me for another seven years until I discovered that Coca Cola tasted even better when mixed with Bacardi. Unfortunately, Churchill's affluent clientele just couldn't understand that his boy from Grantham was happy with a Coke.

'Great show, Vince, what would you like to drink?' seemed the stock greeting. And before I could say, 'A Coke please,' they would be hollering at the sommelier for yet another bottle of champagne. And so it went. I discovered later that some of the girls would tell their guests that I loved champagne after a show. Thankfully I had seen the girls operate the glass on the tablecloth scam so I soon became part of the collusion. Their commission went up and so did my stock. I was accepted as being part of the Churchill's family with the rest room becoming as familiar as my parents' lounge.

For three weeks, hostess Julie was a lady to whom I would say 'good evening' or 'goodnight' from a distance. I was longing to get to know her better but I couldn't muster the courage to approach her. Thankfully she didn't see it the same way.

One evening before the first show, Julie asked me if I would like to join her and her companion Charles for an after-show drink. I said I would be delighted. On joining them I soon became very much at ease with them. They seemed a much classier couple than many of those with whom I had shared an after-show drink. Charles was a man in his late 40s with a very strong southern American accent; it later transpired that he was an oil executive from Texas. He talked softly, didn't smoke and appeared to be a moderate drinker. In fact there was no sign of champagne.

My transport plans for getting home to Larry's apartment after the shows were very inconsistent. It could be with Larry, with Chris, by taxi or on occasions a lift. As I prepared to go on stage for the second show, Julie came into the rest room and asked if I would like a lift home with her and Charles following the show. I told her that would be great and she returned to her table and Charles.

The journey home to Knightsbridge was uneventful. Small talk and show talk and we were home. Charles thanked me again for the show and Julie got out of the car, gave me a memorable kiss on the cheek and pushed a piece of paper into my hand.

As they sped off into the cold Knightsbridge air I couldn't wait to find out what the paper was all about. I read it as I took the lift to the third floor apartment. It asked me to phone her after 12 noon.

It was with great trepidation that I phoned Julie. She thanked me for calling and asked me if she could pick me up for a coffee. I said I would love to have coffee with her and gave the OK on a 3 pm pick up time.

Julie arrived promptly driving her MG sports car. We drove to a coffee bar in Kensington where, over cappuccinos and black forest gateau, she proceeded to tell me how much she enjoyed my singing. The conversation was centred mostly on Julie's hostess activities. She went to great lengths to tell me that she didn't approve of girls who took clients home or to hotels after the club, stressing that the club didn't condone it either. Her relationship with Charles had been going on for over a year and he visited Julie every few weeks for a couple of days. He had told her he wasn't married but she thought he was.

When Julie dropped me off she asked me to bring a tape measure to the club that night. I asked her why and she said I must wait to find out. My dressing room at the club that evening was more like a bespoke tailor's with Julie taking my measurements for reasons she would not divulge. Despite my pestering her she would not divulge her intentions.

After the breakfast show a few days later, Julie arrived in her civvies and asked me to meet her outside so she could give me a lift home. Arriving outside Larry's apartment, she asked me if it was OK for her to come in. Fortunately Larry was in South Africa so the coast was clear. I was summoned by Julie to help her carry 'something from the boot.'

'Something from the boot' turned out to be parcels, bags and boxes all carrying fashion labels from the likes of Cecil Gee (high class men's store), Austin Red, Annello David (quality shoes), to mention but a few. By the time we arrived in the apartment I was totally confused. The goods had to be for me, but why?

With the parcels on the sofa, I collapsed in a chair waiting for Julie's next move.

'Well, go on, open them,' she commanded. Not wishing to prolong either the agony surrounding why I had got the gifts, or what they were, I proceeded to open them. Suits, shirts, jackets, slacks, ties and shoes were laid out as if we were in a high-class fashion show dressing room. My curiosity was now turning into fear. 'What do I have to do?' This was a lot of expensive gear. The expression 'toy boy' had yet to manifest itself. Had it existed I was convinced this would have been the route we were heading down.

After the fashion show, during which I expected my benefactor to get her evil way with me at any stage, I asked her why she had bought them for me. 'I didn't,' giggled Julie, 'Charles did.' 'Charles did? What's he after,' I asked. 'Nothing, he bought them for my brother, not you.' Laughing her head off as she told me. 'Won't your brother be upset?' I asked. 'I haven't got a brother,' she said, and continued to tell me how she had told Charles that her brother was starting a new job and needed clothes. He then told her to get her brother's measurements and they would go shopping for him. 'So there you are, they're for you!'

I continued to voice my concern that people don't normally get such gifts without a proviso. I guess I was hoping she would make a suggestive remark regarding something I could do for her. It wasn't to be. Julie said she loved my singing and I was a very nice guy she wanted just for a friend. With that she kissed me on the cheek and left.

Julie became a very good friend and was a wonderful guide through the crazy journey I had embarked upon.

A Lancaster Bummer!

The song *'Kisses Sweeter Than Wine'* was a number where I would do a sweep search of the audience for celebrities when performing in the West End nightclubs. During one performance I noticed Ronald Shiner, a well-known character actor who specialised in Cockney wide-boy roles. Very few mid fifties British movies were without Ronald's presence.

As I thanked the audience at the end of my show, I smiled at Ronald and the guy sitting next to him who looked remarkably like

Burt Lancaster. When I reached the dressing room I asked the boys if any of them had noticed Ronald Shiner on the front table. The reply from one of them was, 'Yeah! He's sitting next to Burt Lancaster.' 'So it was Burt Lancaster, I thought I was seeing things,' I replied excitedly.

The movie Trapeze, starring Burt Lancaster and Tony Curtis, was one of my favourite movies. I couldn't believe I had just performed in front of Burt Lancaster. Sadly, as the next couple of hours would reveal, that was not the only performance he expected from me that night.

Within 15 minutes of coming off stage I received a phone call from the Maître d'. 'Mr Lancaster has invited you to join him for a drink,' he said calmly. 'Who me?' I stuttered. 'Yes, you Vince,' he said, putting the phone down. The Maître d' took me to Burt Lancaster's table and introduced me. I was in awe. 'No one in Grantham will believe me when I tell them.'

He was not as tall as I thought he would be, and I was very surprised when he commented on how tall I was. He was very polite and asked me what I would like to drink. The waiters, however, now knew my Coca Cola order, which often arrived at a table before I did.

Following an interlude of compliments, he broached the subject of a new movie he was due to make. Explaining it was a movie he was directing as well as taking the lead role in, he arrived at the part I found hard to take in. One of the main roles in the movie was that of a good-looking guy in his late teens to early twenties and he felt I fitted the part perfectly.

I'm sure my reaction appeared to be that of nothing but total gormlessness. I just sat there unable to digest what was going on. Grantham people didn't appear in Holly-wood movies, they only watched them while eating ice cream or snogging.

Burt went over the scenario once again, punctuating it with, 'Do you understand?' Yes, I did understand, but I didn't quite know how to react to it. 'What we need to do is get you to my hotel,' stated Burt. 'I am catching a plane to Los Angeles at lunch-time tomorrow, so we need to talk before I leave.' I explained to him that I had a manager and must discuss the matter with him before I could join him for talks.

'What we'll do is this,' stressed Burt. 'You come back to my hotel now and we'll discuss my plans for you over breakfast, you can then discuss it with your manager.' Of all the nights, neither Larry nor Chris were in the club. During the course of Burt's explanation, Ronald Shiner showed very little interest. It was this lack of interest that alerted me to something not being right. I sensed that this wasn't the first time he had been down this route with Lancaster. I excused myself from the table to visit the men's room.

During my absence I took the opportunity to phone Larry. It was 3:15 am so I knew Larry wouldn't be too pleased with me phoning but I felt it was in both our interests. I started to explain everything that Lancaster had told me. Before I could mention the movie, Larry was wide awake and threatening me if I dared go anywhere near Lancaster's Hotel. 'You get in a taxi and you get home immediately. Don't you dare speak to him again,' screamed Larry. And he put the phone down.

By now, I was more confused than before I'd phoned Larry. I had spurned his advances but it hadn't been to my detriment so maybe I could do the same with Lancaster. I returned to the table to be greeted by a big smile and firm handshake from Burt. Once again Ronald Shiner appeared to not care less what course events might take.

I didn't tell Burt of my phone call to Larry but explained that I had to go home now, but I would be happy to visit his hotel at 8:30 am to talk over his plans for my appearing in his movie. Before I had finished saying 'go home,' Burt, who hadn't yet filmed Elmer Gantry but appeared to be getting into the role, snarled at me and said, 'You don't come with me now boy, you ain't gonna be in the movie.' So that was that! I left the table with Ronald Shiner not even raising an eyebrow. I guess it was a regular event.

Yet Another Bum Scare?

Our Churchill's contract was renewable on a monthly basis and the way business had improved over the previous 4 months, I think Larry must have made a small fortune by hyping up my fee every month. Not that I saw any of it. In fairness, most of the money must have gone on entertaining guests at the club, guests who were supposed to be there to enhance my career. What a dozen sailors and marines could have done for my future I dread to imagine, but they were regular guests of Larry.

On the sixth month of our residency Larry informed me that we were being transferred to Winstons' Club on the opposite side of Bond Street. He was also quick to point out that Harry wanted us to remain with him but Bruce Brace, former Churchill's owner and now proprietor of Winston's, had made Larry an offer he couldn't refuse. I was sorry to leave Churchill's, but then again what testosterone-pumping young lad wouldn't have been?

Our opening night at Winston's was a Monday. It was a refurbished club with a similar appeal to Churchill's. The main difference was the floorshow. Mr Brace appeared to be going for fewer showgirls and more variety.

It was topping the bill and being heralded as the new darling of the West End. I didn't know who the old darling was so I couldn't compare. Having had a sound check in the late afternoon and having left immediately, I had no idea who the other artistes were.

When I returned at 10.15 pm for an 11 pm show, I went straight to my dressing room. At about 10.40 pm there was a lot of distant noise that became like an approaching earthquake. Doors were being banged, high volume screaming was on the increase and the sound of people running made for a scary atmosphere. We realised what was happening when our door bust open and a waiter stuck his head around the door and in broken English shouted 'bum scare.' Surely Larry's arrival couldn't cause that much commotion! No, he meant bomb scare.

We soon discovered that a phone call from a foreign sounding character had informed the management that there was a bomb planted in the club and due to go off at 11 pm. The caller claimed to be Turkish stating his targets were the Greek waiters who were working in the club.

It was at the height of Archbishop Makarios, General Grivas and the EOKA problems, so it made for a scary scenario.

We were ushered out into the street and stood there in our snazzy bathrobes awaiting the bang. It was at this time I noticed a billboard on the front of the club advertising the floorshow. Of course it meant nothing at the time because those below me on the bill were also slaving away to make a name for themselves. Eventually they all did pretty well. Perhaps you've heard of them: Danny La Rue, Ronnie Corbett and Barbara Windsor were their names. Imagine if the bomb had gone off. The BBC would have lost many of its future stalwarts.

Twenty minutes after the bomb should have exploded we were all standing there awaiting instructions when Chris Reynolds and Mike Ward, my press managers, sauntered up. With big grins on their faces, they pulled me to one side and Chris said, 'Fantastic, we timed it just right for the early editions.'

'Timed what just right?' I asked.

'The phone call,' joked Chris.

'What phone call?' I asked.

'The bomb hoax phone call,' giggled Chris.

'You mean you phoned the club?' I screamed.

'Shut up,' they said. 'You'll get us into trouble.'

'I'll get you in trouble,' I mumbled fearfully. 'My brother will kill me! He's a copper!'

Chris then tried to tell me of the great press I should receive the next day. We were eventually escorted back into the club and the show began. Sure enough the next day I made headlines on an inside page. 'Pop Star Involved In Bomb Hoax.' For a minute I thought they had tumbled us but they were only referring to my being there.

The Drunken Rats

Churchill's audiences were never the quietest of crowds and as it was my first encounter with nightclub audiences, I had to learn pretty quickly. Unfortunately I didn't learn quite quickly enough. I did have a few put downs I would use for hecklers and noisy groups and on one occasion a group at a large table not too far from the stage were in a boisterous mood.

Just before my last number I decided to have a go at them and let them know I was the boss.

'Excuse me folks,' I shouted to the boisterous table. 'We have a rule in this club where the person holding the microphone does all the talking! OK?' It didn't make one ounce of difference so I sang my last song and finished the show.

Shortly after arriving in the relaxing room I received a phone call from the Maître d' to go to the front desk.

He took me to the rear of the club and asked quizzically. 'You see that big table on the left. Do you recognise any of the people sitting there?'

'I think so,' I replied nervously.

'Who?' he asked, sounding more like one of my ex headmasters.

When I realised who they were I replied at machine gun speed. 'Sammy Davis, Frank Sinatra and Dean Martin!'

He continued, 'And Peter Lawford and Joey Bishop! Just think yourself a very lucky lad that they were making so much noise, they didn't hear your comments about the microphone, or it could have finished up where the sun don't shine.'

'What are they doing here?' I asked. He told me that Churchill's and the Astor Club were the only West End nightclubs to keep a stock of Jack Daniels bourbon. Especially for Sinatra and his pals.

From then on I was always very careful whom I directed my smart arse ad-libs at.

The Gay Mafia

The Golden Guitar Club in Soho was one

of the first dedicated gay clubs in London. My manager Larry Parnes and my agent Hymie Zahl joined forces to open the club, which proved to be a magnet for the showbiz gay community.

Rumours were rife about Russ Conway, but on the occasions I worked with him he hadn't shown any indication of being gay. We had even travelled together on an overnight sleeper train to Swansea where we were appearing at the Tower Ballroom in an outside broadcast of the Six Five Special TV show.

It wasn't until Granville, a pal of mine from my hometown of Grantham, visited me in London for a few days that Russ showed his true colours. Granville was a good-looking guy with jet black Elvis styled hair and a good dress sense. In showing 'Granny', as he was affectionately known, Soho, I couldn't resist taking him into the Golden Guitar.

The club was not a regular haunt of mine. The innuendos we had to deal with, as being 'Larry's boys', were bad enough without adding fuel to the already glowing fire by frequenting a gay club.

As we entered, all eyes focused on Granny, but none for longer than those of Russ, who was wearing a grin like a Cheshire cat as he beckoned us over to join him at the bar. I introduced Granny to Russ, who looked to be in a state of shock at being introduced to the 'King of the Keys' and the housewives' choice. Once the introductions were over Russ set about giving Granny the third degree and making his intentions obvious. Granny's shock then intensified upon realising that Russ was hitting on him. Feeling very responsible for Granny, I eventually managed to get him away from Russ unscathed and we continued our Soho tour.

A regular at the club was Norman Newell. Norman was one of the Top A & R (Artiste and Repertoire) managers and responsible for recording artistes such as Shirley Bassey, Vera Lynn, Russ Conway, Bette Midler, Petula Clark and Peter & Gordon. His honours included one Grammy, an Emmy and 3 Ivor Novello Awards. He also enjoyed major success as a songwriter with hits such as *Portrait of my Love* and *More*.

Norman was also a raving queen. So much so that when he passed his driving test, the New Musical Express wrote in the back page Alley Cat column, 'Norman Newell passes his driving test... Oh no! Not another woman driver on the roads!'

The NME were subsequently sued and had to pay a considerable amount in damages to Norman. But it didn't compare to the damage Norman could inflict on an artiste's career if he didn't get his way. It was this that sounded the death knell between Parlophone and me.

Over lunch one day, Larry explained that at times I had a bad attitude and it was preventing me having the hit I deserved.

'If you are nicer to Mr Newell and do as he asks, he will make sure you have a bit hit,' said Larry, sounding more like Hatti Jacques in a Carry On film.

I was not as assured as I would have liked to have been and didn't have the guts to tell Larry I had no intentions of hitting the sack with Norman, so I told him I would think about it.

Needless to say a few days later I was summoned to the Golden Guitar to meet Larry. And who should be with him but Norman.

Norman told me he had arranged for me to go away with him for the weekend where we would discuss my future. I asked him sarcastically if it was OK for me to bring a girlfriend, he walked off in a huff, and I never recorded for Parlophone again.

Belafonte's Island in WC1

The Oasis was, and still is, located in the West End of London amid the glitz and glamour of its theatres. An outdoor swimming pool with health-based activities, it was an oasis of leisure.

Whilst promoting my new Parlophone record, *This Should Go On Forever*, I was booked to appear on 'Cool For Cats', a musical television show from ITV hosted by Kent Walton. The show, a 1950s 'Top of the Pops' style programme, was based at a studio in the West End of London where it was recorded, or transmitted live, but on this occasion the Oasis was to be the location for the broadcast.

Closing the Oasis to the general public for the day enabled the TV production team to transform it into a Caribbean style paradise especially for the appearance of top American singing star Harry Belafonte. Harry was visiting the UK to promote his new record, *Island in the Sun* and 'Cool for Cats' was his first UK television appearance.

A few tons of strategically placed sand, a palm tree mounted on top and a couple of fishing nets, with sea shells sewn into them and thrown over a shed, provided the perfect backdrop. Who would know that it was an 'Island in Holborn' within spitting distance of Cambridge Circus and not an island in the sunny Caribbean?

Standing on the diving board over the deep end of the pool, with the man-made version of a Jamaican beach behind him, Harry Belafonte mimed to his recording of *Island in the Sun*.

It was then, as I watched the production

team and Harry set up their shots at rehearsals, that I befriended Barry, the General Manager of the Oasis. Barry's enthusiasm for the show and his determination to make us welcome included him inviting me to use the centre facilities at any time. I took advantage of Barry's offer and soon became a regular Oasis visitor.

During one of my visits, my sunbathing was interrupted by a young girl who asked if I was Vince Eager. Having confirmed I was, she asked if I would sign an autograph for her as she was a big fan. She told me her name was Amanda so I signed her piece of paper and went back to my sunbathing.

Within minutes she returned with a message from her parents inviting me to join them for a drink. I explained that I didn't drink alcohol but would be happy to say hello.

As Amanda's parents introduced themselves as Maureen and David Wise, it soon became clear that it was the mother who was the fan. A ploy used by many mothers to reel in a pop star was to make out it was their daughter who was the fan whereas in reality it was the mother who had the hots.

Maureen went on to tell me that she watched me on the BBC TV show 'Drumbeat' every Saturday and was thrilled to meet me. Within minutes of meeting, they had extended an invitation for me to join them for dinner at their home on the Mile End Road in East London.

It was two weeks later that I found myself at Maureen and David's East End home; taking them up on their dinner invitation. Sitting down for dinner, I had no idea that the dessert on offer would prove to be one of the tastiest I had ever had set before me.

The extra table setting and empty chair next to David should have given me a clue that all was not what it appeared to be. An enjoyable meal peppered with polite conversation took a turn when the doorbell rang and David said, 'Ah! That will be Wendy!'

Within minutes David had returned from answering the door was introducing Wendy as 'my girlfriend Wendy.' I was gobsmacked. My surprise obviously showing, Maureen quickly established that she and David led separate lifestyles and that she had a boyfriend named Martin whom, coincidently, I was a dead ringer for. Martin was serving with the Royal Air Force in Aden and Maureen was missing him desperately, but being able to watch me on TV helped her cope while he was away.

Post dinner conversation was limited to more innuendo than substance as, along with the wine stock, Maureen's missing of Martin decreased. After coffee David suggested we retire to the lounge. Arriving in the lounge I soon discovered that what David really meant was, 'Why don't you and Maureen go to the lounge and Wendy and I will go to my bedroom?'

As I tried to look relaxed in an armchair, Maureen excused herself and left me with the cosy fire and a soft drink. It was at times such as this that in years to come I appreciated the calming qualities of a cigarette and a Bacardi and Coke. With the TV turned off and the magazine rack empty, I pondered the prospect of Maureen's return.

Within 15 minutes Maureen returned, dressed in a garment I had seen worn only by Hollywood screen sirens in X-rated movies. The baby dolls, as I was to learn they were called, revealed much more than the lacy, yet very skimpy underwear, she was nearly wearing.

Maureen pounced. Needless to say I was putty in her hands and did nothing to resist. It was only at the height of passion when she called me 'Martin' that I realised all was not what I thought it was. Not wishing to kill the moment I said nothing but Maureen was keen to get onto the subject once the passion had subsided.

'I hope you don't mind me calling you Martin when we're making love,' said Maureen apologetically, 'but you're just like him.' I told her I didn't, which prompted her to offer her services any time I wanted to drop by.

Hastily, she added that she didn't make a habit of doing this sort of thing, as she was madly in love with Martin and they were getting married on his return from Aden.

Maureen's home became a regular stop over for me in the coming weeks and proved a very influential part of my reaching maturity. I reluctantly brought it to a halt when the words 'Vince' and 'love' crept into our post-session conversations.

Consequently *Island in the Sun* holds happy memories of more than palm trees and sun-drenched beaches in the Caribbean when I hear it!

A Triumph for the Herald

While on a photo shoot for a girlie magazine, I struck up a friendship with the photographer Allan. It was for a cartoon style piece where I came to the rescue of a fan whose boyfriend had cheated on her and I put everything to rights by taking her to Battersea Funfair.

It was a long hot summer's day and it took a lot of patience from Allan and me. He must have taken over 400 photographs of me on my own or with the jilted girlfriend, with most being some sort of pose orchestrated by him or the director. At the end of the day he offered me a lift back to the apartment in Knightsbridge.

We decided to stop for a coffee en route and soon discovered we had quite a lot in common. Allan was from Melton Mowbray, only fifteen miles from my hometown of Grantham and he especially liked Lonnie Donegan, Elvis Presley and cars. During the coffee break he mentioned that he was going home to Melton Mowbray for an overnight stay the following day and very kindly offered to drop me off in Grantham and bring me back to London the day after.

Our journey was all about cars. Allan was driving a most beautiful S Type Jaguar. It turned out he was very much in demand as a photographer of cars and Jaguar had done him a deal. I fell head over heels in love with the Jag and was determined to get one.

During the journey Allan gave me a brochure he had produced for Standard Triumph Cars. It contained top-secret photographs of a soon-to-be-launched new model, the Triumph Herald Coupe. He promised to send me a copy of the brochure when it became available.

On my return to London my quest became to get my hands on an S Type Jaguar. I told Larry of my yearning and surprisingly he had a sympathetic ear.

Larry pointed out that my dreams could be shattered by the insurance premium.

Larry's secretary, Muriel, was given the task of getting insurance quotes and it didn't take long for me to realise the Jag was out of the question.

Apparently a 19-year-old rock 'n' roll singer who had just passed his driving test did not appeal to the automobile insurers unless accompanied by a very large cheque. A cheque that would prove to be more than the price of the Jaguar.

With my dreams of owning a Jaguar in tatters, I recalled Allan having told me that the Triumph Herald's innovative five-section body would make it a cheaper car to insure. Maybe that was the way to go. I showed a photo of the Triumph Herald Coupe to Larry and he promised me he would look into it.

And look into it he did, as I found out on my 19th birthday, June 4th 1959. I proposed to my girlfriend Hazel Kendal. She accepted and we were engaged. We had already arranged to go out for dinner that evening to celebrate my birthday so now it would be a double celebration. I arranged for Hazel to come to the apartment and we would leave from there.

In the afternoon, Larry arrived at the apartment in a very good mood. He asked me if I was having a nice birthday and he hoped I hadn't made any plans. I was already feeling very hesitant about telling him

94

of my engagement to Hazel and just told him that I was taking her out for dinner. His reply was we could all go out for dinner later.

Hazel arrived at 4 pm and I immediately showed Larry Hazel's hand and the ring. His mouth looked like the Blackwall Tunnel. 'You mustn't let your fans know,' he garbled nervously. 'It could ruin your career. Hazel, put the ring on the chain around your neck then no one will know.' Close to tears, Hazel put the ring on the chain as Larry hurried to answer the ringing telephone.

Checking that the engagement ring was on the chain, and couldn't be seen, Larry told us to follow him. He led us to the lift, down to the ground floor, out of the building onto Gloucester Road and around the corner into Queen's Gate.

The flash of a camera greeted our arrival into Queen's Gate. The paparazzi weren't as prolific in 1959 so I immediately knew it was one of Larry's publicity stunts.

As I realised that I was part of one of Larry's publicity set-ups, my eyes slowly readjusted from the flash, the clearing blur revealed the outline of a beautiful powder blue and white Triumph Herald Coupe.

A somewhat out of tune 'Happy Birthday dear Vince' came forth from Larry, his publicity guru Chris Reynolds and a reporter, clutching her pad and pen and looking more like a groupie in search of an autograph.

When my eyes finally cleared, I was able to take in the enormity of the situation. I had just received the best birthday present ever and yet was not as happy as I should be. It always seemed that whenever Larry did something, which represented kindness or generosity, there would be an ulterior motive.

In the car, behind the car, leaning against the bonnet, draped across the roof, mouth wide open, smiling, every position and reaction was captured by the photographer. The reporter was obviously a cub, possibly on her first job, as she didn't ask any searching questions and never picked up on Hazel's presence or questioned who she was or why she was there.

Once the press had gone I examined my beautiful new shiny car. Or was it? As I was about to take it for a spin, Larry told me that it had to go back to the showroom and I would get it back in a couple of weeks. 'They are in big demand and this one is a demonstration model,' he explained.

The following morning the Daily Herald newspaper boasted the page three headline, 'A Triumph for the Herald,' with a sub headline 'Pop Star Vince Gets A Bumper Birthday Present.' A photograph of me leaning out of the car window with a big grin, accompanied the story of how Larry had surprised me by giving me the car for my birthday.

It didn't mention that shortly after the photo was taken I got a bigger surprise when Larry told me the car had to go back to the showroom.

Larry had arranged to borrow the car for the day, in order to get publicity for both the car and me.

Larry had done it again. No press without pain.

Up the Unction

Wee Willie Harris was managed by Les Bristow, an ex-wrestler and Cockney to the core. Les had master minded Wee Willie's overseas success in Europe and South America and would travel with Willie on all his trips.

It was on his return from one trip to the Lido in Venice, Italy, where Willie had become a major attraction, that Les so nearly came to a sticky end at the hands of his long-suffering wife Norah, who was the manageress of a restaurant opposite the 2 i's Coffee Bar in Old Compton Street, London.

Having returned from Venice the previous day, Les had slept in and Norah had gone to the restaurant in the early morning to prepare for the lunchtime trade. Les had a relaxing day at home and went to the West End in the evening to have dinner at

Norah's restaurant. En route Les called into the 2 i's and invited me to join him.

As Les opened the restaurant door we were greeted with a much more hostile reception than anticipated. Norah was entrenched behind the coffee espresso machine where she began to hurl dinner plates at Les.

With the launch of each plate she would use the first syllable of an expletive to vent her fury on Les for having brought home from Italy, and given to her, as she referred to it, 'a dose of the fuck-ing-crabs!'

Les and I beat a hasty retreat across to the 2 i's where he was expecting sympathy from the regulars. Unfortunately Norah had phoned the 2 i's ahead of Les' arrival and warned people to keep their opinions to themselves, otherwise they would encounter a similar fate to Les.

Everyone knew of Norah's temper and determination and decided to err on the side of caution.

Les received just sniggers as he tried to blame the 'dose' on a one night stand with a showgirl at The Lido after his drink had been spiked. He then began making en-quiries about how he could get rid of the crabs. He phoned a doctor Paul Lincoln used for his wrestlers, and a man who was not averse to twisting the truth if it served his purpose, to see if he could help. 'Blue Unction, Les, that's what you need. You can get it from the all night chemist in Piccadilly Circus.' With that Les and I stepped out in the direction of Piccadilly Circus and the all night chemist.

It was about 9 pm and the chemist was a hive of activity. Les knew most people in the West End who worked the night shift and the chemist shop was no exception. He approached an assistant he knew and whispered in his ear the magic words. 'Blue Unction.' The assistant took one step back, looked across the crowded shop floor and shouted to the colleague furthest away, 'Can you bring me a bottle of Blue Unction?' With a face as red as the Blue Unction was blue, Les shouted across to the assistant. 'Yea, I've got a dose of the fucking crabs!' The shoppers erupted into laughter as Les tried to cover his embarrassment by making a speedy exit.

Les had overlooked that Norah also knew most of the people who worked the night shift in the West End. Her second phone call, following her warning to the 2 i's, had been to the all night chemist, the only place you could buy Blue Unction at 9 pm in Central London.

When Ronnie Met Billy

A Furyous Christening

Sharing a penthouse with my manager Larry Parnes didn't make him any more endearing and a healthy heterosexual flatmate was all I yearned for. I just wanted someone to hang out with, and it was an event on Wednesday 1st October 1958, in Birkenhead, that was to turn my yearning into reality.

Following my sound check at the Birkenhead Essoldo, Marty Wilde's drummer, Brian Bennett, suggested we went for a Wimpy burger. As we stepped out into the dampness of a very overcast October Merseyside afternoon, a slightly-built young man wearing a gabardine overcoat with the collar turned up and looking very much like a cross between Elvis and James Dean, walked towards Brian and me and, in a Liverpool accent asked, 'Excuse me la, is Mr Parnes here?' I replied, 'Yes, why?' He said he had recorded some self-penned songs onto a tape and sent them to Larry but he hadn't received a reply. He wanted to know if Larry liked them.

I went back into the theatre and Larry was in the dressing room Marty and I were sharing. I explained the situation to Larry and he asked me to fetch him in.

On seeing the young man enter the dressing room Larry's face just lit up. He was immediately in awe of what he was looking at. Larry introduced himself and asked the guy his name. 'Ronald Wycherley,' the young man replied. 'I understand you sent me a tape of some of the songs you have written,' asked Larry. 'Yes,' mumbled Ronnie, 'but I didn't get a reply.'

'I don't think I've received them,' said Larry. 'Would you sing one for me now if I get a guitar for you?' Ronnie agreed nervously. With that, the Hofner Committee guitar belonging to Marty's guitarist Kenny Packwood was commandeered. Ronnie took his coat off at Larry's request and he was ready to go.

Standing apprehensively in the middle of the dressing room, Ronnie strummed a few chords to check all was OK with the guitar, then played a chord and started to sing, *'Rise in the morning, you're not around...,'* the peace and quiet that was the dressing room was shattered by the screaming of young girls outside the window. Those of us inside were astounded by what we were hearing and seeing. Larry couldn't take his eyes off Ronnie. This guy wrote this song? And he's got a great voice! And he's fantastic looking! I could imagine that's what was going through everyone's mind as Ronnie brought the song to an end. After a brief moment of disbelief we all broke into a round of applause. 'That was very good Ronnie. Please, sing us another one,' asked Larry. Ronnie then proceeded to play and sing *'Margo Don't Go'* which left us as much in awe as the first song.

The applause that followed, coupled with the screams from outside, indicated for those who didn't already know it, that we were in the presence of someone very special.

Larry first asked Ronnie if he would like to be a professional singer, to which the shy young man simply replied, 'Yes.' 'Tell me again, what was your second name,' asked Larry. 'Wycherley' mumbled Ronnie. 'Well,' said Larry, who was starting to take on his rather camp maternal role, 'we have to find a suitable name for you. Ronnie Wycherley is a nice name but doesn't really describe you. I think you look furious at times when you're singing. So Fury should perhaps be your second name. As for your first name, you have a boy next-door appeal, so we need something like Tommy, but you can't use that because of Tommy Steele. Maybe Bobby or Billy. Yes, Billy, that describes you perfectly. Billy. Billy Fury, we'll call you Billy Fury.' Already I was jealous of him. What a great name. Why couldn't Larry have christened me Billy Fury?

That was it! As cold, calculating and brilliant as it could be. Ronald Wycherley was no more. We were in the presence of the future great Billy Fury.

'I think you should sing on tonight's show. All you have to do is stand there and sing the two songs you have just sung for us. You don't have to do anything else.' Larry said excitedly. With that, Billy was soon kitted out with Kenny Packwood's guitar and a yellow and black style cowboy shirt, from another of the Wildcats, in readiness for his debut.

Concerts were not an ideal medium for getting a message across. The screams and hysteria from teenage audiences over-powered any well-rehearsed musical content and made sound checks and sound systems appear superfluous. All that was really necessary was for the teen idols to turn up, stand there and be screamed at – and then everybody could go home.

It was to this backdrop of audible mayhem that the compere, a young man named Jimmy Tarbuck who was also being given a try out by Larry, did his utmost to get the message across about the new teenage sensation who wasn't on the printed programme or posters. Here was to be the bonus of all bonuses and the audience wouldn't know it.

Although he couldn't be heard, the compere's enthusiasm was enough to let the audience know that something special was about to happen. The only indication was when he raised his left arm in the direction of side stage and on walked this very nervous boy looking like a cross between Elvis and James Dean.

Any decibel meter that may have been in operation would have been rendered useless by the screaming which greeted Billy. On reaching the microphone, he gave a wry smile, looking down at Kenny's guitar and started his intro into *'Maybe Tomorrow.'* The audience was ecstatic. Billy was without a doubt the hit of the show. To stand there with nothing other than a microphone on a stand, a guitar and a pin spot and receive that reception was awesome. Larry couldn't get the ink dry on the contract soon enough.

Having arrived at the Adelphi Hotel in Liverpool, Larry spent most of his time in deep conversation with Chris Reynolds or on the telephone to London. It was obvious that plans were well underway for Billy to be introduced to the world.

Chris Reynolds appreciated Larry only for what he could get out of him, as indeed most people did. Chris was a great friend to Larry's boys and would get very upset at the manner in which Larry often treated us.

As Marty and I sat eating in the Adelphi Hotel bar, Chris came in nursing a large brandy. 'Larry is smitten with this new guy,' whispered Chris. 'He's fixed up a deal with Decca and he's having a poster made for tomorrow's show in Stretford. Larry's putting him on again.' With the possibility of Larry coming over to join us we said goodnight and retired.

Stretford, Manchester is Coronation Street country. It was the friendly folk from this area who were to be first in line for the Billy Fury experience. The poster in the centre of the foyer gave them an indication as to what was in store for them. It read, 'Appearing tonight, for the first time, The New Teenage Rage,' a mantle I had been wearing for the Extravaganza tour, 'BILLY FURY'. Again Billy was a bit hit.

The audience loved him. Following the show we headed for the Midland Hotel, Manchester, where for some of us things took a dramatic turn for the worse.

Marty, Chris, Larry, Billy and I were sitting in the lounge enjoying a nightcap. We had an early start the next morning as we were all flying back to London. Marty and I were sharing a room and we were the first to say goodnight.

Following our ablutions, we started to discuss what Billy was letting himself in for by sharing with Larry. We knew as we had both been there. Marty and I started a running commentary taking a line each:

'Billy's in the bathroom,' said Marty.

'Larry is waiting under the sheets clutching the Vaseline,' said I.

'Billy is brushing his teeth for the 25th time,' giggled Marty.

'Larry asks Billy what's taking him so long,' I said.

'Billy comes out of the bathroom.'

'Larry pulls the sheet back for Billy to get into bed.'

'Billy picks up the table lamp and jumps on the bed.'

'Larry chases Billy,' and so it went, with Marty and I getting more and more excited and animated, jumping from bed to bed as our respective turn came to deliver a line. Eventually we calmed down and went to sleep.

The next morning at breakfast we arrived in the dining room to find Chris Reynolds sat on his own at a table for five. We joined him and ordered breakfast.

Chris asked us if we had seen Larry. We told him we hadn't. 'You two are in big trouble,' said Chris while trying not to laugh. 'Why?' we asked in unison. With that Larry walked into the dining room with Billy. Instead of joining us at our table for five, they sat at a table for two that couldn't have been farther away without being in the street. It appeared we had been well and truly ostracised.

Chris continued to relate our tale of woe,

of how Larry and Billy left the bar to go to bed shortly after us, and how Larry had forgotten his room key – to his room directly opposite ours. So he decided to come to our room and use our telephone to get the key sent up. Then, upon arriving at our bedroom door he overheard our running commentary on the imaginary events in his and Billy's room.

Explaining the eavesdropping disaster, Chris found it harder and harder not to burst into laughter. Marty and I however were not seeing the funny side.

As Chris finished his summary, Billy walked up to our table and very nervously informed Marty and me that Larry wanted to see us one at a time. 'He wants to see you first, Marty,' mumbled Billy. With that, Billy disappeared and Marty joined Larry at his table.

Larry's dialogue with Marty was intense. You could see he was furious. I was hoping, with Marty being the senior player, he would be getting the brunt of Larry's anger. Perhaps Larry would have calmed down by the time my turn came. I was soon to find out.

As Marty eased his gangly frame out of the chair and began to walk back to our table I could see the fear in his eyes. A frowning Marty told me it was my turn. With that he gave me a 'good luck, you're going to need it' look.

As soon as I was within earshot of Larry his tirade began. It was one-way traffic. I didn't stand a chance. Larry went on to relate the story as Chris had told it, the only difference being the ending. Larry told me he had received an offer of £80,000 for Marty's contract, which he would be selling, and as for me, I was finished in show business. With that he dismissed me.

It wasn't long before we were aboard a flight from Manchester Ringway to London's Heathrow. Billy was making his first flight and it wasn't one he would forget. Turbulence had the plane bouncing around like a cork in the ocean. My first act, as Billy's companion, was to get him a sick bag, then another and another. He was throwing up for the whole flight. His once pale complexion had faded to pure white.

At Heathrow we were met by one of Larry's drivers and taken to Larry's Knightsbridge apartment and my London home. Once inside the apartment Larry gave Billy the guided tour.

'This room will be yours, Billy. My room is the next on the right and Vince's room is at the end of the corridor,' said Larry in his usual motherly manner. 'Vince will show you around the rest of the apartment as I have to go to the office and get things moving for you.'

I had just received the first indication that perhaps I wasn't finished in the business after all. Having expected to be frog marched and put on any train heading anywhere, I was relieved to have been given what appeared to be a stay of execution and a new flatmate.

All the Nice Boys Loved a Sailor

Describing the months leading up to Larry's departure to his new Marble Arch apartment as a roller coaster ride, would be an understatement. Larry's emotions would swing like the pendulum on a grandmother clock. One minute he would be acting the role of a good friend and mentor, the next he would be breathing fire and acting like a spoilt child.

As the new kid on the block, and with my relegation, Billy was very much in demand. Recording *Maybe Tomorrow* and the run of promotional work he was involved in took up most of his time.

Initially my role was to escort Billy and show him around, and with neither of us having a driving license or access to a car it didn't take us long to get to know many of the West End taxi drivers. It also enabled us to get to know some of the dancers and escorts from certain West End clubs.

Billy's contract and my own were very different and were to become the subject of both future legal and domestic wrangling. As we were classed as minors, our respective parents had the responsibility of signing on our behalf. Billy's was the first of Larry's contracts not to operate on a percentage. Mine was a 60/40% split with me receiving 60%. Expenses etc. were apportioned in various ways.

I was also to discover that Larry would receive all record royalties with me not receiving a penny until twenty years later. Billy's contract was an increasing annual basic salary with Larry picking up most of the expenses. His first year was £1,000 (£20 per week), the second year £2,000 (£40 per week), the third £3,000 per year and so on.

As I received a salary only if and when I worked I was often without a penny to my name. Billy however received his £20 salary on a weekly basis. Unfortunately he would often have to pay for the taxis out of his own pocket and he could finish up waiting weeks to get his expenses. Consequently more often than not we didn't have enough for a cup of coffee.

Larry enjoyed cruising Piccadilly Circus and Leicester Square in the hope of picking up sailors or marines. When returning to the apartment late in the evening, service personnel coats and hats hanging on the clothes rack in the hall would often greet us. Larry would also chat up prospective lays by promising them they would get to meet Tommy Steele, Marty Wilde, Billy or me if they came back to his apartment.

On one occasion Tommy was summoned to the apartment late one night in order for Larry to prove to a couple of sailors that he was his manager.

Larry introduced the sailors by saying, 'Tommy, I would like you to meet two very good friends of mine,' and turning to the sailors asked, 'What were your names again?'

Obviously not all the guys who came back to Larry's apartment gave in to his advances. I overheard one guy threatening Larry with a hammering if he didn't get to meet Tommy.

Getting Our Own Back!

Lying before us, appropriately face down, was Larry Parnes, the man who controlled a big chunk of British pop, and our destiny. He was a man who was a ruthless businessman, an entrepreneur second to none and a man who would manipulate anything and everything to get his evil way with his chosen ones. Billy and I were two of the chosen ones and up to that point we had either spurned or avoided his advances.

Larry was in pain, and had asked Billy and I to ease it with Algipan, which had been prescribed by his doctor. 'To be applied sparingly on the area to be treated,' read the prescription notes on the box. 'Where does it hurt Larry?' I asked.

'Just above my waist-line in the middle,' mumbled Larry from within his pink lace-edged pillow. Gripping the tube, I began to squeeze, and squeeze, and squeeze. Within seconds the entire contents of the tube had been squirted onto his back.

As Billy and I massaged the cream into Larry's lower back, we figured the pleasure of the hands of two young males massaging close to his buttocks would soon disappear, when the effect of applying the whole tube of cream would take effect – and it did.

Larry groaned a little, 'That's very warm,' he mumbled. 'Oooh, it's getting very hot Vince.'

'Perhaps it's meant to, Larry,' I replied, as I tried not to laugh.

'Oooh, it's really hurting. How much cream have you put on Vince?' asked Larry in a muffled voice.

'The whole tube Larry,' I replied.

With that, Larry was off the bed and running towards this shower as if he had a Roman candle up his backside. 'Call the doctor, quickly,' he screamed hysterically.

Being private, the doctor who had issued the prescription appreciated Larry's business. I think Larry was his pension plan. By the time he arrived, Larry was writhing in a bath full of cold water. 'Why didn't you read the prescription notes?' asked the doctor. 'There weren't any,' I replied innocently.

By now Larry was screaming for help. Two injections and painkillers were all that the doctor could administer to ease Larry's obvious pain. Having accomplished what we set out to do, Billy and I left Larry's Marble Arch penthouse, anxious to report to friends, families, and colleagues as well as Larry's adversaries – of his misfortune.

In order not to implicate ourselves too deeply, much of what really happened was left to the imagination. However, the smiles that accompanied our explanation indicated that, put before a jury, we could have been found guilty of grievous bodily harm.

UFOs in Knightsbridge?

As well as being perfect for our Scalextric car racing game, the huge marble table adorning the lounge of our apartment was also great for building Airfix model aircraft. Billy was a very patient guy and he would spend hours building model planes from kits.

Billy would display his planes on the ledge of the lounge bay window, which had a door leading onto the balcony overlooking Gloucester Road. The person least impressed with his handiwork was our cleaner Janet who was always complaining about how they collected dust.

Billy built over fifty planes during our penthouse stay and he would take great delight in placing them all on the marble table with the smaller models at the front and the bigger ones at the rear. He would often pick one up, run around the lounge whilst making a plane engine noise and use the table as an airstrip.

The planes were excellent quality with some having wheels on the undercarriage which allowed them to be pushed freely across the marble-topped table. It was one of the planes falling off the table after taxiing that led to one of Billy's most infamous, and dangerous, pranks.

Following a successful landing, one of the larger planes fell off the tabletop and tumbled towards the floor, breaking its wing on the arm of a dining chair. As Billy rescued the pieces he decided it was beyond repair and, opening the door leading onto the balcony, he pulled his cigarette lighter from his pocket, flicked the lighter and set fire to the plane. I had built planes myself as a kid but had no idea as to how volatile they were.

As soon as the flames took hold, Billy

launched the plane and it descended at a great rate of knots to Gloucester Road below where it hit the pavement and shattered. Thankfully it was late at night with few people around and there were no repercussions.

The plane descending at such a pace was an anti-climax to what Billy had hoped for. He said, tongue in cheek, he was hoping it would have flown further.

Close to the balcony, was Larry's state of the art Hi-Fi system with an in-built record storage rack. Larry's selection of records ranged from demos to top singles and album hits by the likes of Johnnie Ray. A selection that mirrored his lifestyle as much as his profession.

The record, which was Larry's pride and joy, was a promotional recording made by Dean Martin and Jerry Lee Lewis promoting one of their movies called 'The Caddy'. They had made it when they finished the official sound trailer for the movie, along with a few bottles of booze in the process. It was disgusting.

'C is for – c??t,' said Jerry amidst fits of laughter from him and hilarity from others present.

'A is for arse,' replied Dean in much more sombre tones.

'And D is for dick,' screeched a drunken Jerry.

And so it went. It got worse and worse as the trailer progressed until it finished in hysterics amidst obscenities, the likes I have never heard before, or since!

As Billy pondered the failure of his flying inferno, he started to finger through Larry's records as if searching for something specific. He suddenly stopped. He'd found it. He picked up the X-rated promotional recording of the film 'The Caddy', by Dean and Jerry, walked towards the balcony giggling, 'I bet this will fly further,' and threw the record like a Frisbee into the black night over Gloucester Road.

'Dean and Jerry' did indeed fly much further than the ill-fated plane, so much so that it landed on the roof of the building opposite. And so a new sport was born. When old or unwanted records came into our possession we would have record tossing contests off the balcony, the highest points being awarded for landing on top of a moving double-decker bus as it passed by below.

Thankfully, our supply of useable records was restricted and we eventually moved before our collars could be felt.

Billy the Kid

On the few occasions Billy and I were solvent, we would treat ourselves to all manner of things – from Airfix plane kits to air rifles. Our biggest social investment was the purchase of a Scalextric car racing game and it didn't take us long to discover that the Italian marble top table in our apartment made the perfect base for high-speed racing. The air rifle Billy bought however, proved to be less fun, especially for me.

During my period of being in Larry's bad books, he would often ask me to drive Billy to appointments. It was while getting ready for a trip one day that 'Billy the Kid' decided to test his prowess as a gunslinger.

Of the six rooms that led off the main corridor in the apartment, my bedroom was at the end facing the lounge, a distance of about 45 feet.

As I turned the handle and opened the door towards me, I heard a click followed by a thud then a pinging noise. They were sounds I hadn't heard before and prompted me to close the partially open bedroom door much quicker than I had opened it.

Opening the door again, only with much more trepidation, I heard the same sound; this time I felt something brush my leg. Looking down I discovered an air rifle pellet nestling in the thick shag pile carpet. It was Billy's doing. He was firing at me every time I tried to open the door.

I shouted to Billy to pack it in and let me out. My demands were met by a laughing that always gave Billy away. He had a habit of putting his tongue between his teeth when he laughed which at times would make him sound a little girlie, something he most certainly wasn't.

After a few more shots in my direction Billy relented and let me open the door. I guess being the big animal lover that he was, he would rather have a human target for practising than one of his feathered or furry friends.

Evenin' Both!

The period Billy and I spent together in Larry's Penthouse at 7 Gloucester Road was, at times, very emotional. Being recognised one minute, as we were, even more so when we were together, and then figuring out how we could get some cash together to eat, left us somewhat bemused. How could we be screamed at, autograph hunted and chased by girls, yet often couldn't afford a bus or tube?

It was obvious that Larry's objective was to have total control of everything about us, from our professional lives to the most intimate actions of our personal lives and the best way to achieve that was to restrict our access to cash and prevent us from becoming independent.

Of the initial, 'Larry Parnes stable of singers', Billy and I were the only artistes not living at home. Tommy Steele, Marty Wilde, Joe Brown, Colin Hicks, Duffy Power and Dickie Pride were all Londoners who lived with their parents and slept in their own beds most nights. Billy and I however didn't get the opportunity to talk to our parents very often as they were without telephones and had to rely on the public phones to call us. Larry's attempted control of Marty and Tommy would often create hostility from their families.

There were innumerable tabloid stories relating to Larry falling out with Tommy's mother, Mrs Hicks and I understand he often felt the wrath of Mary's mother and father, Mr and Mrs Smith.

The Italian Restaurant, situated on the ground floor of the building topped by our Penthouse was, in many ways, more responsible for the success of Messrs Fury and Eager than Parnes himself, as they kept us alive! Their generosity in keeping us in complementary Italian food was much more appreciated than anything Larry did for us, but it wasn't just their complementary pastas that kept us going. The kindness and advice they served up was often more fulfilling and went a long way towards making up for us not being able to talk to our families on a regular basis.

Forever may the legacy of their kindness remain, as their Spaghetti Bolognese and friendliness became a benchmark for my future love of Italians and their food.

Desperate situations often demanded desperate measures when it came to resolving our financial shortcomings. Meeting the girls from Murray's Cabaret Club in the Freight Train Coffee Bar at 2 am. required three prerequisites: money, transport, and a late departure from the apartment. Thankfully we found a way of obtaining them all in one operation.

Before retiring, Larry would place his money and car keys next to a photograph of crooner Johnnie Ray on his pink, lace covered dressing table. It was only a short crawl over the thick, white shag pile carpet from Larry's bedroom door to the dressing table. A crawl on all fours that Billy or I were happy to make, in order to execute our three-point plan and meet the Murray's girls.

Larry's regular snoring pattern kicking in was akin to a starter's pistol being fired; it let us know when it was time to go. One of us would open the door gently and the other would crawl to the dressing table and take a couple of £1 notes from Larry's usually thick, wad of money plus his car keys. Mission accomplished, we would head around the corner from the apartment to Queens Road where Larry's pink and grey

Vauxhall Cresta was parked.

Billy having no driving experience whatsoever, but me having a provisional driving licence, automatically made me the designated driver.

Once we had arrived in the West End, time would determine what we would get up to. If it was close to midnight we would cruise around and call into various coffee bars for a coffee or a Coca Cola and check out the girls. If it was closer to 2 am we would usually head directly to Chas McDevitt's Freight Train Coffee Bar where we would await the arrival of the girls from Murray's.

It was on one such occasion, when cruising past the 'Expresso Coffee Bar' the location for Cliff Richard's movie Expresso Bongo, that our late night sorties came very close to being exposed.

The one problem I had with driving Larry's Vauxhall Cresta car was the gearshift lever located on the driving column. It was as if there was no reverse gear and no matter how hard I tried I could never find it. This meant that random parking was out of the question and I had to ensure that when parking, I could get out without having to engage reverse gear.

As we passed the Coffee Bar, a policeman stepped into the road ahead of us, raised his arm and beckoned us to stop. Having wound down the window, and being fans of the BBC TV series Dixon of Dock Green, 'Evening all,' was what we expected. Not, 'Now then my two rock 'n' rolling friends. What are we up to this morning?'

Being recognised was a lottery. If someone liked you then it usually ended in smiles, but if they didn't, especially a cop, you could be in for a hard time. On this occasion it ended in panic as PC Plod brought to my attention that we were driving the wrong way in a one-way street and that we should turn around. Turn around? You show me where reverse is mate and I'll give it a go, I thought! Billy and I gave the constable nervous smiles as I told him that I would turn around after the bend in the road ahead. With that we wished him goodnight and drove away slowly. As we rounded the corner ahead, the constable disappearing from my rear view mirror was the cue for me to put the pedal to the metal.

Murray Girls! Murray Girls! The Too Good to Hurry Girls!

When we weren't performing in Sunday concerts, Billy and I would invite girls to the penthouse at 7 Gloucester Road, Knightsbridge. We both hated the 'Larry's Boys' tag and did everything we could to show that we were healthy, active heterosexuals. It must have been the only time Larry's bed had seen heterosexual action.

As Billy and I didn't drink, there was very little booze, but a few of the girls would carry aphrodisiac inhalants they obtained from American businessmen who visited the club. With Viagra not having yet been invented, some of them would arrive from the States with a little bottle they would sniff before trying it on with the girls. It was some form of aphrodisiac and it did work. Although we didn't need it, the girls insisted we try it and it certainly gave you an edge in the longevity department.

The club was closed on Sundays so if you were dating, or wanting to date any of the girls, Sunday was the day – otherwise you would be expected to visit the club and pay through the nose for the girl's company. Two of the girls who graced us with their presence at the penthouse, but separately, and who both later went on to achieve international notoriety, were Christine Keeler and Mandy Rice Davies.

We hadn't seen them at work in Murray's, but we soon discovered Christine was a stripper when she gave us an impromptu performance. Mandy came to the apartment at a later date but wasn't as entertaining as Christine had been.

It was a few years later during the Profumo scandal that one of Larry's former road managers, Peter Dixon, reminded me of their visits to the apartment.

Following out of town concerts, Chas McDevitt's Freight Train Coffee Bar in Wardour Street was where many of the musicians and artistes would head for. The coffee bar developed a reputation for celebrity spotting and consequently for picking up girls. It was also where the hostesses from Murray's Cabaret Club headed to relax when the arduous task of emptying the wallets of their wealthy American clients was done and dusted.

The girls were very generous to us; always plying us with coffee or Coca Cola if we were skint, which was more often than not.

It was not uncommon for us all to leave the Freight Train at 4 or 5 am and head for Southend. American ten-pin bowling was emerging as a popular sport and bowling alleys were opening up all over the country, one of the biggest being at Southend. Southend Bowl was open 24 hours a day and had a breakfast special. If you booked a certain number of games you got a free breakfast. It was perfect. Have a bowl and breakfast and head back to Knightsbridge where we would sleep until late afternoon.

We became such regulars at the Southend Bowl that people would come to see us play and get autographs. Bill Bingham, the bowl manager, said thank you by making all our bowling and breakfasts complementary.

Maybe This Morning?

Making a long distance telephone phone call in the 1950s entailed being connected via a variety of operators at difference telephone exchanges en-route. When I phoned my father from London at his workplace in Grantham, my calls would go via the Knightsbridge, Peterborough and Grantham telephone exchanges. Depending on the nature of the calls, operators would often listen in, and if the conversation was really interesting or it was someone they knew, they would tip off their colleagues so they could all listen in.

It wasn't until girls from the Grantham and Peterborough telephone exchanges started turning up at social events and shows I had arranged to go to, that I realised what they were up to. It was due to their listening in to one such phone call that Billy and I met up with Hilary and Margaret, two lovely girls from the Peterborough exchange who seemed determined to get their hands on us, and they succeeded.

They arrived at a Sunday party we had arranged and Hilary and Billy hit it off immediately and became an item.

Hilary would then meet Billy at shows, or

come down to London for a weekend, and it was on one such occasion when Hilary missed her last train back to Peterborough that Billy faced a dilemma.

Billy had met, and got on very well with Hilary's mother, but he knew she wouldn't be too happy if Hilary didn't make it to work on the Monday morning, so a drastic situation demanded drastic action.

Larry was in Switzerland for a few days and his pink Vauxhall Cresta car was parked in its usual place in Queens Gate. Billy and I had used the car on many occasions to go to the West End without Larry's knowledge, so why not now. The car keys were on Larry's dressing table so Billy, who had now learned how to drive, grabbed the keys, grabbed Hilary, and headed for Peterborough.

What happened next, according to Billy, was that he had a puncture on the A1 and discovered he had no spare tyre. As it was 3 am and they were miles from anywhere, they decided to walk.

A short distance down the road they came across a small garage which was closed. There was a cottage on the land adjoining the filling station, so Billy decided to try and wake the occupants by throwing pebbles at the window. Apparently it didn't take long before the window opened and a gruff male voice shouted, 'What the fuck do you want?' Billy, in his most polite and calming tone,

129

explained what had happened and asked the man if he knew where they could get help.

Hilary then chipped in and told the grumpy man, 'He's Billy Fury the singer!'

'You're Billy Fury? What you doin' out ere at this time o' night?'

'We're driving to Peterborough and we've got a puncture,' replied Billy.

'How do I know you're Billy Fury? Sing me a song,' he demanded.

Billy sang, *'Rise in the morning. You're not around etc,'* in singing the first few lines of his hit *Maybe Tomorrow*, neither Billy, Hilary, nor the man at the window, had realised how appropriate the lyrics were.

The man then interrupted Billy's serenading, telling him he sounded like Billy Fury and that he would come down. Once he was standing next to Billy, and realised it was him, his demeanour changed and he was joined by his wife who offered Hilary a cup of tea while Billy and his newfound fan set off to fix the puncture.

After gluing a patch on the inner tube, the man told Billy that it was only a temporary measure and he must put in a new inner tube as soon as possible.

A week later Billy and I were confronted by a steaming Larry who was furious at having had a flat tyre in Leicester Square at midnight and then finding out that it had only recently been fixed. On occasions

Larry would loan his car to 'friends' he had met while he was out cruising around the West End, so maybe even he thought it was ironic that it should happen while looking for 'new friends'. Obviously Billy and I never admitted to anything.

Blood Brothers

'Wince, do you have any sticking plasters?' screamed 'Boots', our German tour manager, as he rushed into my dressing room. 'Doze fucking idiots have cut der fucking vrists and are bleeding.'

We were backstage at the Grand Theatre Wolverhampton before our Sunday night concert and the start of our second week of a month-long tour. Boots was Tommy Steele's regular tour manager but Tommy was on holiday so Larry had seconded Boots to us for a month.

There was a world of difference between touring with Tommy Steele and touring with Messrs Billy Fury, Dickie Pride, Duffy Power, Georgie Fame, Joe Brown, Tommy Bruce, Vince Eager *et al.*

Boots just couldn't get to grips with our life styles, and walking into Billy and Dickie's dressing room and finding the pair of them cutting the palms of their hands with a razor blade in order to become blood brothers, proved to be the last straw.

Patience Was a Virgin

Greasy spoon style all night transport cafés were the life blood of late night travellers. There were no fancy names or giveaways to encourage custom. Just the unhealthiest food money could buy. It was a cholesterol kicking combination of fried eggs, fried bacon and fried bread, all dripping in fat and swilled down by a mug of heavily sugared tea. Yes, this was the basic diet of those who found themselves on the Queen's highways and byways between the hours of midnight and 7 am.

In order for a transport café to achieve five-star status, an essential item of furniture required was a jukebox. The chances were that some of us who were travelling to and from shows would have a record out and it could be featured on the café's jukebox. If it was, we would get a big kick out of hearing it played, especially if chosen by a burly grease-laden lorry driver addicted to transport café fry-ups, and not a weak-kneed teeny bopper.

Tony's café on the A1, south of my hometown of Grantham, was certainly worthy of five stars. It was one of the most popular, and the one I knew best as I often went there with my driver and road manager Noel when visiting my family.

On an early morning return to London from Doncaster, Billy Fury, Tommy Bruce, Dickie Pride and our musicians and I made the mandatory visit to Tony's. At 1 am the café was very busy and heads turned as we walked in. We were well known to most transport drivers and were on Christian name terms with some.

As we stood in line waiting to place our order, Tommy became impatient and mumbled in his inimitable gravely voice, 'C'mon darlin' Tom Tom's gonna waste away.'

It was at this point that Billy, who was just ahead of Tommy in the queue, turned, and giggling said, 'Just remember Tommy, Patience is a virgin,' and continued giggling. Tommy's retort was, 'You mean patience is a virtue Bill.' 'No, she really is a virgin Tom,' replied Billy who knew exactly what he had said and was by now laughing his head off.

Only a few of us knew that at the time Billy was seeing a girl named Patience.

Larry's Song

Having boarded the tour bus at Marble Arch we headed for our show at the Woolwich Granada. On the back seat of the bus, and in their usual prankish mood were

Billy Fury and Dickie Pride.

As we passed through the Elephant and Castle, Billy and Dickie burst into uncontrollable fits of laughter. They then started humming the hit tune to *Jimmy Brown* by the Three Bells, which was punctuated by loud whispering and giggling. As we neared Woolwich we discovered the reason for their antics as they burst into song.

The Elephant and Castle had obviously got their artistic juices flowing as they sang a song they had composed about Larry. The gist of the song was Larry's lifestyle, and his lusting after young boys on his late night cruising around Piccadilly Circus and Leicester Square.

The last line was to the tune of *Jimmy Brown*, 'So they buried his big arsehole, in the Elephant and Castle, farewell to the biggest queer.'

They never did record it!

Treading the Boards

No Arm in It!

Leaving the West End night clubs of Churchill's, and then Winston's, was a wrench. I had learnt a lot about stagecraft and life during those six short months. But it was Larry's opinion that a rock 'n' roll variety show, similar to the full week theatre presentations, could work on a one-nighter basis and I was to be part of that show.

He called the show Extravaganza. Marty topped the bill, with The John Barry Seven, magician Mike Coyne, girl singer Pat Laurence, comedy duo Daly and Wayne and myself. The tour was on the Essoldo Theatres' circuit and the opening show was at the Burnt Oak Essoldo in North London. Years later I was to discover that Elton John had appeared on the Michael Parkinson Show and revealed that it was seeing the Extravaganza show on that particular night that made him want to play rock 'n' roll.

One of the early dates was the Loughborough Essoldo in Leicestershire. A town not too far from my hometown of Grantham Lincolnshire, and the first opportunity for my family and friends to see me perform as 'Vince Eager: The New Teenage Rage'.

I decided to get a train to Grantham the day before and travel with my parents to the theatre on the day of the performance. All the other artistes would travel in The John Barry Seven coach. An old British European Airways coach, which looked much like a semi double-decker bus with a very high back and a massive luggage area. It was perfect for touring a show.

Upon arriving at the theatre I bumped into Larry's publicist Chris Reynolds running through the theatre foyer. I wanted to introduce him to my folks but he appeared to be preoccupied with something more important. A few minutes later I saw Marty with bandages on his hands. I asked him what the problem was and he said he would tell me later.

When I finally met someone who was prepared to explain what was going on, it transpired that during the journey from London to Loughborough there had been a small fire on the bus. It was brought under control following a short roadside delay and they continued the journey to Loughborough. Chris Reynolds decided however to phone Larry and inform him of what had happened, as there was a possibility they could arrive late at the theatre.

Larry took no time in instructing Chris to wrap Marty's hands in bandages, then phone his Fleet Street contacts and inform them that Marty had put out a blaze on the tour bus and saved the lives of those travelling with him. Chris duly obliged and, sure enough, many of the following days national newspapers carried the story.

Larry's initials were L.M.P. Laurence Maurice Parnes, which prompted his nickname of 'Parnes, Shillings and Pence', but I preferred, 'Larry Manufactures Publicity'.

I Got It at Curry's

Debutantes' coming-out parties were great gigs. The daughters of the rich and famous would have parties in their honour to celebrate their coming of age and mark their introduction to society.

Anywhere from The Grosvenor House Hotel in Park Lane, to a giant marquee in mummy and daddy's back garden acted as the venue for these lavish events.

Big bands, orchestras, jazz units and string quartets had been the norm for many years. The more famous the entertainment, the more credibility the coming out would have.

In the late 1950s the daughters had more to say in the choice of musical entertainment. As the big bands and classical style music became less in demand, the pop stars began to take centre stage.

In 1959 I was booked for a party in Eton

139

on the Hill, the home of Eton School. I was informed that the party was for the daughter of the Chairman of Curry's Electrical stores and was taking place at their home.

On occasions where the party was at the home of a debutante, bedrooms would often be allocated as changing rooms. For the Curry's party my band was given one room and I had another to myself. At the time it was of no significance but later it proved to be very significant. We finished our set to a great reception and were waylaid by young ladies in crinoline gowns baying for autographs and kisses as we returned to our changing bedrooms.

On reaching my bedroom cum changing room, I went straight into the en-suite bathroom to get out of my sweaty clothes and freshen up with a shower. With just a towel around my waist I emerged from the bathroom to be greeted by two young ladies who were in the bed. Their crinoline gowns strewn on the floor, they pulled back the bedclothes to reveal themselves wearing only their underwear, which was sufficient for me to show them why Larry had named me Eager.

I could never say no to a curry!

'One Night' with Danny Rivers

Danny Rivers was not a Larry Parnes' artiste – but should have been. He had a great voice and was a great rock 'n' roller, and nobody in the business had a greater sense of humour. The fact that he didn't get a fair crack of the whip recording-wise was maybe due to his carefree attitude and somewhat rebellious nature.

When their contracts ran out, Marty and Joe, and many other Parnes' artistes, joined the George Cooper Organisation, an up and coming management agency that cared for their artistes, and it was during a George Cooper Sunday night concert at the Dudley Hippodrome, near Wolverhampton, that Danny gave his most memorable performance.

There, as at many venues, George asked me to be the company manager and compere in addition to performing.

Dudley Hippodrome was a very rare venue in that it had a bar in its Green Room (a room where artistes could relax), which was open on a Sunday. Being partial to a tipple, it was here that Danny headed after rehearsals.

The first house was at 6 pm, with the second at 8.30 pm. Danny's spot was in the first half of the show and his opening song was the Elvis Presley hit, *One Night*.

When introduced, Danny would be discovered centre stage, lit by a tight spotlight, and sensually gripping the microphone stand. As the song progressed, he would slide slowly down the microphone stand, finishing prostrate as he ground his hips suggestively against the microphone stand and the stage. He would then slowly raise himself up from the stage, while caressing the microphone stand, with the audience screaming hysterically.

After his first house performance, Danny retired to the Green Room bar, and as his time to go on stage for the second show drew closer the result of his heavy drinking took effect.

I knew nothing of this, as I waited side-stage to introduce him. I only knew that he wasn't there. I asked our mutual pal Michael Cox, (who made the hit record *Angela Jones)* if he would fetch Danny as he was due on. Danny eventually appeared with his shirt outside his pants and without his jacket and tie, and he was also having trouble walking.

I then asked Michael to try and find Danny's jacket in time for his performance and padded out his introduction with a joke, in the hope that it would give them time to get the jacket and make Danny look presentable.

'Please welcome the star of "Oh Boy" and top recording sensation, the fantastic, Danny

Rivers,' I shouted out to the hysterical audience. With that, a spotlight picked up Danny, who was hanging onto the microphone stand, this time not sexually, but for dear life to stop himself from falling over!

As the band played the introduction to *One Night*, Danny could no longer hang onto the microphone stand and sank slowly to the stage, where his writhing became even more animated than usual, and the audience's screaming grew louder than ever.

At the end of *One Night*, Danny remained laying on the stage. In normal circumstances he would get up to start his next number, but not this time. He was incapable. The band started his next song but Danny stayed down. There was a slope, which ran down into the footlight well from the stage, and it was covered in a linoleum-type material. As Danny was singing and trying more and more to get a purchase on the slope with his foot, he slipped further down into the footlights and I had to instruct the electrician to turn the footlights off. At 250 watts a light he would have been roasted alive! Danny remained in the well for his entire act as he sang every song lying down.

The situation presented me with two problems. First, how to get him off the stage without the audience knowing, and secondly, how to stop Michael and myself from peeing ourselves with laughter as we looked on.

We devised a plan to give a full blackout and close the curtains at the end of his act. I would then go on stage and stand extreme stage left in a tight pin-spot to introduce the next act and Michael and a stagehand would then slide under the curtains, grab Danny's feet and pull him back behind the curtains.

It went like clockwork, but I dried up with laughter during my introduction of the next artist as I watched Danny sliding face down and feet first under the curtain.

Home of the Brave

'You and your band are going to Scotland for four weeks,' said my manager Larry.

With most of my TV appearances in the late 1950s being on the BBC, there was a brief period when my profile in Scotland was greater than that of both Marty Wilde and Cliff Richard. Apparently it was due to television transmissions and where they were, or were not, received.

When ITV was launched it took a few months for their transmitter to be operational and for their signal to reach Scottish viewers, consequently the viewers had to be content with what the BBC had to offer. Marty and Cliff were mainly on ITV's 'Oh Boy' Show whilst I was a regular on BBC's

'Six Five Special' and 'Drumbeat.'

We had been booked to tour Scotland by Duncan McKinnon, a ballroom promoter based in Melrose on the border region of Scotland. Larry told us to call at Duncan's office in Melrose on the way to our first appearance in Cowdenbeath, a Scottish town which, up until then, I could only associate with the football results on BBC Radio's Saturday evening 'Sports Report.'

My band, The Quiet Three, consisting of Kenny Packwood, guitar, Tex Makins, bass and Jimmy Nicol, drums, and my road manager, Noel Wallis and myself arrived in a farmyard in the beautiful Scottish Borders which bore the address given to us as Duncan's Office. As we pulled into the yard chickens scattered everywhere. It transpired that chickens were Duncan's main business.

No kilt or sporran, but with a very strong Scottish accent and looking more like a character out of the Archers than a rock 'n' roll promoter, Duncan welcomed us to Scotland and invited us into, what he referred to as 'the inner sanctum', his office. Consisting of a desk with a few papers scattered on it, and what looked like a wardrobe in the corner, it was a far cry from Larry's austere Oxford Circus set up.

After fetching in a few chairs, Duncan opened the wardrobe door to reveal shelving from top to bottom, which accommodated malt whiskey. Tex, Jimmy and Kenny suddenly developed smiles, the likes of which I had never seen before.

Every bottle label was facing forward and revealed that they contained Glen Grant Malt Whisky. We discovered later that Duncan was a major shareholder in the company.

Thinking they had died and gone to heaven, the boys happily accepted Duncan's offer of 'a wee dram,' but due to Noel having to drive, and me not drinking alcohol, we declined. As the afternoon rolled on with the atmosphere becoming more and more relaxed, Jimmy reminded us that his supply of drum sticks was getting low and that he needed to stock up before the gig.

Duncan told us of Browns, a well-known music shop in Edinburgh that stocked everything musical. He offered to phone the shop manager, who was a personal friend of his, and arrange for him to stay on after closing time in the event that we were late. With 'The Quiet Three' in a far from quiet mood, we set off for Edinburgh, and Brown's Music Shop some 40 miles away.

It was past 6.00 pm and Brown's was closed, fortunately Duncan's telephone call had alerted the manager to our late arrival and we were invited into the shop.

The percussion section was in the basement, and that's where Jimmy was ushered.

Noel and I went with Jimmy, whilst Kenny and Tex remained upstairs in the brass and woodwind department. Over-indulgence in Duncan's malt whisky presented the basement stairs as an obstacle which Kenny and Tex saw as being un-negotiable.

We emerged from the basement with Jimmy's drumsticks to find that Tex and Kenny had returned to the mini bus. Thanking the manager for waiting for us we boarded our mini bus and set off for our first-ever Scottish gig, Cowdenbeath Roller Rink.

We had only travelled a short distance when laughter and indescribable sounds emerged from the back of the bus. I was in the front with Noel and turned around to find out what the commotion was. There was Tex, endeavouring to get a tune out of a brand new trombone, and Kenny by his side holding a brand new clarinet.

It was then revealed that Tex and Kenny had taken advantage of the lack of super-vision in the shop and had just walked out with the instruments and put them in the bus. As we were due in Cowdenbeath within the hour, it was decided we could do nothing until the following morning when I would phone the shop.

Our first night was a sell out and a big success and I was surprised that Duncan wasn't there. His assistant Scotty later informed me that the boys weren't the only ones to have fallen under the influence of Glen Grant!

The following morning I was awakened at 9.15 by a phone call from a less than happy Duncan.

His Glen Grant hangover, coupled with a phone call he had received from Brown's Music Shop manager, resulted in him being anything but the happy generous soul of the previous afternoon. On pain of death if I didn't, Duncan instructed me to contact the manager at Browns and arrange for the return of the 'borrowed' instruments.

The phone call to Browns' manager found him quite cool and indifferent to what had happened. It was only when we returned the instruments later in the day that he explained it was something of a regular occurrence when visiting musicians had been excessive in enjoying the local hospitality and then visited the shop. He then reeled off a list of names, some of whom were household names. His favourite story was of TV trombonist George Chisolm who, under the influence, walked out of the shop with a trombone concealed under his raincoat. George apparently awoke the next morning having slept with the instrument. He then returned to the shop enquiring if the trombone belonged to them.

Duncan didn't mention the incident again

and the manager of Browns' made us very welcome on the many other occasions we visited the shop. It was this initial experience of the friendliness of the Scots that was to make Scotland a very happy hunting ground for Vince Eager & The Quiet Three for years to come.

Big Hearted Sullivan

I was in the process of putting together a new band when I was tipped off about a great guitarist playing at St Mary's Ballroom in Putney on Saturday nights so I decided to check him out. Approaching the ballroom I heard guitar playing which I would have bet on as being Denny Wright from Lonnie Donegan's Skiffle group, but on entering the ballroom I soon discovered it wasn't; though he certainly played like him.

Following an outstanding set I was taken backstage where we were introduced. His name was Jim Sullivan and I told him of shows I had coming up supporting Marty Wilde and offered him the job. Jim accepted and a few weeks later we rehearsed with Bobby Woodman on drums and Tex Makins on bass.

Before the dates with Marty we had a few ballroom dates on our own which gave us a great opportunity to get to know each other and settle in.

During this period, the national and musical press filled many column inches reporting on a feud between Marty and me.

It transpired, as was expected, that our manager Larry was the perpetrator of the story with claims we had fallen out having ordered similar gold lamé stage jackets.

Then false quotes were reported from Marty and me, which turned the whole thing messy. Just what Larry wanted to help promote the shows.

Our first date with Marty was at the Gaumont Theatre in Bournemouth. Following my first half act I was told that Marty had walked across the back of the stage with a towel over his head during *'It's Only Make Believe'*. Larry was there and said he didn't see it and he told me to stay away from Marty until he had determined what had happened.

Later in the show Marty approached Big Jim and asked him what I was paying him. Jim told him £20 per week and Marty offered to double it. It was an offer Jim couldn't refuse and a couple of weeks later he joined the Wildcats. Though very disappointed, I didn't blame Jim or Marty for what happened. Marty had the big hits and Jim helped him to have many more.

There were a number of stories cultivated regarding bad blood between Marty and me, which were totally unfounded. We were both very easy going guys and I have never badmouthed him and I'm sure Marty has never badmouthed me. I have always had the greatest respect for him as a fellow pro and a friend.

Forty years later I booked 'Big Jim', as he had become affectionately known, to appear with me at the Eddie Cochran 40th Anniversary Festival in Chippenham. As both of us had been heavily involved with Eddie during his ill-fated 1960 UK tour, both personally and musically, we were thrilled to be there.

Topping the bill were Bill Haley's original Comets. With a combined age of over 350 years, the five of them were still going strong and wowing the audiences.

Along with my sons' band 'The Avengers', Jim and I were due on stage at 7.30 pm so we agreed to arrive at 5.00 pm in order to give ourselves plenty of time to relax before the show.

As I walked into the arena at 4.30 pm, I discovered Jim relaxing with his lovely wife Norma at a table in the refreshment area. I commented that we were both early to which Norma replied, 'Vince, you have no idea how excited Jim has been about getting here.'

Norma then went on to explain that the Comets' guitarist, Fran Beecher, was Jim's idol and, as a youngster, Jim would copy his solos from the Haley recordings. As this would be the first time Jim had seen Fran live, Jim was hoping to get to meet him afterwards; he was beside himself with excitement. To say I was gob smacked is an understatement. Here was the man who had played on over 1,000 hit records, toured the world with Tom Jones for 5 years, turned down a job offer from Elvis and had been with the James Last Orchestra for 15 years, and he was excited at meeting Fran Beecher.

On hearing this I arranged with the promoter John Knight for us to meet Fran when we came off stage.

As we entered the Comet's dressing room Fran Beecher immediately stood up and walked up to Jim, grabbed him by the hand and before Jim could say anything Fran told Jim he had always wanted to meet him. 'I've watched you so many times on the Tom Jones TV show in America, and with James Last, and you are the greatest,' said Fran.

Jim was speechless! He stood there with an embarrassed grin on his face as Fran continued to shower him with compliments. It was supposed to be Jim paying homage to his hero. Not the other way round. Within minutes the mutual admiration society had reached a peak with each of them asking to have a photograph taken with the other.

Jim also congratulated the Comets on still

going strong after 50 years. 'How do you do it?' he asked.

Fran replied that as this tour of Europe lasted over seven weeks, three of them had been in hospital for 'a service' before coming over.

Two had triple heart bypasses and a one had a hernia operation that they insisted had put them in good shape for the tour.

Not only is Big Jim Sullivan one of the world's greatest guitarists, and nicest people, he's also the most humble.

A Pit of Gold!

The first time I met Joe Brown was at a Sunday night concert at the Romford Odeon. Larry had brought Joe into the backing musicians' line-up for the show to assess his musical prowess. I was closing the first half and had my regular group The Quiet Three backing me, with Joe as a guest guitarist.

Joe stood there like a matchstick with the wood shaved off. It someone had told me that this scrawny, blond, brush-haired Cockney, though he was actually born in Lincolnshire and always refers to himself as being a 'Yellow Belly', would become one of Britain's greatest ever and best-loved performers, I would have said they were nuts.

Likewise, if Larry had had any idea of the

mischief Joe and I would get up to in the years to come he would never have introduced us.

The Romford Odeon was a big theatre that would often feature classical orchestral and ballet productions. It was one of the few cinema/theatres that had the facilities to accommodate such big productions, and part of the stage facilities included an extension to the forward stage area. This was achieved by raising the floor in the orchestra pit and meant that the moat-like area separating the audience from the stage had gone. The stage now finished flush with the first row of the stalls and this was a godsend to artistes who involved the audience. I was one of those acts and I couldn't wait to get at them that Sunday night.

I featured a song by a good friend and great performer, Johnny Kidd, entitled *Please Don't Touch*. It was a big hit for Johnny, and one I loved performing. At the afternoon rehearsal I decided I would jump off the stage into the centre aisle and work in the audience for the finale of my act.

Come the first house performance, the audience were up for the show. I was closing the first half and was determined not to let them down. We also had a VIP guest in the audience. 'Oh Boy' producer Jack Good had come to review the show for his regular 'Disc' magazine column, so I had to be on form.

It's Only Make Believe had once again got the audience on my side and I could pretty much do what I wanted with them. The atmosphere was electric and during the guitar solo in *Please Don't Touch*, I launched myself like an Olympic long jumper into the glare of the spotlights and down into what I thought was the centre aisle, a journey that took far too long for comfort. As the glare of the spotlights disappeared, I felt as if I was falling down a mineshaft, with what light there was disappearing behind me. Suddenly there was an almighty crunch as I hit some immovable object with the velocity of an Exocet missile.

As I got to my feet I felt a pain shoot through my right ankle, but the adrenalin kicked in and numbed it. Gazing up through the smoky haze I saw the spotlight moving overhead as if searching for a target. Gazing down on me were a couple of people I recognised who had been sitting on the front row of the stalls only a few minutes earlier and I suddenly realized I was on the floor of the orchestra pit. They had dropped the forestage without telling me. I felt an object to my right. It was the organ stool, so I put my throbbing right foot on it and forced myself up. As I grabbed the edge of the orchestra pit and pulled myself up, the spotlight picked me out like a rabbit in a car's headlight.

The audience gave out an almighty cheer

as I straddled the ledge and then finally stood in the centre aisle where my leap of faith should have taken me in the first place.

It was then that I realised that I was still singing! As the audience clapped in time to the music I made my way back to the stage thinking of my ironic choice of song, *Please Don't Touch!*

My arrival back in the dressing room, coupled with the sudden drop in my adrenalin level, soon had me realising all was not well with my ankle. I took off my shoe and the football-sized swelling became all too obvious. The general consensus was that I couldn't perform in the second show. However, Larry didn't name me 'Eager' without good reason, so off came the shoe on my left foot. I would perform in my bare feet!

Joe has told this story many times both on-stage and in his great biography, 'Brown Sauce.' He also related the story once on the Simon Dee Show on BBC TV. *Yes Tonight Josephine* was the song Joe seemed to think I was singing at the time, but fellow musicians and audience members have confirmed it was *Please Don't Touch*. 'A pile of gold laying in the orchestra pit,' was Joe's description of me lying on the orchestra pit floor, referring to a gold lamé suit he said I was wearing. A gold jacket it may have been, but even I thought a gold lamé suit would be taking my admiration of Elvis a little too far.

My missile-like antics hurt at the time but didn't do me any harm in the long term. Jack Good gave me a great review and I made a couple of the national newspapers.

Twelve Minutes or No Minutes!

With over 50 TV appearances, three single records, an album and a string of successful theatre dates to my credit, 1959 proved to be a great year. 1960 however was proving to be a different kettle of fish. The ill-fated Eddie Cochran & Gene Vincent tour, Euro-vision Contest problems and my futile efforts to get Larry to allow me to record a big ballad, all happened within the first three months.

Due to him using Eddie Cochran's tragic death to promote his own interests, Larry Parnes no longer figured in my long-term plans and I wanted out of our management agreement. I had however, agreed to appear on his Idols on Parade autumn theatre tour as one of the dates was the Grantham Granada, my hometown theatre where it had all begun. The people of Grantham had been fantastic in supporting The Vagabonds and me so I was really keen to do the date.

Larry was also paying £2,000 for the 10-week tour, much more than he had paid me before.

Mark Forster, who worked in Larry's office, told me it was because he was trying to sweeten me up following my outburst over his handling of Eddie's death, but I was still determined it would be my last tour for him.

The autumn tour contract stipulated a thirty-minute appearance, the same as during my previous summer season with Billy Fury in Great Yarmouth, which had gone very well.

With not having a big hit record to my name, my group The Quiet Three and I worked very hard on my live show, which included the piano, guitar, comedy and audience participation, and I felt the only artiste who had the edge on us was Joe Brown and the Bruvvers. Joe was always looking at ways to improve his stage show and I thought, and still do, that he is awesome.

Two weeks before the start of the tour I received a letter from Larry's office with the running order for the show. It had me down for 12 minutes and not 30 minutes as contracted. I immediately phoned Larry and told him of the mistake. His reply was that as he had more artistes on the bill everybody's performance time would be cut.

I told him that if I couldn't do the 30 minute act I had done in Great Yarmouth, I would pull out of the tour. 'OK,' he replied.

'You're off the tour!' and he put the phone down.

I spent the following few days sounding out colleagues close to Larry as I fully expected him to meet me half way and perhaps offer me 20 minutes, but he never contacted me.

The realisation that I wouldn't be performing in Grantham left me gutted. Having just had such a great season at Yarmouth I was desperate to take my act to Grantham and show them what I had learned.

When I announced my withdrawal from the show it was met with howls of derision in certain quarters of Grantham. From the minute the show posters were put on display, certain elements of the population started to deface them. Being nervous of performing before my hometown crowd was one of the rumours circulating as the reason for me pulling out.

Fellow Granthamian, and good friend and road manager, Noel Wallis proved to be a big asset as he knew the town and he knew the truth. He also defended me vigorously wherever and whenever necessary, helping me through a very difficult period.

I made a statement to the local press that I would be playing the theatre in the not too distant future, and as I was involved with the local Handicapped Children's Society, I would donate my fee and 10 complimentary tickets to them.

My visits to Grantham during the following two years were greeted with the occasional snide remarks from a few people, but I did eventually arrange a date at the Granada in a show with The Temperance Seven and Shane Fenton and the Fentones.

When offered the date, I was told I would be doing 25 minutes. I was quite happy with that, but had an idea as to how I could extend my act to 30 minutes. The night after Grantham we were scheduled to play the Granada in Mansfield, Shane Fenton's hometown. I phoned Shane and asked him if he fancied doing a 30-minute spot in Mansfield.

He said he would love to but we were limited to twenty-five. I then suggested that if he were to give me five minutes in Grantham, he could have it back in Mansfield. That way we both get to do 30 minutes in our respective hometowns. He agreed.

I have never felt as nervous as I did before the show. There were two performances and both were sold out. When I was introduced the audience were quiet, but polite. No hecklers, but no cheers either. Thirty minutes later I walked off to an amazing reception.

My parents were booked for the second show so I arranged to meet them between shows in a nearby hotel. They looked pensive and my father was knocking them back.

'How was it then son?' he asked, but before I could answer him a workmate of his came up and said. 'That's the way to show 'em lad. You were fantastic. No more name-calling. You've shown them!' Word must have got out because when I was introduced for the second show the reception was fantastic. And they've been great ever since.

It's My Father!

It was an idyllic setting. Nestled at the foot of Mount Snaefell on the Isle of Man, it seemed the perfect place to spend the summer. Or was it?

Michael Cox, Danny Rivers and I decided to share a rented bungalow for our four months' summer season at the Crescent Pavilion in Douglas. It didn't matter that it was twelve miles from Douglas. It had three bedrooms. One each!

Arriving in Douglas, we drove off the ferry in convoy. I led the way in my sporty ice blue Triumph Herald Coupe, with Michael as passenger and navigator, followed by Danny in his brand new red Mini. Leaving the port area we picked up the signs and followed the Manx TT motorcycle course towards our destination.

The winding road passed through such places as Quarter Bridge, Union Bridge and

Glen Vine, all familiar names to Manx motorcycle TT race fans and soon to be all too familiar to Danny Rivers, especially Quarter Bridge.

The white bungalow looked picture postcard perfect as the bright sun picked it out at the foot of Mount Snaefell. Being 50-yards up a track, it would have to be a hell of a party to get the neighbours complaining here. You couldn't see them. Sadly it didn't take long for us to discover that looks weren't everything.

Danny's attempt to drink from a bottle of Yates' wine, eat fish and chips, caress a young lady, and steer his Mini car around the Manx TT course with his knees all at the same time was to play a major part in our decision to move from the wilds of Mount Snaefell to the relative comfort of Douglas holiday camp.

Everything was going fine until Danny's knees lost their grip on the steering wheel as he approached Quarter Bridge, the consequences being that the car went through the bridge instead of going over it.

As Danny's back seat resembled a Yates' bottle bank, he decided to get rid of the incriminating evidence immediately after the crash by throwing the empty wine bottles over the bridge and onto the embankment below. Unfortunately the boys in blue discovered his jettisoned stash and used it against him in court where he was found guilty of driving whilst under the influence.

The argument between Danny and Quarter Bridge, the 24-mile daily commute, less one car, sleeping in a cold damp bed, and waking up in dense morning mists in a bungalow that seemed to move further up the mountain every day, made the decision to seek accommodation in Douglas an easy one. Our almost futile search for alternative accommodation eventually led to a suggestion by the theatre manager to contact the Douglas Holiday Camp. They had hundreds of chalets and would maybe do a deal as we were there for such a lengthy period.

The camp manager, Mr Dixon, was extremely helpful and eventually said we could stay for the entire season on a sleep-only basis, subject to two of us sharing a chalet for three of the weeks at the peak period.

As we settled into our 'Hi De Hi' environment the perks rolled in. Free meals, free drinks, free laundry, accommodating chalet maids, chalet upgrades, it was fast becoming Utopia. Mr Dixon, being a shrewd operator, soon saw the opportunity to capitalise on our gratitude.

After a day of heavy rain he asked me if we had settled in and were being well looked after. This was accompanied by a wry smile and an indication that he was referring to the perks we were enjoying.

It was then followed by, 'What would be the possibility of arranging for some of the show musicians to play in the camp ballroom on rainy mornings?' He added hastily, 'I'll arrange for them to have complimentary food and drink while they're here.' I replied that I would put it to the musicians and our manager, George Cooper, and let him know. The alternatives to staying in bed on rainy days in Douglas involved spending money. Consequently the guys were keen to accept the offer of playing for a couple of hours for food and booze.

Having received George's blessing, a deal was struck. It was agreed with Mr Dixon that the musicians would play only when it was raining, and a maximum of two mornings a week, plus he would let me know before 9.30 am so that I could contact them.

One of the biggest entertainment attractions on the island was The Ivy Benson Orchestra, the all-girl orchestra with the reputation of enjoying their own company more than that of their male suitors. The girls were playing at the Palace Ballroom and on our first visit to see them it didn't take Michael and me long to discover that at least two of the girls appeared to prefer male company. The girls were Heather, the pianist, and Gill, a saxophonist. Having taken the girls to dinner after the show, Michael and I then took them back to the camp.

Next morning a banging on the chalet door awakened me. As I shouted 'Come in,' I pulled the sheet over Heather's head to avoid any embarrassment, the door opened to reveal Mr Dixon.

He said it was raining and asked me if I could arrange for the band to play. I told him I would phone them. 'Thanks Vince, I'll see you later,' he said winking yet again, as, at the same time he clutched his right upper arm with his left cupped hand giving the international sign of sexual encouragement between males.

'That was Mr Dixon, the camp manager,' I told Heather as I pulled back the sheet to reveal her flushed yet smiling face.

'Yes, I know, he's also my father!' chuckled Heather.

Heather was a beautiful and talented girl in every way, yet that brief, almost calamitous encounter with her father took the impetus off what I think would have been the beginning of a long relationship.

'ELVIS the Porn Show'

After my audition for the role of the mature Elvis in 'Elvis the Musical', I was offered the role of understudy to PJ Proby. PJ had a reputation for being unpredictable and a bit of a hell-raiser so I didn't fancy the idea of being on standby and having to go on stage at a minute's notice, and declined.

Six months after the show opened rumours were circulating the PJ was hitting the bottle and had fired a gun through his dressing room door. I received a phone call and was offered the role, but commitments prevented me from taking it. A year later it came up again and I took over from Bogdan Kominowski.

From 1980 to 1984, I toured the UK, Europe, South Africa, Australia and Canada with the show, but the memory that will remain with me forever is from the New Theatre, Cardiff.

The show was technically very involved and I witnessed many technicians being brought close to tears as they battled to fix slide and film projectors that had failed just before a show. There were no laptops or computer-generated assistance in those days, as seat of the pants technology was used to project the 300 slides and film, which acted as the backdrop to the award winning show.

American Trilogy was the song usually used for the technical rehearsal and the New Theatre in Cardiff was no exception as, other than the young Elvis and the middle aged Elvis, it featured the entire company plus the projection equipment.

During the flute solo in the song, the musicians, singers and I would turn around and look upstage to the three giant screens behind us, where a film of Elvis's funeral cortège was shown on the centre screen, and photos of fans crying and laying wreaths at the gates of Gracelands were shown on the side screens.

Well, that's what it should have shown. Instead, as we turned around we were greeted with the most explicit pornographic pictures imaginable. Needless to say the entire company were unable to continue as they collapsed into fits of laughter.

There was however one person who didn't see the funny side. That was Martin, who was in charge of the projection equipment and the setting up of the slides before a show. It was Terry, the sound engineer, who had switched the slides and then wanted him to remove them and return them to him. 'There are ten slides so make sure you get them all,' Terry shouted to Martin, who was feverishly going through the trays in search of the offending slides.

As we stood by for the curtain to go up on the evening's performance, Martin was still desperately going through the carousels. 'I can only find eight,' Martin said nervously to Terry via the intercom.

'OK,' replied Terry. 'You'll have to keep an eye on the screen during the show, and when the slides come up advance them very quickly and make a note of where they are.'

With the anxiety showing more and more on Martin's face, and in his voice, Terry gave in. The show being compromised played a much bigger part in Terry's decision than his concern for Martin's health.

It was fortunate for Terry that he was at the rear of the stalls operating the sound desk and in contact with Martin via the intercom. Being any closer could have cost him his life!

Empy and the Fab Four

Who would have thought it, the Emperor of China singing *The Wonder of You* to his beautiful daughter the Princess Balrubador, with vocal backing courtesy of the 900 members of Bath Theatre Royal audience? Of course, it was pantomime, Oh yes it was!

Following *The Wonder of You* was a comedy routine that involved the Fab Four consisting of Henry Kelly, (Wishee Washee), Francis Matthews (Widow Twankey), Barry James (The Policeman), Mark Curry (Grand Viziar) plus yours truly, The Emperor of China, or Empy.

However, this was the last night and anything went. The warning from the Director not to deviate from the script fell on deaf ears. In true last night pantomime tradition everybody ignored the directive, and instead of taking a bow, turned to their right in a well rehearsed manner, and walked off stage leaving yours truly standing there all on my lonesome.

As *The Wonder of You* had turned into something of a showstopper, their idea in leaving me high, dry, and on my lonesome was to pay me back for its success.

What they didn't know was that I was more at ease on stage on my own than with a bunch of thespians.

As they exited stage right, I leant over the footlights and whispered to the musical director, *The Wonder of You*. No sooner had I said it than the orchestra launched into the introduction, which includes the audience singing along, when encouraged.

The audience were in fine voice and their generous participation heralded the hasty return of the not so Fab Four who were screaming as they rushed on stage, 'Oh no, not that again.' Sadly for them it wasn't their decision; the audience were into the swing of things and realized that the Fab Four had inflicted a dirty deed on Empy, so they should pay for it.

As the song progressed the audience's enthusiasm grew more and more until, at the end, they all stood up and were cheering for an encore. Much to the consternation of the Fab Four the orchestra struck up yet again and to the cheers of the audience I sang it again. I think we could have gone on all night but twice served its purpose as the Fab Four ate humble pie.

The Preacher was a Rat

The producer of 'Elvis the Musical,' Paul Elliott, was also Britain's most prolific pantomime producer with as many as 32 productions running nationwide and many of the artistes in his new upcoming Elvis tour had spent their Christmas working in one of his pantomimes.

One such person was Gareth Marks, son of comedy character actor Alfred Marks. Gareth had been appearing in Dick Whittington at the Belfast Opera House for Christmas, which coincidently was the first theatre on the Elvis tour.

Our first night in Belfast was a sell-out and expectations were high. From the opening chord of: *That's Alright Mama,* it was clear that 'Elvis the Musical' was in for another great run. Either side of the stage pulpits were built out over the orchestra pit. The one stage left was mainly for the Preacher, played by Gareth Marks, and the one stage right was for me, the mature Elvis.

As I came to the end of *In the Ghetto,* a very

serious moment in the production which I sang from the pulpit, Gareth's first entrance as the Preacher was to slowly climb the steps of his pulpit, timing his arrival at the top to coincide with the finish of my song.

As I finished my song, the audience not only applauded but also started to hiss and boo, and then burst into fits of laughter. I couldn't believe what I was seeing and hearing. It was my third year in the role of the mature Elvis and I had no idea as to what was going on.

Gareth then pulled a funny face, made a few strange signs and continued with his dialogue, which was a cue to my exit. As I walked behind the backdrop to the opposite side, I found the stage manager and company manager falling about with laughter.

'What's the hell's going on?' I asked.

'Don't you know?' asked Tony the company manager who was giggling like a big girl.

'Know what?' I replied.

Tony explained that when Gareth appeared in pantomime at the theatre a few weeks earlier, his role was King Rat and every time he made an entrance the audience were encouraged to hiss and boo him.

Thankfully it was a one off and didn't happen during our twelve days in Belfast.

The Day 'The Hawk' Swooped

I first met Ronnie 'The Hawk' Hawkins in January 1960 when he came to the UK with Eddie Cochran to appear on Jack Good's Boy Meets Girl TV show. Eddie and Gene's manager, Norm Riley, managed him and I got to meet up with him on the occasions he came to our show.

As Eddie had done, Ronnie congratulated me on my version of *It's Only Make Believe*. I was thrilled when he told me it was the best version he'd heard and I should give America a shot.

The next time I saw Ronnie was over 20 years later in 1981 when, following the breakdown of my first marriage and feeling pretty depressed, I headed for Canada to spend some time with my brother.

Looking through a local Toronto newspaper I came across an advert for the launch of a new model of car and discovered Ronnie was appearing with his band in a specially erected entertainment marquee. My brother told me it was only a few miles away so we decided to give it a visit.

We caught the last ten minutes of Ronnie's set and then, with my brother being a cop, pulled a few strings and went back stage. As I walked up to Ronnie he smiled and said, 'Hey, It's the Only Make Believe man, Vince, how you doing?' We talked for a few minutes and then Ronnie invited my family and I to see his show the following Saturday at the El Mocambo nightclub in Toronto.

The El Mocambo was the club where the former Canadian Prime Minister's wife, Margaret Trudeau had a liaison with the Rolling Stones and the incident catapulted the club into the world media spotlight making it one of the world's leading rock 'n' roll venues.

Arriving at the club the following Saturday we were met by Ronnie who took us up the stairs to a smoke filled music lounge. Not only was it smoke filled, it was packed, and all the tables and chairs were occupied.

Ronnie asked us to stay near the bar while he organized seating for us. My brother and I looked at each other bemused as Ronnie disappeared into the smoky haze. Seating? The room is wall-to-wall people. Where the hell is he going to seat us?

A few minutes later a big cheer mixed with howling filled the lounge as all eyes focused on the stage. It was Ronnie. He grabbed the microphone and shouted, 'Hi folks! Can I have your attention for a moment please? A good pal of mine from the UK has just arrived with his family. He is the guy who inspired David Bowie to enter showbiz,' that was the first I'd heard of me inspiring Bowie, 'and he's an awesome singer who's gonna get up with the band and me later. If some of you good folks could offer his family your seats it would be much appreciated.'

With that, everyone in the room stood up as one and offered us their chairs. We could take our pick. It was very embarrassing, but much appreciated.

I did 30 minutes with Ronnie later in the evening and received a great reception.

During the coming weeks I became part of the Canadian rock 'n' roll scene as I did dates with Ronnie, Long John Baldry and my good pal from my Drumbeat TV show says, Roy Young.

It certainly laid the foundations for my visit to Canada a couple of years later when I appeared in Toronto, Ottowa, Montreal, Vancouver and Edmonton in 'Elvis the Musical'.

Farewell to the King

After a show supporting Lonnie Donegan in July 2001, Lonnie suggested we should do something together sometime.

In August of 2002, a good pal of mine, Harry Whitehouse, informed me that he had spoken to Lonnie's manager who would like me to sing with Lonnie at the Royal Concert Hall, Nottingham in October. By coincidence, the hall occupies the site where the Nottingham Empire stood, the venue of

Lonnie's very first variety stage appearance and the site of our first meeting 45 years earlier.

The duets I had performed with Eddie Cochrane, Gene Vincent, Marty Wilde, Cliff Richard, Billy Fury, Mike Stoller and others were about to fade into insignificance. This was Lonnie. For me they just didn't come any bigger. This would be the big one, the dream coming true.

On arriving at the stage door I was told by Lonnie's manager, Mike Stevens, that Lonnie couldn't make the rehearsal as he had a back problem and was resting at the hotel and he suggested that I rehearse a few numbers with Lonnie's band but without Lonnie.

After the rehearsal, Mike asked me if I could do him a big favour. He told me that Lonnie's back was worse and he could perhaps do only half a dozen songs sitting on a stool and asked me if I would do extra numbers to help out. I agreed but was gutted; I knew it meant no duet.

Twenty-five minutes before he was due on stage, Lonnie walked in. He looked relaxed, calm and complained little of his back other than to blame it on a long car journey. He made light of the oral and anal painkillers the doctor had given him and joked that he thought they would start to take effect when they met in the middle.

He asked me to be ready side stage following *The Grand Coollee Dam* when he would introduce me and I would sing a couple of sings while he had a breather. The thought of not performing a duet with him was a major disappointment, but filling in for him was still an honour.

After he related the story of how I had gone backstage to see him 45 years earlier, he introduced me. As I walked towards him, bowing humbly in recognition of his greatness, I fully expected him to shake my hand and exit the stage. But no! We shook hands and he stood his ground. For the next 10 minutes I enjoyed the most thrilling experience of my professional life as I sang *Bring a Little Water Sylvie* and *Midnight Special* with my King.

Immediately following my contribution I watched the rest of Lonnie's performance from the circle. Having been on-stage for one hour and forty minutes he chose *This Could Be the Last Time* as his closing number. It raised the audience to its feet as one. The applause was enough to shake the foundations of both the Concert Hall and the Empire Theatre.

During his bows I returned side stage. When he came off I thanked him for the best show I had seen him perform and for allowing me to be a part of it.

Peter Oakman, Lonnie's bass player of 40

years, placed his arm around Lonnie's shoulder and said, 'If that's what pushing a tablet up your arse does for you, Lonnie, you should do it before every show. You were amazing.' Then Lonnie put his arm around my waist and said, 'That was great, let's do it again'. I hugged him and left.

Five days later I was on holiday, sleeping in the Lanzarote sun when I received a phone call from my son Christie. He told me that Lonnie had passed away. It transpired that it was not a bad back from sitting, but a blood clot.

At Lonnie's funeral his eldest son Peter gave a eulogy and in it he made reference to his father's popularity when he related how, as the curtains closed after every performance, Lonnie would always receive a standing ovation. He then asked the mourners to join him and his family in giving Lonnie one last standing ovation as the curtains drew around the coffin.

In his eulogy, Joe Brown commented that the casket was not big enough for the massive talent it contained.

Floral tributes from The Rolling Stones, Paul McCartney, Adam Faith, Marty Wilde, Joe Brown, Elton John, to name but a few, summed up the love and respect Lonnie enjoyed within the music industry.

The thrill of having my sons Christie and Simon in the audience to witness my duets with Lonnie was almost equal to that of performing the duets themselves. They knew he was my King!

The Yanks Invade

My Heroes Arrive

I had just met one of my childhood heroes, George Formby. I was using his dressing room at the Queen's Theatre, Blackpool for a Sunday night concert, when he knocked on the door and asked me if he could get something. I was in awe and lost for words, other than to ask him how he was. Then he was gone.

It was only a few weeks earlier that I had heard from my manger Larry Parnes that I would be supporting another of my heroes on his British tour, Gene Vincent. It was my admiration of Gene that had prompted me to use Vince for my stage name.

Larry was gracing us with his presence for this particular show, not something he normally did, especially so far from London. He came to my dressing room just after George had left and was in a good mood. He told me there was to be an addition to the Gene Vincent tour due to start the following month. Eddie Cochran had been added. I think he expected me to be over the moon. However, in spite of my being a big Cochran fan, I had certain reservations. Larry had promised me I could close the first half, plus

I opened my act with the Cochran Classic *C'mon Everybody*. Double whammy, I thought.

On our return to London I met Larry to discuss the tour. It was a great bill. Eddie Cochran and Gene Vincent had both been a big influence on me from when I first saw them in the movie 'The Girl Can't Help It' at my local Granada Cinema in Grantham.

I told Larry I still wanted to close the first half and understood I couldn't perform *C'mon Everybody*. To my surprise he agreed, although from the billing it should have been Eddie closing the first half and Gene the second.

The Gaumont Ipswich on Sunday, 24th January 1960 was the start of the tour. My group, The Quiet Three and myself were a very confident outfit. They were three of the best musicians on the circuit and played a major role in my putting a strong act together.

I arrived in Ipswich just as the sound check was about to finish. The Wildcats (backing Eddie and Gene by arrangement with Marty Wilde) were doing their final check. I followed them with my check, which took only a couple of minutes.

The running order showed that I followed Eddie's 25-minutes act in the first half. I decided to get ready and watch for 20 minutes from the rear stalls before I was due on.

As the curtains opened, following Eddie's introduction by compere Billie Raymond, the audience went hysterical. Eddie stood centre stage with his back to the audience, in the spotlight, wearing an orange shirt with black leather trousers. He played the intro to the Ray Charles classic *What'd I Say* and before singing, '*Tell your momma, tell your pa...* etc' he spun around to screams of hysteria from boys and girls alike. It was sheer magic. The guy looked brilliant, he played guitar like I never heard anyone play and his voice was brilliant! What had I done? I had to follow him. It was my own stupid fault for having a big ego and mouth to match when I insisted that Larry let me close the first half. After 15 minutes of Eddie's act I returned backstage to meet my fate.

Eddie must have been thrilled with the reception he received. As he came off he exited in front of the curtains, as I was waiting behind, so I couldn't compliment him on a great show.

The reception I received was much better than I had expected and the crowd did indeed lift me. *It's Only Make Believe* has always been one of my biggest numbers and it's where I did my 'Johnnie Ray' and milked the lyrics for all they were worth. Tonight was no exception. Tears and all! It was received with a standing ovation, which I couldn't quite believe, and from there it seemed I could do no wrong.

I came off stage on such a high. Gene had yet to perform, but I felt I had done a pretty good job of holding my own with Eddie.

Sitting in my dressing room during the interval there was a knock on the door. The door opened and there stood a very handsome, heavily made up guy, in his dressing gown. It was Eddie.

'Hi Vince, I'm Eddie Cochran. It's a pleasure to meet you,' he said, as he made his way into my dressing room.

'Likewise,' said I rambling on nervously and telling him how much I had enjoyed his act.

'Your version of *It's Only Make Believe* is the best I have ever seen or heard. You're one hell of a performer, man,' said Eddie.

This had to be the best mutual admiration society of all time. I just couldn't believe he had been generous enough to come to my dressing room, let alone be so enthusiastic with his praise. Eddie stayed with me until the end of the show; we then went side stage to watch Gene.

Gene didn't get the same audience reaction as Eddie, and Eddie went on to tell me that Gene was in pain with his leg, which he'd injured in a motorcycle accident. I had already met Gene when he did his 'Welcome to Britain' appearance on the Marty Wilde Show at Tooting Granada a month earlier and he had told me then that his leg was proving to be a problem.

It was to be Gene's injured leg that, on occasion, would take up much of Eddie's time as he tried to help his friend.

Three Steps to Heaven

The new Triumph Herald Coupe that Larry had given me for my 19th birthday, which I found out later I had paid for, had design problems with the door and windscreen seals. Consequently every time it rained the foot-wells filled up like paddling pools. After many visits to various Triumph dealerships, the car was recalled and Standard Triumph Motors loaned me a Standard Vanguard saloon until it was fixed.

It was a much better car for when Gene and Eddie travelled with me, as it had a bench front seat with a steering column gear change and consequently lots of room for Gene to stretch out his injured leg.

When travelling with Eddie and Gene it was hard to imagine them as two of the superstars of rock 'n' roll. They were both very fond of Britain, Eddie especially so. He could not get over how green the countryside was. Given that they were over here from January to April, four of the most miserable months of the year, my mind boggled as to what their reaction would be to our summer greenery.

Their love for England and its countryside was almost equal to that of my inquisitiveness towards America, and it was during one of our car journeys that the seeds were sown for me to visit America and stay with Eddie on his ranch in California. As the subject was discussed it became more and more exciting for me. On the agenda were hunting mountain lions, since Eddie had a love for guns; we were also to cut an album in Eddie's studio, and he had fixed me up with a date withy Connie Stevens of '77 Sunset Strip' fame.

During our chats about dating girls, Eddie never once mentioned Sharon Sheeley. Songwriter Sharon arrived at the very end of the tour and Eddie was obviously very upset at her decision to come over. I think Eddie looked upon her as being more of a stalker than girlfriend. They certainly weren't engaged, as she would later have people believe.

Eddie had become a very dear friend and a fan, and was surprised that I hadn't enjoyed more chart success than I had. He felt that he could turn that around by recording an album with me. As well as being a multi-talented musician (he played guitar, piano, drums and bass), he was also a songwriter and a producer. In short, he did everything and I was very excited at the prospect of recording with him. When Eddie and Gene did travel with me, they would love to visit the greasy spoon style transport cafés. Their records were often played on the juke boxes and they would get a kick out of watching the drivers pick a track and then sometimes mime the words or tap their fingers as they listened and relaxed.

On occasions, my parents' home in Grantham was a stopping off point when we drove up the A1. My mother made the best apple tart imaginable, and when leaving London to go to a show Eddie and Gene would enquire: 'Are we stopping at your Ma's for some apple pie?'

While we were in Grantham I got a great thrill from showing them the Granada Cinema where I had first seen them on the big screen some four years earlier in 'The Girl Can't Help It.'

Eddie would often take my Levin guitar from the boot of the car and play it on the back seat. It was on the A1 to Grantham where I first heard *Cut Across Shorty*. When Eddie had finished playing it he said, 'And this is the B side,' he then played *Three Steps to Heaven*.

It was Eddie playing these songs, and telling Gene and me that *Cut Across Shorty* was to be the 'A' side, that played a major part in my decision to leave the Larry Parnes' stable.

Gene's Leg Problems

The producer of the TV shows 'Oh Boy' and 'Boy Meets Girl', Jack Good, proved his genius when he dressed Gene in black leather and gave him direction on how to use the microphone stand in conjunction with his bad leg. It was so different. Listening to Gene talk about it I got the feeling that it helped redress the balance, as his leg had by now become something of an asset.

Gene felt he had been dealt a bitter blow when, in 1953, a lady driver shot a red traffic light, hit Gene's motorcycle and shattered his left leg. Gene's physical condition certainly affected his mental state.

During our show at the Gaumont Theatre in Worcester, Eddie told me that Gene was in terrible pain and he wasn't sure he could finish the performance. After the show we returned to the hotel where a bottle of bourbon was opened and Eddie accompanied Gene in a tipple as I looked on. Not being a drinker it gave me the opportunity to distance myself from their problems as Gene was definitely trying to drown his sorrows and kill the pain; Eddie was stressed, as he felt responsible for Gene's well being while they were in the UK. Gene sat in an armchair in his hotel room, grimacing with pain, and we all felt that removing the irons from the injured leg may give him some relief.

Eddie unstrapped the irons, showing that the heavily scarred leg had no flesh on it to speak of, just skin wrapped around a bone reminiscent of the pictures of starving people's limbs we later became accustomed to seeing in famine stricken lands. The emptying of the bottle of bourbon heralded Gene passing out and Eddie and I laid him on his bed, covered him up and we left the room.

Gene's health problems, and subsequent drinking, prompted Larry to reverse their positions in the show in making Eddie the headliner. It wasn't just the quality of Gene's performances; it was the inconsistency that was the problem and the main reason for him being relegated in the show's running order.

There were times when Gene would pull off amazing shows and appear to be at peace with his audience; on other occasions his demons would surface and he would bring all his problems to bear by being curt, unfriendly and occasionally walking off stage.

There were occasions on the tour bus when Gene would isolate himself and play with a knife or a gun. It was rumoured he smuggled the gun into the country by concealing it on the iron supporting his bad leg.

Gene would often sit on his own on the

tour bus and looked menacing as he fondled his knife or his gun. It was always Joe Brown who was elected to sit with Gene to try and persuade him to put them away. Gene appreciated Joe's great guitar playing, his Cockney accent, and his humorous approach to life and he always had time for him. There's always the possibility that Gene had seen Joe lose his temper and all the firearms in the world wouldn't stop him having a go!

The Medical

After the opening night of Eddie and Gene's tour, Larry could see that I had struck up a friendship with them, and he told me to be at his office the following lunchtime as they were to have medicals for an insurance policy he was taking out for the tour.

I met Eddie and Gene at Larry's office where we hopped into a taxi and headed to a surgery in the St Paul's district of London. When we arrived I discovered that Larry had also arranged for me to have a medical. It appeared that Eddie and Gene were to be insured for £10,000 each and me for £2,000.

Due to Gene's medical history his examination lasted a lot longer than Eddie's and mine. Gene told us he was asked questions about his psychological background. Apparently the damage to his leg had left him with mental problems that culminated in his being admitted into an American sanatorium. It was via Eddie, and Gene's manager Norm Riley, that Eddie had agreed to stand as guarantor for Gene's visit to the UK. We found out later that due to Gene's mental problems his insurance premium would be twice that of Eddie's.

As the advance bookings were so good, Larry had extended the tour to April 16th, an additional 6 weeks. The policies were originally for 7 weeks, so when the extra weeks were added to the tour, Larry extended them to midnight on Easter Sunday 17th April 1960, the day Eddie and Gene were due to return to America.

As Eddie died at midday on Sunday 17th April, and the insurance didn't expire until midnight, Larry received £10,000 for the loss of Eddie's life and an undisclosed sum for Gene's injuries. Thankfully, the insurance company didn't have to pay out on me!

Easter Sunday 1960

Eddie, Gene and I were due to fly to America from Heathrow on Easter Sunday, April 17th, 1960. As they were in Bristol until Saturday 16th April, and I was in Scotland until Thursday 13th we made arrangements to meet at Gene's flat in Fulham at 8.30 am on Easter Sunday. We would then travel to Heathrow together in convoy where my road manager Noel Wallis would drop me off.

Our flight originated in Frankfurt and was due to leave Heathrow for New York around mid afternoon. My plans were to stop over in New York for five days and spend some time with my brother, who was due to drive down from Toronto in Canada to meet me.

Noel and I arrived at Gene's flat at 8.15 am. There was no reply from the flat and we became concerned. I phoned the Stratford Court Hotel in Oxford Street and spoke with Eddie and Gene's manager, Norm Riley, who was staying there. Norm suggested that perhaps the boys had got involved in a party, as it was the last night of the tour, and had decided to go straight to the airport.

We arrived at the airport at about 10.30 am, checked my bags in and went for a coffee. It was during this time that I was paged. Larry's Press Officer, Dennis Atherton, was on the line. He sounded very calm, and somewhat unconcerned, as he informed me that the boys had been involved in an accident as they travelled by taxi to London. He said that Gene was in a bad way but Eddie was not too badly injured and he should be released from hospital within 24 hours. He suggested that I fly to New York as planned and he would contact me with Eddie's travel details.

Within thirty minutes of returning to the coffee lounge I was paged again. This time it was Larry who sounded very stressed and very angry. He told me that it was Eddie who was seriously ill and he had been in the operating theatre all night and Gene had minor shoulder and head injuries. He then castigated me for considering flying to America in the knowledge that my best pal was seriously ill.

I was shattered by the news of Eddie's condition and tried explaining to Larry that Dennis Atherton had told me earlier that Eddie would be fit to travel in 24 hours.

I asked him for the address of the hospital and cancelled my flight. My road manager Noel, who thankfully had stayed to see me off, then drove me down the A4 to St Martin's Hospital in Bath.

We arrived at St Martins shortly before 1.30 pm. Thankfully the nurse on reception recognised me and I was taken to meet one of the surgeons who had operated on Eddie. He explained that Eddie was in a critical condition and unlikely to survive the day, and, if he did survive he would be left with the mind of a child of four. The surgeon then wrote out a phone number that I could phone at any time to get news of Eddie's condition. As we were advised not to visit

Gene, who was resting, we decided to head back to London.

When leaving the hospital via the main doors and walking down the steps, Larry and some of the guys from the Parnes stable including Billy Fury, Dickie Pride and Duffy Power greeted me. The press were surrounding them, with Larry working to get any publicity he could. He told the press that the irony was that the 'A' side of Eddie's next record was to be *Three Steps To Heaven*. I was furious. The 'A' side was to be *Cut Across Shorty*, and more importantly Eddie was still alive. I was sickened by what Parnes had said and Noel and I left the group on the steps and headed back to London.

At about 4.20 pm we were driving through Chippenham and I decided to phone the hospital and get an update on Eddie's condition. The news was that he had just passed away. I was absolutely gutted. Immediately I asked the question, 'Why Eddie?' Gene had so many demons, and at times gave the impression he would rather not be here.

With no plans for the next five weeks I headed for Cheam in Surrey to visit some very good friends who, I knew, would give me support and a shoulder to cry on. It was also somewhere Larry couldn't find me.

The next day's newspapers were full of the East Sunday accident and Eddie's death. The first headline I read was, 'Pop Star Pal

To Fly With Coffin To States.' This referred to my supposedly having said that I would accompany Eddie's body to his home.

I had avoided the press and said nothing to anyone. It was once again an insight into Larry's unscrupulous methods of gleaning publicity and it heralded the final chapter of my dealings with him.

Jerry and The Jacket

As our coach left Charing Cross on its journey to Newcastle on Tyne, all on board were full of anticipation for the fourteen days ahead. It was the start of a tour that looked as if a blind man sporting a pin and a map of the UK had scheduled it. Up north. Down south. Back up north. Across to the west. Over to the east. Back to the west. It was a ridiculous itinerary, which would determine us being on the coach for many hours on some days and throughout the night on others.

The star of the show, controversial American rocker Jerry Lee Lewis, was travelling with promoter Don Arden in a limo to the first date at Newcastle City Hall on 29th of April 1962. Jerry's previous tour in 1958 had ended in disaster when after only two performances, he had to flee the country with the cause of the disaster, his new 13-year-old wife and cousin, Myra, who was due to accompany him. Their recent marriage was legal and above-board in their home state of Mississippi, but certainly not in the UK. It provoked outrage in the national press and most people were shocked that the tour had been allowed to take place at all. With poisoned quills at the ready, the British press were anticipating bringing Jerry Lee to his knees yet again.

The show's line up consisted of Jerry Lee Lewis, Johnny Kidd and the Pirates, The Echoes, The Viscounts, Buddy Brittain, Mike Read and yours truly.

Following our arrival at Newcastle City Hall, The Echoes, the backing group for Jerry Lee, The Viscounts and myself, were soon set up and ready to rehearse with Jerry Lee. All that was missing was Jerry Lee. He was due to be there at 4.30 pm, but come 5.30 pm there was still no sign of him. As the minutes ticked towards curtain-up time of 6.30 pm we all became more and more concerned at the thought of him not turning up and the tour being cancelled.

Don Arden, father of Ossie Osbourne's wife Sharon, was known as the Godfather. If you delivered, so would he. If you didn't, then anything could happen. I had a good working relationship with Don but I knew many who didn't.

As 6.30 pm arrived and there was still no

sign of Jerry Lee and Don, the decision was taken to start the show in the hope that they would soon turn up. The sell out audience gave the first half artistes a fantastic reception, but I wouldn't want to be the one to tell them that Jerry Lee wouldn't be performing. Jerry's fans were likely to turn nasty.

The interval arrived, but Jerry and Don didn't, and you could now cut the backstage atmosphere with a knife. Not only were our fears of the tour being cancelled becoming a reality, we were also beginning to fear for our safety. I had been involved in the Dundee Caird Hall riots of 1960 when Eddie Cochran, Gene Vincent and I had to be smuggled out of the Caird Hall, and that riot was due to the audience having a good time!

The Echoes were perhaps the most concerned at Jerry Lee's no show as they were due to play for him, yet they hadn't even met him. As they launched into the first number to start the second half of the show, the stage door opened and in strolled Jerry Lee and Don looking relaxed and oblivious to the drama.

Swaggering to the side stage area, Jerry Lee calmly shouted to The Echoes, 'Gimmie a twelve bar shuffle in C.' With that, drummer Laurie Jay shouted 'One, two, three, four,' and they started what could have been the intro to many rock 'n' roll songs.

Jerry swaggered onto the stage and acknowledged the screaming fans as an arrogant monarch might acknowledge his subjects. Sitting at the piano, he immediately latched onto the rhythm set by The Echoes and started to play the pounding foot stomping intro to *'Whole Lotta Shaking.'* Needless to say Jerry was an outstanding success and the audience went wild.

A few days later we were at the Colston Hall, Bristol. During the afternoon I wandered into the city centre where I bought a classy looking brown leather jacket. As I walked into the theatre Jerry was walking down the corridor and said, 'Nice jacket, man,' in his wonderful southern drawl. I thanked him and set off for the dressing room Johnny Kidd and I were sharing.

In the interval Jerry's road manager Henry Henroyd came to my dressing room and asked me if he could borrow my jacket for Jerry Lee to try on. Jerry had told Henry that he liked the jacket and that he was thinking of buying one the next morning. Henry took the jacket and said he would bring it straight back.

During the second show interval two fans came to our dressing room to get autographs from Johnny and me. As Johnny was signing I noticed that one of the fans was wearing a jacket exactly like mine. 'I've got a jacket just like that,' I told the fan. 'Jerry

Lee sold me this one' he said. 'He didn't like it and said I could buy it for £20 if I wanted it.'

With that I ran out of the dressing room and down the corridor screaming, 'You bastard, Jerry.' As I got to his dressing room I walked straight in as he was getting ready to go on stage. 'Where's my bloody jacket?' I asked him. 'What jacket's that?' he replied. 'The brown leather one that Henry fetched for you,' said I. 'Henry ain't shown me no leather jacket,' he mumbled whilst putting his socks on.

I found Henry side stage setting up for Jerry and asked him about the jacket. 'Of course he's got your bloody jacket. I put it on him to try.' With that I returned to my dressing room and Henry went to see Jerry. A few minutes later Henry returned to my dressing room where he returned the £20 to the fan and asked for the jacket back saying there had been a mistake. Henry apologised on Jerry's behalf but Jerry never mentioned the jacket, and neither did I. He was nicknamed 'The Killer' for a reason!

The Girl Couldn't Help It!

The 1956 movie, 'The Girl Can't Help It', introduced me to rock 'n' roll icons Gene Vincent, Eddie Cochran and Little Richard.

It also introduced me to the leading lady, Jayne Mansfield. I wasn't into blondes with squeaky voices – not that I dwelled on her face for too long. I was more into brunettes and rock 'n' roll.

Almost twenty years after seeing 'The Girl Can't Help It', and having worked alongside and befriended Eddie and Gene, I was invited to the York Press Ball at the Cat's Whiskers Ballroom in York where Jayne Mansfield was to make a guest appearance at midnight.

The Press Ball in most communities was the fund-raising social event of the year. It was when the power of the press was brought to bear on the local business community as they acquired the best there was available for the event. Be it the venue, tombola prizes, entertainment or celebrity guests, the press balls would always outdo the competition by a mile.

In acquiring the services of Jayne Mansfield, the press ball committee had arranged for a liquor-stocked limousine to pick her and her entourage up from the Contessa Night Club in Middlesbrough, where she was appearing earlier in the evening, and then drive her post-haste the 50 miles to York.

As nervous press ball committee members strode the foyer and the corridor leading to the VIP suite, the air of anticipation of Jayne's arrival grew more and more intense. The echoing voices of Keith Harris and Orville, the star cabaret for the evening, were drifting from the ballroom but doing little to bring a smile to the faces of the agitated committee members.

As midnight drew nearer, the anticipation of Jayne's limo arrival far outweighed that of any of Cinderella's golden coaches. Midnight struck and it was now Saturday.

The reception for Keith Harris and Orville as they finished their act was intended to preclude that of Jayne's entrance. Not any more.

As 12.15 am arrived every contingency plan in the book had been scrutinised but none would suffice. The pumpkin into a limo hadn't materialised. They were Jayneless.

Just as all hope appeared to have disappeared, a screeching voice echoed through the foyer, 'They're here, the limo's here!'

All eyes were focused on the limo door as it opened slowly to reveal a female who looked more like 'Barbie the Hooker' doll than a Hollywood screen goddess. Her hair looked like an explosion in a mattress factory and she was clutching a champagne glass that, it would appear, had been replenished many times during the 40-mile journey from Middlesbrough.

Stepping gingerly from her somewhat tarnished golden coach, it soon became apparent that Jayne's difficulty in walking a straight line was the result of a battle between her pink-satin 1950s-style-figure-hugging, ankle tight pencil skirt and the copious amounts of champagne she had consumed en route.

As she entered the foyer her unsteady bouncing gait was giving cause for concern as for the safety of her two biggest assets. They appeared to be making determined efforts to escape from their 34FF lace prison.

The arrangements were to take Jayne directly onto the ballroom floor where she would sing a song and present the tombola prizes. Unfortunately her condition determined otherwise and she was shown to the VIP suite in the hope that a strong black coffee and a cold damp cloth might restore her to something resembling a presentable condition.

I had returned to the VIP suite just before Jayne entered. She was wearing a dress with heart shaped holes cut out of it. I'm sure it didn't have the effect the designer was hoping for. So tight was the dress that the heart shapes only revealed heart shaped flesh being forced out. Gross!

Discussing 'The Girl Can't Help It', and hearing of her experiences with Gene and Eddie in the making of the movie now seemed out of the question.

It was Jayne's efforts in making her way to the ladies' toilet that left me with my hands full.

As she staggered from side to side in her efforts to get to the toilet, she bounced off a wall, the force of which ejected her boobs for all to see. As her manager ran to the rescue he shouted at me to give him a hand. In all honesty a hand wasn't big enough – they were enormous! Pulling on the elasticised top with one hand, while endeavouring to force the rebellious pair back to where they came from with the other, would have been more appropriate in a porn game show than at a city's premier charity event.

Jayne did eventually make the ladies' room, and at the presentation of the tombola prizes she was given a wonderful reception by her adoring fans who had no idea what a handful she had been earlier.

Davy Jones Was Browned Off!

In 1960 my manager Larry Parnes produced a summer show at the Britannia Pier, Great Yarmouth. Having enjoyed success earlier in the year with the ill-fated Eddie Cochran and Gene Vincent tour, he decided to stay with the American theme by booking an unknown black American artist named Davy Jones. The show as billed as, 'The Anglo-American Beat Show' and the remainder of the bill consisted of Billy Fury, Dickie Pride, Keith Kelly, Johnny Gentle,

The Barron Knights and myself, with me and my group The Quiet Three closing the first half and Billy closing the second.

Although my relationship with Larry was at its lowest, I enjoyed a great season in part due to the song, *It's Only Make Believe*. My performance of the song was what had prompted Eddie Cochran to come to my dressing room in the interval of his opening night concern in Ipswich earlier in the year to compliment me.

There was one occasion during the summer at Yarmouth when, due to the fantastic audience reception, I had to sing *It's Only Make Believe* three times on the trot. After the show Billy Fury said I should record it as it would be the hit I was looking for. He suggested I tell Larry that I wanted to record it as it was going down a storm with the audiences.

On Larry's next visit he reluctantly agreed that *It's Only Make Believe* was a song that suited me and that the audiences loved it, but he thought it was too soon after Conway Twitty's hit version, which would stop it being a hit.

The Yarmouth summer season was unusual, in that we performed afternoon shows only at 2.30 pm from Monday to Friday with two shows on Sunday nights.

As the weather was not great that year, plus our targeted audiences were teenagers who would rather be at a concert drivelling over Billy Fury, than sunbathing with their parents, we did very good business.

The one person who couldn't care less about the weather and sunbathing was Davy Jones. The black American singer was always cracking jokes about sunbathing and couldn't believe the obsession some of us had with it. 'You'll never see anyone sunbathing in Alabama,' he would shout in a very southern drawl at bathers.

It was when Billy, Noel, Davy and I called into a chemist's on our way to the theatre early one afternoon that Davy really got his anti-sunbathing point across.

As we paid for our goods, Davy picked up a bottle of Bergasol Sun Lotion from the counter and coyly asked the sales girl if he could try it. Looking bemused, she told him he could, and unscrewing the top Davy lifted the bottle to his mouth. Unnoticed by the sales girl, Davy discreetly covered the top of the bottle with his thumb and placed the bottle to his lips.

'No! No! You don't drink it!' screamed the sales assistant.

'Honey,' replied Davy, slowing removing the bottle a few inches away from his pursed lips. 'How'd you think I got to be this colour?'

Pop's Pranksters

The Great Itching Powder Plot

Cardiff always proved to be a popular date on the theatre itinerary. The New Theatre, the pro digs, the nightlife, the horse riding, the girls and the joke shop all contributed towards Cardiff's popularity with the touring shows. Our visit with the Idols on Parade Show proved to be no exception.

Having gone through our Monday routine of arriving at the theatre, checking into the pro digs and booking the horses, Joe and I decided to check out the joke shop. We were like kids in a candy shop. Within minutes we had stocked up on itching powder and the foul smelling 'Stinko'. A victim for the Stinko was already in place – John, the company electrician. He had bad breath anyway, and was always hustling in on girls who were only interested in the likes of Billy, Mark, Tommy, Joe or myself. The plan was to set him up at a party we had all been invited to a club called '77 Sunset Strip' on nearby Barry Island.

John was prime for a Stinko attack. Having been told on many occasions by associates to sort out his bad breath and BO, he failed to see the problem and consequently did nothing about it, so we felt 'Stinko' could perhaps bring the subject to the fore.

Shortly after arriving at the '77 Sunset Strip' club Joe and I conceived a plan. As John moved in on a group of girls near the jukebox it appeared that the girls were beginning to pick up the drifting odour of his BO and bad breath and it didn't take long for him to become a lone figure standing in front of the jukebox.

It was on the cue of the girls moving out, that Joe and I moved in. As we sauntered up to the jukebox, Joe stood on John's left and I stood on his right. Joe placed his right arm around John and placed his right hand on John's right shoulder and I mirrored Joe's actions by placing my left arm around John with my left hand on his left shoulder.

We had already taken the tops off the Stinko bottles and placed a finger over the end to conceal the obnoxious smell they gave off. Glancing across at each other behind John's back as he perused the jukebox selection, Joe and I acknowledged each other's nodding and our plan was executed, as we gently poured Stinko on each shoulder. Once we had dispatched the contents of the bottles, we patted John on his back, made our excuses and beat a hasty retreat.

From our position at the bar it didn't take long before we were rewarded for our efforts. John walked away from the Jukebox and took up a position at the bar next to a group of people. No sooner had he arrived than everyone at the bar moved out as if a hand grenade had been tossed among them.

It was a blessing in disguise when one of the dancers took pity on John and explained what was going on. Thankfully it had the desired effect in the coming days when John invested in some long overdue deodorants and mouthwash.

Up on the Downs

The artistes who performed at weekly variety theatres often had nothing much to do during the daytime. You'd arrive in a town late on a Monday morning, do your orchestral/technical rehearsal and that was it. For the remainder of the week every daytime hour would be free and you could do whatever you wanted. As long as you were in the theatre before the half hour call was made, the daytime was your own to do with as you wished.

There were no local radio stations and very few TV stations, where you would be required to go and plug the show or your latest recording. The occasional invitation to have drinks or lunch in the Mayor's parlour, with a local newspaper in attendance, was usually determined by whether the councillor's wife and secretary fancied you or not!

So it was the golf course or the cinema where many would while away their spare time.

Mornings didn't really exist in a pop star's world. Occasionally a theatre would allow rehearsals for a couple of hours in the morning, but to be honest there weren't many of us who saw the postman. We may have seen the milkman as we got back to our digs, but not the postman.

Golf didn't appeal to Joe or me. Our interests were horse riding, ice-skating and practical jokes.

Before a week in a town or city, I would do a check-up on the horse riding and ice-skating facilities closest to the theatre.

Our first love was horse riding, so that was always the first call I made. I would book for the Tuesday afternoon ride and ask them to hold two horses every afternoon for the rest of the week. The booking for the remainder of the week would be confirmed on the Tuesday.

It gave us the opportunity to check out the horses, the ride and to find out what restrictions there were regarding galloping. Some wouldn't even allow you to gallop, only a trot or a canter for a few minutes and then walking. If the set-up wasn't suitable and we didn't want to ride there again we would make an excuse about having to rehearse or do interviews for the rest of the week and cancel the booking.

During a week at the Brighton Theatre Royal I had made arrangements to ride out of a stable in nearby Hove. The lady I had spoken to on the telephone was without doubt the horsiest person I had ever spoken to. She was so Fenella Fielding.

The question I always asked when making enquiries was, 'Where will we gallop?' Not, 'Are we allowed to gallop?' I think we both fancied ourselves as Lester Piggott but wouldn't admit it.

The plum-in-mouth Hove lady, explained that we would be allowed a short gallop on the downs but as we hadn't used her facility before, one or two of her stable girls would escort us. The thought of a couple of stable girls on the Sussex Downs compensated somewhat for the limited and escorted gallop. I booked it.

On arriving at the stables on the Tuesday lunchtime, we soon discovered why, whenever you enquired in Brighton about Hove, you soon got the impression that it was the snobby part of town.

The owner of the stables looked even more Fenella Fielding than she sounded on the phone. Crop in hand and slapping her jodhpurs, she marched towards us looking like a madam in a bondage movie. Her glaring look reminded me of a Gestapo guard I had seen in a war film. This woman was not to be messed with.

She gave Joe and me a very stern head to toe inspection and without muttering a word walked off towards the two jodhpur-clad young ladies who were bridling up two beautiful horses. The impression we had was that we had failed miserably. Joe was, and still is, brilliant at turning on the charm and with a big grin, his cockney twanged voice asked politely, 'We alright then?'

Madam turned around and replied, 'Yes! But I will be sending one of my girls with you.' 'I bet we get the bleedin' ugly one,' mumbled Joe. And with that the less desirable looking of the two young ladies stepped forward leading two horses. 'Told ya so,' was Joe's retort as we each took a set of reins with a horse attached.

'Jenny will take you onto the Downs and she will tell you when you can trot and when you can canter,' instructed madam. 'What about galloping?' we asked in unison. 'If Jenny feels the horses are up to it, you may have a short gallop,' she replied haughtily. 'That's what she bleedin' finks,' muttered Joe as we mounted our trusty steeds.

With that, the Hove mews rang out to the echoing sound of two uncontrollable pop stars and one very naïve young lady. All in for an afternoon they wouldn't forget.

The horses were well above our usual standard of old nags from a farm or run down riding stable. As we were led through the back streets of Hove to the Downs, a journey that was taking about twenty minutes of our valuable two hour ride, Jenny became more relaxed and talkative, telling us all about how great it was to ride the Downs, and that she helped out at the stables as it was the only way she could get a regular ride due to the cost.

On arriving at the Downs, Jenny told us we could trot for five minutes but then we must walk again. Reluctantly we set off into a trot and exactly on five minutes Jenny shouted, sounding more like madam, 'Now walk!' We gathered our reins and, for what felt like an eternity, walked our trusty steed across the Sussex Downs.

Joe and I began looking more and more at each other, obviously thinking the same thought, 'When are we going to get to canter let alone gallop?'

With that Jenny shouted, 'OK, a five minute canter. Go!' and off we went. It was but a few moments before the inevitable happened. The canter became a gallop and Jenny was screaming, 'No! No! Canter – not gallop!'

We reluctantly reined in and after a few moments we were walking again and feeling very cheated. Jenny then went to great lengths to point out that the heat was not good for the horses and madam would be furious if they returned with a sweat.

For another fifteen to twenty minutes we boringly made our way, the beauty of the Downs somewhat making up for the slow progress.

Eventually it was 'Joe charm time', 'C'mon Jenny, let's have a gallop darlin',' pleaded Joe. 'OK', says Jenny apprehensively, 'But you must walk the horses when I tell you.'

Before you could say rock 'n' roll, we were gone. Galloping as if our lives depended on it.

It was fantastic! Joe and I were neck and neck as we covered the downs at a rate of knots, occasionally glancing behind us to catch a glimpse of Jenny bringing up the rear on her pony but fading more and more into the distance as we gathered momentum.

As the distance between us grew, Joe and I gave no thought to Jenny's pony not being able to keep up with us. With the wind in our ears conveniently drowning out any instructions Jenny may have been shouting, we carried on galloping.

Eventually the galloping took its toll and the horses began to sweat up. As we reined them in Jenny and her pony came alongside us. Her pony was in a sweat and she was in tears.

Jenny was hysterical. 'She'll kill me, she'll kill me. When she sees how badly the horses are sweating she'll never forgive me. She'll never let me ride her horses again.'

Her obvious despair soon wiped the smiles off our faces. We hadn't heard her cries to stop, and we knew why. We didn't want to. Jenny's predicament now became our priority. How can we get the horses to look as if they haven't been galloping or sweating up?

As Joe and I reluctantly dismounted Jenny suggested that if we walked the horses they might dry off before our return to the stables. So much for our three-hour ride, more like a 45-minute ride and a 2 hour 15 minutes walk back to the stables.

Having stopped at a drinking trough on the way back, the horses looked presentable when we arrived back at the stables. By going on about how hot it was on the Downs, and the fact we were very worried they were sweating up even when only trotting, we had a trouble-free return and no reprimand for the lovely Jenny.

A Shot in the Dark

In 1960 I bought a blanked-off .38 Smith & Wesson revolver to use in my act, when I would pretend to shoot my drummer Jimmy Nicol during a drum solo.

It was in Middlesbrough during the tour of the Idols on Parade show however when the revolver was to play the starring role in yet another Brown/Eager top prank production.

The ingredients were the revolver, Roger Greenaway, a shampoo sachet, a strip of Sellotape and a helping of tomato ketchup.

The only person privy to our dastardly deed would be Mark Wynter, hit recorder of *Venus in Blue Jeans*. As Joe and I were sharing a dressing room with Mark we had to let him in on the prank.

Roger Greenaway was one of the Bristol-based Kestrels vocal group.

They were four very talented, and soon to become prolific, singer-songwriters who also included Roger Cook, Roger Maggs and Tony Burrows. As well as having their own spot in the show, they also backed Joe in the first half finale, *Henry the Eighth*. Roger Greenaway was the total opposite to Joe and myself, quiet, diminutive, and a real gent. We were mouthy and lanky – but we were gentlemen too!

The plan was for Joe to pick on Roger as if he felt Roger was upstaging him and trying to hog the spotlight. As the tour progressed, we arranged for the accusations and threats to become more and more intense, although Joe was, and still is, the complete perfectionist and was prone to losing his rag anyway.

As the strains of *Henry* faded, the safety curtain (usually made of metal as a fire precaution) would come down for the interval and any noise on stage would be muffled by the curtain. With the curtain down, Joe

would leave the stage screaming and shouting at Roger while the rest of the company
were trying to stick up for Roger without
making Joe worse.

One of our dancers was a well-endowed
young lady named Frankie who tended to
be the mothering type and at times a little
nosey. She was a young lady who, along with
the other female dancers known as the
'Valentine Girls,' wore white blouses for the
first half finale, and she was the one we were
hoping would fall for our prank.

The stage manager, Sue, was a nice lady,
but struggled with keeping the peace over
Joe's accusations against Roger, and it was
she who was to play a major part in the lead
up to the execution of the dirty deed.

During the previous week I would stand
side stage as Joe was performing Henry, and
talk to Sue. I told her that I was excited as a
friend was taking me grouse shooting on the
Yorkshire Moors during our stay in Middlesbrough and that I was bringing my own gun
along, and I'd show it to her the following
evening.

The next night, before the performance of
Henry, Joe and I taped the shampoo sachet
filled with tomato ketchup across the palm of
Roger's hand. Just before the interval curtain
was due to come down I strolled casually to
the prompt corner where Sue was, with my
.38 Smith & Wesson in my hand. 'Here it is,

Sue. This is the gun I'm using for hunting grouse tomorrow. But be very careful, it's loaded,' I told her. It was indeed loaded, but with a blank, and in the darkness of the side stage area you couldn't see that the barrel was blocked off.

As Sue was holding the heavy revolver and commenting on its weight, Roger walked off stage in our direction followed by Joe shouting, 'That's it, you little bastard! I'm not telling you any more.'

As Roger passed Sue and I, Joe lunged forward and shouted, 'Give me that bloody gun, Sue, I'm gonna kill the little bastard!' I shouted 'No, Joe! It's loaded!' With that, Roger turned round to look at us and Joe shot him.

The noise of the .38 going off was very loud. As it did, Roger clutched his chest and fell to the floor. The blood-filled shampoo sachet strapped to his hand burst with the desired effect, ketchup oozing through his fingers onto his shirt. 'Oh my God. Roger, he's shot you!' Frankie screamed. She knelt down and pulled Roger towards her well-endowed bosom with the ketchup bleeding onto her pure white-clad boobs.

There was pandemonium. Everybody thought they had witnessed a murder. Sadly our enjoyment was short lived, as Roger, with his head nestled between Frankie's knockers, burst out laughing. Frankie was covered in ketchup and didn't find it one bit amusing; neither did the stage-door manager who had called the police, who subsequently reprimanded me for using my revolver.

When I'd bought the gun I had to license it and take it to a police station every couple of months to prove it was in my possession and still blanked off, but using it in this way breached the terms and conditions of my licence and I came very close to losing it, and being arrested.

Freddie the Starr

In the late 1950s and early 1960s, performing in Liverpool was amazing. The Scousers were such enthusiastic and knowledgeable audiences yet they were very gladiatorial in showing their appreciation. If you could cut the mustard they would show their appreciation beyond belief with cheering, clapping, standing up and shouting out their adulation. But if you couldn't meet their standards, they would dissect your performance with the most hurtful, and yet at times hilarious, verbal onslaughts imaginable.

A singer's life was perhaps the safest of all, performing a selection of songs in segue often being the safest bet. Comedians would often be confronted by an audience who were individually, let alone en-masse, funnier than they were.

Having performed at the Liverpool Empire and other venues many times in my formative years as a 'teen idol', I became familiar with the Scousers. It was at the height of my cabaret years as a solo artiste (where I would use the house musicians) that I discovered I had the ability to give as good as I got.

Heckling from late night supper and club audiences everywhere was generally alcohol-driven, and often incomprehensible, so consequently the hour of day would often determine how funny you were, or weren't. Both my rapport and my confidence grew as I added more patter to my act. I didn't tell jokes. I preferred the more topical approach, which generally teased the mind of the prospective heckler.

Whilst performing at the Shakespeare Club in the late 60s, I was holding my own, when a voice hollered, 'Sing some Elvis numbers, Vinnie!' My reply was. 'Why should I? He never sings any of mine.' It was corny, yet the standard reply to a song request and it usually got a bit of a laugh.

When I came off stage a blond haired guy came up to me at the bar and said how much he had enjoyed the show, even though I hadn't sung any Elvis numbers. 'I'll buy you a drink, Vinnie, then you can give me a lift home,' he said.

'Home?' I asked. 'Where's that?' 'Through

the tunnel,' he replied.

Before I could question him further about the lift home we began attracting attention at the bar as customers came up for autographs. But not only mine as some were asking the blond nutter who, by now, was making out he was Elvis Presley or Norman Wisdom by shaking his leg or falling against the bar.

I looked at his autograph and it read 'Freddie Starr.' I had no idea who he was.

When the autograph hunting subsided Freddie began to tell me of his love for Billy Fury and Elvis Presley and how he would love to be a rock 'n' roller. He already had a group in Liverpool, which were very popular, hence the autographs. I eventually agreed to give Freddie a lift home and we set off to the other side of the River Mersey.

We arrived at Freddie's house at about 1.30 am. I parked my car on wasteland opposite the house and went in for a coffee. Freddie couldn't wait to put on some sounds.

When he did it was wall to wall Billy and Elvis. He was singing and gyrating to the records at the same time, often having me in hysterics like never before. He was hilarious.

At 3.30 am. I told him I must go, as I had to drive to Manchester where I was staying with relatives. 'Stay here Vinnie,' said Freddie. 'We have a spare room.' The idea sounded great, so I accepted.

I had been in bed for about 30 minutes and at the stage where you hit the deep sleep, when a loud, yet whispering voice, awakened me saying, 'Vinnie, Vinnie,' at the same time as I was being rocked from side to side by someone pushing my shoulder. Yes it was Freddie.

'Quick Vinnie, get dressed. We've got to say goodnight to George,' said Freddie.

The following minutes passed with Freddie getting more and more irate as I questioned him about George, while remaining in my bed.

I eventually succumbed, got out of bed, and under instructions from Freddie, put on my pants and shirt with shoes and no socks. 'It won't take a minute,' he said.

We crept down the stairs, opened the front door and were greeted by the first light on the horizon as it lit up an eerie mist on the wasteland opposite where my car was parked.

Crossing the road Freddie continued to rant on in his loud whisper as he addressed George. 'Where are you George?'... 'What are you doing George?' 'I've brought Vinnie to see you, George!'

I was now beginning to stumble on loose bricks and debris as we ventured deeper into the heavy mist. I mumbled the questions to Freddie of 'Who? What? Where?'

Eventually Freddie turned around and

whisper-shouted to me, 'There he is.' He then turned back and shouted, 'Hi George, it's Freddie, I've got Vinnie with me.' I saw nothing, but the excitement in Freddie's voice certainly indicated that he had.

Freddie continued to talk to 'George' in a somewhat comforting manner before turning to say, 'Let's get back to the house.'

By now I was wide awake and totally confused. As we crossed the wasteland to return to the house I asked Freddie who George was. 'He's the brickyard ghost,' replied Freddie. 'I say goodnight to him every night because he gets really upset if I don't.'

With Freddie you never have a ghost of a chance!

Freddie Took the Piss!

The 'Bolton Casino' on Compton Way, Bolton, was a lovely old cinema conversion and a great gig. Having closed the first half my evening was finished. I was about to head for home when I heard a whisper that Freddie was late. It was now 10.10 pm and Freddie was due on stage at 10.15 pm. But it was Freddie, so everyone assumed he would arrive eventually, wow the audience, and be forgiven.

The compere asked Freddie's band if they would go on and play a few numbers until he arrived. They agreed, and went on. I decided to wait at the bar. It wasn't a long wait. Roars of laughter greeted his entrance, as in a light brown mackintosh he did a Norman Wisdom style entrance down the left-hand aisle of the auditorium. Stumbling and staggering, he eventually made his way to the stage where he 'Wisdom walked' his way to the gold drape back curtain that ran the full width of the stage.

It was here that Freddie looked over his shoulder and adopted a stance as if he was standing in front of a gent's urinal. We soon found out why. Freddie thought he was in a gent's urinal, as he leant slightly backwards while proceeding to turn the light gold curtain a darker shade as he peed against it.

The audience were in stitches. Without exposing himself Freddie tidied himself, turned around, did a Normal Wisdom walk down stage and got on with his act. As usual he had the audience in the palm of his hand and they loved him.

You couldn't take the piss out of Freddie, but he could take the piss out of himself.

Freddie's Act Stunk!

'Wigan Casino' didn't have a romantic ring to a club itinerary, and it was even less romantic when Freddie Starr appeared there.

The Wigan and Bolton casinos were big dates in the late 1960s and early 1970s cabaret diary. I worked them about twice a year and always enjoyed a great working relationship with their staff and audiences. A Lancashire brewery owned them and the main man for booking, as well as for deciding whether you came back or not, was Frank Simcox. As long a you did your job and you kept your nose clean, a nicer man than Frank could not be found on the circuit. Freddie, however, tested Frank's patience more than any other performer.

Had Freddie not had his amazing talent and been the favourite performer of most audiences, chances are he would never have played a venue more than once.

One such occasion was when Freddie and I shared a bill at Wigan Casino. It was just before Christmas and as there was only one dressing room that, with a few people in, could be become very cosy, especially if you were sharing with the Dagenham Girl Pipers as we were this particular week.

The cabaret room was long with the stage in the middle of one long wall and the dressing room entrance on the opposite long wall. Consequently when artistes were introduced they would open the dressing-room door, run across the dance floor and up the steps onto the stage. When you arrived on the stage the audience were either side of you, with a few on a balcony above.

The Dagenham Girl Pipers closed the first half by performing on the dance floor, as there were way too many pipers to fit on the stage. At the end of their act they marched off the cabaret floor straight into the dressing room where Freddie was dressed in his bath robe and doing his Cassius Clay (Muhammed Ali) impression with the occasional bagpipe sound thrown in. The girls stopped in their tracks as they witnessed this lunatic of a performer cavorting around in his bathrobe.

Freddie was never happier than when he had an audience, and it mattered not how many or where, he would perform. As he wound up his Cassius Clay sparring session he danced across the dressing room floor to the entrance and punched the door, his fist going straight through the door and out the other side. He coolly stepped back, reeled off a Cassius Clay style poem, and sat down. Acting as if nothing out of the ordinary had happened. Freddie sat and watched the girl pipers collect their belongings and head for Bolton Casino. Certain acts would double between the two venues, performing in the first half in one and then driving across to perform in the second half at the other.

With the pipers gone, Freddie decided to examine the damage to the door. After a very casual inspection he said, 'Come on Vinnie, I know what we can do.' All of a sudden it was a 'we' situation. Now what was I letting myself in for? Freddie led me down some stairs where there were boxes stored at the bottom. 'I noticed these boxes when I came in. I think they're Christmas deccies. Let's see what they have in them,' he said. One of the boxes was opened and we pulled back the flap. Inside were artificial Christmas wreaths.

Freddie grabbed two of them. 'These will do great,' he chuckled, and with that we ran back to the dressing room where he hung one on the outside of the door and one inside, both covering the offending hole.

Just before the second half started Frank Simcox paid us a visit. I later found out from Frank that he dropped into the dressing room every night when Freddie was performing but never with any other artiste. These days it would be referred to as 'damage control.'

'Nice decorations Freddie,' said Frank. 'Yeah! Vinnie found them in a box downstairs and put them up,' replied Freddie. Frank looked at me with a wry smile and mumbled 'Very nice Vince. Merry Christmas,' and left the dressing room. With that Freddie was like a tornado. He got dressed and was on stage before you could bat an eyelid, or give him a bollocking for involving you in his misdemeanours.

A few nights later when the girl pipers came off stage, Freddie grabbed my arm and said, 'Come on Vinnie, let's have a laugh with my band.' It was the interval and there was no one on stage. With the girl pipers not using the stage it meant Freddie's band could be set up and ready to go for the second half.

As we arrived on stage Freddie asked me to slacken the strings on a Gibson semi-acoustic guitar that was on its stand. 'What for?' I asked, as he began to undo the belt on his trousers. 'Pass it here,' said Freddie, now with his pants around his ankles and crouching. He then grabbed the guitar, laid it on the floor and proceeded to defecate through the sound hole.

I couldn't believe my eyes. I stood there, totally gob-smacked.

'Re-tune the guitar, Vinnie, while I put my kegs on,' he mumbled. 'No chance Freddie,' said I. 'You tune the bloody thing.' With that, I left the stage with Freddie clutching the guitar in one hand and his pants in the other.

Five minutes later Freddie came walking into the dressing room as if nothing had happened. 'The guy from the duo is tuning the guitar and I've asked the lighting guy to put the stage lights full up. That'll make it nice and warm,' he said, and then continued to get ready for his show.

It was only a matter of minutes into his performance that suspicious glances between the musicians and rabbit style twitching nostrils, indicated that the stage lights were having the desired effect on the smouldering stools.

The musical content took on a life of its own, as the band appeared to play faster in order to get off. Freddie however was his usual unpredictable self and appeared totally unconcerned for the guitarist who was undoubtedly suffering the most. They did finish the performance and from what I could gather it was not the first time Freddie had pulled this stunt, and I'm sure it won't be the last.

Jim Fixed It

Once it was converted into flats, the Aaland Hotel in Coram Street, off London's Russell Square, became home to Jimmy Saville, The Hollies and me. Jimmy occupied the ground floor apartment – convenient for parking his bicycle in the hallway. I had the floor above Jimmy and The Hollies were above me.

Jimmy used the bicycle to travel to record his shows at the Radio Luxembourg studios in Curzon Street, Mayfair or the BBC studios in Portland Place.

Before Jim fixed anything for me I very nearly had to fix him, when my fiancée Sandra, soon to be my first wife, stayed in my apartment overnight prior to my arriving back from Canada the next morning.

As with any attractive young lady, and irrespective of whether she was spoken for or not, Jimmy would try his luck. Sandra was offered every incentive under the sun to join Jimmy in his apartment. Thankfully Jimmy accepted the big 'no' he received from Sandra as an answer and let the matter rest.

As the highest-paid disc jockey of the early 1960s Jimmy was fast becoming a wealthy man. Cycling satisfied his two main obsession, his health and his wealth. Keeping fit helped him stay the pace at his main interest in life, the ladies. Among his few indulgences were his cars, a burgundy Rolls Royce and an electric blue E-Type Jaguar.

He befriended the owner of a Green Hut, one of the watering and feeding holes for taxi drivers. Green Huts were usually found in the squares throughout London and were the exclusive domain of relaxing taxi drivers ... and Jimmy Saville. There was nowhere cheaper to eat, so Jim loved them.

I occasionally went with Jimmy in one of his cars as he headed for the closest Green Hut, only 125 yards from our flats. As Jimmy relaxed inside, dining and spinning his yarns, his beloved Roller or E-Type would be parked outside. Next to the black cabs.

Due to Jimmy introducing me to the taxi drivers and the operator of the Green Hut, I was allowed to go in on my own and enjoy a chat and good inexpensive food.

As it happens, Jim did fix it for me!

Jimmy Slept Here

Every Wednesday during the summer season Jimmy Saville would travel to a dance night he hosted at the 40 Ballroom in Torquay. Most people would take a train or get a driver to take them. Not Jimmy. He had a beautiful mobile home, which he preferred to hotels, as there would be no nosy questions from reception staff if he turned up with a lady on his arm.

On one occasion Jimmy was returning to London overnight when he encountered dense fog on the moors. At the first opportunity he pulled off the road, parked on the grass and got his head down.

In the morning a loud banging on his mobile home door awakened him. Jumping out of bed, he answered the door to a tirade of abuse from an elderly gentleman who was upset that Jimmy had parked on his front lawn. The tirade soon turned to smiles when the gentleman realised he was giving a verbal battering to the one and only Jimmy Saville.

Within minutes Jimmy was dressed and enjoying a cooked breakfast in the comfort of the bungalow. With his usual charm Jimmy entertained the elderly couple, then said his goodbyes, stating he would return.

Jimmy did return to pay his respects to the elderly couple and was shown two ruts in the middle of the front lawn where his wheels had spun as he tried to drive off the mist-sodden grass.

The ruts had been filled with concrete and a sign placed between them reading, 'Jimmy Saville Slept Here.'

How's about that then, guys and gals?

The Gentle Giant

Having enjoyed athletic success as a schoolboy I jumped at any opportunity to participate in sporting activities.

During our summer season in the Isle of Man, my good pal and tennis partner, Michael Cox, hit recorder of *Angela Jones,* asked me if I would like to play for the Showbiz 11 Charity Football Team in Douglas as they were playing the Manx Police Football Team. Michael was a regular player but due to our Manx season he was unable to play in that season's Sunday games.

Other than having my shorts pulled down to my knees by Michael as we stood in line, a tradition when introducing first timers before their maiden appearance, the match went without incident. I played at centre half and thought I had a good game considering the size of the copper I was marking. After the game the team Manager Franklyn Boyd invited me to play when I was available.

Unfortunately the next occasion didn't arise until the following January when the team were playing in Swansea. I had appeared there in pantomime the previous Christmas and looked forward to meeting some old friends.

Our team included Tommy Steele, Toni Dahli, Jess Conrad, Michael Cox, Stan Stennett; the opposition, who were the Welsh Managers Select 11, was made up of legends of Welsh football such as John Charles, Mel Charles and Ivor Allchurch.

John Charles was considered by many to be the greatest footballer ever and a true gent. He was also built like a tank. No neck. Just shoulders that finished at his ears.

Due to his tank-like qualities he was certainly not to be messed with and it was decided that I would be too lacking in experience to handle John and should be switched to another position. In what appeared to be a tactical move, I was moved to right back.

Our goalkeeper was Jess Conrad. Everyone loved Jess, but nobody more than Jess himself. He spent little time watching the ball, as he was preoccupied talking with the girls behind his goal and signing autographs for them.

It was with a certain amount of anxiety

that Jess accepted me playing at right back. It was a position close to the girls and one that was a threat to his touchline popularity. I was also being asked to sign too many autographs.

Jess was never backward at coming forward and was always vocal at half time regarding team tactics. When he told our team manager Franklyn Boyd to move me to centre field and help mark John Charles, Franklyn didn't realise that it was because I was more of a threat to Jess and his touch-line harem than John Charles was to our goal.

The bruising I picked up bouncing off John Charles when trying to tackle him would have been an added bonus for Jess.

The Studio

Peace to All Men and Larry

An uneasy Christmas peace was declared between Larry Parnes and Jack Good in late December 1958, which resulted in Marty returning to the 'Oh Boy' TV show in the February.

Along with Marty's return, Billy Fury, Dickie Pride and I also had dates to appear on the show. For Billy and Dickie it would be their first. And for me it was to be my third, and my last.

One Monday morning in early February I called into Larry's office on Oxford Street in London. It was the usual 'in vain' visit of hoping to collect outstanding money, or even a sub.

I think Tommy Steele and Marty Wilde were the only ones exempt from having to wait in the office for a handout. On one occasion Joe Brown travelled up to the office on his motorbike and became so frustrated at having to wait, that he put his crash helmet on and started banging his head against the door shouting: 'Gimme some bleedin' money, Larry.'

Surprisingly, for a Monday morning Larry wasn't in the office, but his long suffering

PA, and London mother to Billy and me, Muriel was. She certainly had our best interests at heart and these days she would have been classed as a mole.

I had recently had one of my regular fall outs with Larry and communications were at an all time low so what Muriel told me didn't come as a surprise.

Apparently there was an audition for a new BBC TV pop show in progress at a rehearsal room in Baker Street and the producer, Stewart Morris, had asked for me to attend but Larry had told him I was unavailable. Muriel then said that other than Tommy and Marty, all of the other boys represented by Larry were at the audition as Larry was hoping to get them all involved in the upcoming, follow-on series to the Six Five Special and Dig This.

Having given me the address, and telling me not to tell Larry where I got the information, Muriel gave me the money for a taxi.

As I arrived at the rehearsal room, I could hear the strains of *Good Golly Miss Molly* being belted out for an upstairs room and it didn't sound like anyone from Larry's stable.

Being lured up the stairs by the rocking rendition of Little Richard's classic, I entered the rehearsal room where I was greeted by Billy Fury, Dickie Pride, Duffy Power, Johnny Gentle, Adam Faith, John Barry and many others I didn't recognise, all sitting around the perimeter of the rehearsal room as if it were a doctor's waiting room. The blonde haired guy playing the piano, and bringing *Good Golly Miss Molly* to a rousing conclusion, turned out to be Roy Young, soon to become a good mate and international star.

Sitting at a table in the middle of the room was a smiling Larry, three efficient looking ladies and a stocky guy who appeared to be calling the shots. He turned out to be Stewart Morris the producer and it was he who spotted me first, and smilingly pointed me out to Larry, who very quickly lost his smile.

I sat with Billy and Duffy and they told me they had yet to audition. Expecting a long wait I decided to go out for a Coke. Walking towards the door I was beckoned over by one of Stewart's assistants who whispered, 'You're next.' So I returned to my seat.

Teddy Bear and *It's Only Make Believe* were my choice of audition numbers. Both numbers appeared to go down well with Stewart and his team but were greeted with scowls from Larry.

A few days later I was summoned to Larry's office, where a smiling Muriel greeted me. 'You can go straight in,' she said winking.

Larry told me how hard he had worked in persuading Stewart Morris to use me on the Drumbeat show.

'Stewart was very reluctant to use you,'

said Larry unconvincingly. 'He didn't even want you at the auditions, so you're a very lucky boy.'

Larry then went on to tell me that I had been signed for three months and I would front the show. I asked him if any of his other artistes would be doing the show and he said all of them. The only two who did were Marty and Billy. When Billy did the show he had a problem as Larry gave him wrong information regarding the song he was singing and Billy had problems with the lyrics. Steward Morris was so upset he gave Billy a public dressing down and Billy did only the one show.

I did three months, which was extended to six.

Did the 'Idol on Parade' Get Laid?

The guest artistes on one episode of BBC TV's Drumbeat pop show were Tony Newley and Petula Clark. Although having just turned 20, Petula was already enjoying a prolific career in both movies and recording. She also had a reputation for enjoying male company.

My publicity manager, Chris Reynolds, was a fanatic when it came to Petula and he would have married her at the drop of a hat given the opportunity. He was stalking the studio for the whole of the period Petula was on set.

During rehearsals, Chris noticed that Petula appeared to be enjoying the company of Tony Newley and at every opportunity they would pair off together and engage in what appeared to be more than casual conversation.

Many of the dressing rooms at the BBC Riverside Studios, from where Drumbeat was broadcast, had an air-conditioning pipe running from wall to wall and into the adjacent dressing rooms. If you stood on your dressing room table and held a glass to the air conditioning pipe you could hear perfectly what was going on next door and in the adjacent dressing rooms.

As I approached my dressing room, Adam's head appeared from behind his door and he beckoned me excitedly into his room. 'Quick, stand on the dresser,' said Adam, with a broad grin. I grabbed the glass he handed me and held it against the AC pipe. 'I think Pet and Tony are having it off,' he chuckled. As the grunting and groaning appeared to be coming from Pet's dressing room, and she and Tony had shown a definite liking for each other, there seemed to be no argument to that conclusion.

I jumped off the dressing table and rushed to find Chris in the hope that our discovery would put an end to his Petula Clark obsession. On finding him, I grabbed his arm and took him to the dressing rooms, trying to explain our discovery on the way.

When we arrived in the dressing room corridor, we encountered a red faced, yet smiling, Tony Newley leaving Petula's dressing room. In spite of all the evidence Chris decided that we had fabricated the whole story in order to turn him against her.

As Adam and I watched the live transmission on a monitor in his dressing room, Tony was singing his latest record release, *Idol On Parade* live to fifteen million viewers, so we joined in singing our own lyrics consisting of 'Idol who got laid...'

When Petula sang her latest recording, *Where Do I Go From Here?* we fell about laughing, as we had an idea where she had been, but no idea as to where she was going. Or who with.

Hello My Darling

The BBC TV series Drumbeat proved to be a great success and was extended for a further three months with Adam Faith, The John Barry Seven, Danny Rivers, Sylvia Sands and Bob Miller's Millermen and myself all remaining with the show.

It was during this period that Charlie Drake was a guest on the show singing his latest record *Splish Splash*. Charlie was fast becoming one of Saturday night television's favourites and he was high in the BBC's shopping list to sign up for his own series. Unfortunately, Charlie's diminutive size was to lead to a confrontation of gigantic proportions.

The guest artistes would have their first rehearsal with either The John Barry Seven or Bob Miller's Millermen before lunch on the day of transmission. This would conclude with the resident artistes being called in to rehearse the finale and the guest artiste would then be given their position in the finale line-up. As I was 6' 5" tall, my position was always in the middle with regulars Adam Faith, Sylvia Sands or the guest standing to my left or to my right. As Charlie was positioned to my left by the floor manager, he looked up at me and immediately broke away from the line. Grabbing the floor manager by the arm Charlie pulled him away and began remonstrating with him. The floor manager then turned and shouted, 'Break for lunch everyone. Back at 1.30 pm please,' as Charlie continued his tirade. A tirade he continued until we were all out of the studio.

Drumbeat was usually transmitted from the BBC Riverside Studios Hammersmith but on occasions from the Lime Grove Studios in Shepherds Bush. As Shepherds' Bush had a better selection of restaurants, lunch break would be called and the artistes were soon out of the studios heading for their favourite eatery. Mine was a small Italian bistro in a cellar close to the studio. It was also where our producer Stewart Morris and his staff could be found.

After lunch I left Stewart and Yvonne at the table and headed up the narrow staircase to return. Three steps from the top I was confronted by Charlie who was about to descend for lunch. Even though he was standing three steps higher than me our eyes were level. He looked angry as he yelled at me to go back down the stairs so he could come down. I told him that I was only three from the top and I was coming up.

Charlie ranted on, saying that if I didn't I would be in trouble so I'd better go back down. Ignoring him, I pushed my way past and returned to the studio.

Shortly after I arrived back at the studio, I was summoned to the production office where Stewart Morris explained that the BBC were desperate to sign Charlie as part of their Saturday night programming and he didn't want us to be the ones held responsible for any slip-ups. 'I know you weren't responsible for the problems on the bistro staircase. But would you help us all by apologising to Charlie?' asked Stewart.

Stewart had stood by me during my on-going battle with Larry and had become someone I trusted, so I agreed.

I went to Charlie's dressing room and knocked on the door. Charlie's manager, who greeted me with a smile, opened the door. Charlie, who was sitting on a chair in front of his dressing table, stared menacingly at me as I told him I was sorry for the misunderstanding on the restaurant staircase. 'OK.' He grumbled, turning to face his mirror as if I wasn't there.

Stewart thanked me later in the day and added that I would benefit from my apology.

Two months after the final Drumbeat show I received a phone call summoning me to BBC HQ for a meeting with light entertainment director Harry Carlisle who offered me the Eurovision Song contest the following February.

Null Points for the Suit

'If you're nice to people and you're a good boy these are the sort of rewards you get,' said Larry in his usual motherly tones as he broke the news to me that I had been chosen for the British heats of the 1960 Eurovision Song Contest.

The song was *Teenage Tears*, not my style and better suited to Adam Faith with its gentle melody and plucking violin strings. But in spite of the weakness of the song,

Larry was convinced he had the formula for our Eurovision success.

'Every year the ladies wear cocktail dresses and the men wear dinner suits,' said Larry excitedly. 'You will be different. You'll wear a modern Italian style suit and we'll get it made at Cecil Gee's,' a men's clothing store on Shaftsbury Avenue that had me drooling every time I passed the window.

Before I knew it I was in Cecil Gee's and Larry was explaining to the manger what he wanted me to wear. My face had been on TV every week for almost a year so deals were not hard to come by. An outfit that should have cost over £120 was complimentary and all the manager wanted was a store mention in my press release.

With a made-to-measure grey shark-silk Italian box suit, a grey silk Italian shirt and tie and a hand made pair of grey patent winkle picker shoes from Annello & David Footwear, I was set. I couldn't wait to try them on.

There were two heats to be held over a two night period on the 2nd and 4th February 1960. The first heat on the 2nd consisted of David Hughes, Don Lang, Benny Lee, Lita Roza and Malcolm Vaughan. The second heat on the 4th was Pearl Carr and Teddy Johnson, Ronnie Carroll, Bryan Johnson, Marion Keene, Denis Lotis and myself.

With the knowledge of what happened in

the first heat I felt quietly confident. However, the favourites, and runners up of the previous year's final, Pearl Carr and Teddy Johnson, were in my heat and to be feared.

I was third to sing, and to the lush string backing of the Eric Robinson Orchestra I stood resplendent in my Italian suit and gave it my best shot.

Sadly, it turned out that the judges in the various UK regions were far more interested in my suit than the song as they pulled my appearance to pieces.

'A disgrace to the nation.' 'How dare he dress in such a slovenly manner when representing his country?' 'This is indicative of today's youth and their rock 'n' roll culture,' and 'No respect for their elders,' were just a few of the comments made. My final placing was sixth out of six and my points total was zero, or 'nul points' in Eurovision jargon.

Letters supporting the judges flooded in and when I toured Scotland a few weeks later, I was attacked by a burly kilt-wearing Scot as he tried to use me for a re-enactment of Bannockburn, while hurling abuse at my anti-national dress sense.

Why?

'It's Muriel, Vince!' my landlady Mrs Ryan shouted up the stairs. Being more like my mother than my manager's secretary, Muriel would often phone me just to check that I was OK and behaving myself.

On this occasion Muriel had called to tell me that I was to fly to London the following Sunday morning. Due to the strict Scottish licensing laws, Sunday was usually a day of rest and if you wanted a drink in a hotel or bar you had to prove you were a *bona fide* traveller. This meant that if you lived, or were staying, next door to a bar or hotel, you couldn't drink there but would have to travel a distance of at least three miles to have a drink. You had to drive in order to drink.

Muriel told me that Dick Rowe, my A&R Manager at Top Rank Records, had a song he was convinced could be the big hit we had been searching for and that I was to phone him to discuss the details.

Dick appeared full of confidence as he told me he had secured the exclusive British rights for a song called *Why*, currently number one in the United States by Frankie Avalon. I was to fly to London and record it on the Sunday so that it could be rush-released.

On my arrival at Heathrow, I was greeted by my press manager, Chris Reynolds, who took me to Great Cumberland Place and the Pye recording studios. Chris, like Dick, was a big believer in me and was convinced that it was Larry's interference that was preventing my recording success. With Larry's penthouse apartment being directly opposite the recording studios we expected him to appear at any time during the session.

Guitarist Bert Weedon and drummer Tony Crombie were the first people I saw upon entering the studio. They were both guys I knew, not only from the recording studio, but also from theatre work.

As the musicians set up and did their sound check, Dick took me into the production office to listen to the two tracks he had found for me.

Why and *El Paso* were the tracks in question, with Dick being especially excited with *Why* and confident we would make number one.

The session went really well with *Why* being much the easier of the two songs to record. Having fourteen verses and a running time of over five minutes, *El Paso* proved a very different proposition.

Dick assured me that *Why* would be the elusive big hit and that Top Rank would have the single in the shops within three days.

Chris congratulated me on a great session and echoed Dick's enthusiasm. He did however voice his concern at Larry not showing his face at the session by saying, 'Larry lives directly opposite the studio and I know he's got nothing on today.'

Due to my early flight back to Edinburgh

the following morning, Chris suggested that we went for a Chinese meal and then back to his apartment in Victoria's Dolphin Square, where I would be staying overnight.

The Lobster Pot on Edgeware Road in London, was a celebrity hot spot and the Chinese restaurant where the rich and famous were pampered. As Chris and I salivated over our spare ribs and Singapore noodles, our appetites suddenly went and our mouths dried up as the television in the corner broadcast Anthony Newley singing *Why*, on Sunday Night at the London Palladium.

Our appetites gone, we sat and watched as Anthony finished and then he announced, 'That's my latest recording ladies and gentlemen. It's also been recorded by two other artistes but they don't need the money and I do, so please buy mine.'

'I bet Larry knew about this,' said Chris. 'That's why he didn't visit the studio today. What a bastard!'

My return to Scotland the next morning was a sombre affair. Not having had the opportunity to phone Dick Rowe, all manner of conspiracies were mulling around in my head, with Larry involved in all of them.

When I did finally get in touch with Dick he sounded as gutted as I felt. He didn't think however that Larry was aware of Anthony Newley's cover version.

Nothing Like a Dame

The occasional 'bloody' and 'damn' was as bad as the language ever got within the circle of my family and friends. My uncle Fred used the strongest language but he was a jovial cockney loved by everyone and he could say anything he wanted.

On occasions I would hear the 'F' word used when I was an apprentice joiner, but I had never heard a lady use it ... until I worked with Shirley Bassey.

We were recording a Christmas special for ITV, which involved a dance routine using hoola hoops. The hoops had been the summer rage in 1958 and eight girl dancers were rehearsing a routine where, as they rotated their hips, the hoops would rotate around their waist. But I don't think any of us saw it quite the way Shirley did.

With the routine nearing its finale the intensity grew as the girls struggled to keep the hoops going and to stop them from dropping around their ankles.

At the end I was stood next to Shirley on the edge of the dance floor when she looked at me and, without batting an eyelid, said, 'It looked as if they were having a damn good fuck but not enjoying it, didn't it darling?'

My mother was a big Shirley Bassey fan so

I kept the story to myself. There was nothing like a Dame!

What Dixon Didn't Know

When the BBC television show 'Six Five Special' finished, musicians from bands such as Tito Burns and Tony Osborne would head for the pub opposite the studios where they would enjoy a pint. Sax and vibes player Tubby Hayes, drummer Phil Seaman, tenor player Ronnie Scott and so it went; the cream of the crop would be there relaxing and living life to the full.

Sadly a few of them indulged in more than just a pint to give them a buzz. Phil Seaman and Tubby Hayes were both recognised as being at the top of their game musically, but also in abusing their bodies.

I once saw Phil Seaman perform at the Chez Joey club in Manchester with a hypodermic syringe behind his ear. He had shot-up prior to going on stage and it was the audience who noticed the syringe and burst into fits of laughter.

It was one evening after the 'Six Five Special' however, when Tubby Hayes was to make a more spectacular public *faux pas* than Phil Seaman had. Tubby had gone to his dressing room where, it's alleged, he indulged in some form of narcotics. After leaving his room to come across to the pub, he took the wrong turning.

At the time, Dixon of Dock Green was being transmitted live from the adjacent studio, but due to not being fully *compos mentis,* Tubby opened the wrong door and found himself wandering through the set of 'Dixon of Dock Green', which was being watched by over 10 million people.

Appearing oblivious to what was going on, Tubby continued to stroll across the set, carrying his saxophone case, and out of the studio to the pub, where he received a tumultuous round of applause for his walk-on-performance. His colleagues having seen it all on the pub television.

I Could Not Be Moved

It was during a sound check at the Granada Theatre, Kingston that I realised my fellow Yellow Belly and partner in crime, Joe Brown was not just special, he was very special.

All of us on the bill had finished our sound checks when Joe returned to the stage carrying a 12 string guitar, an instrument I hadn't seen him play before. He then started to play a song which was so far removed from the earlier sound check numbers of rock 'n' roll, but would have been perfect for a Harvest Festival service. It was *All Things Bright and Beautiful.*

No one imagined he would include the tune in his act that night, let alone stop the show with it. But he did! It was typical of Joe's ever-growing talent and appeal. He was, and still is, always looking for a fresh approach.

A song proving popular in my act at that time was a revamped spiritual from my skiffle days, *I Shall Not Be Moved.* I had given it a Gary US Bonds party feel and Joe commented how much he enjoyed it and that I should record it.

Joe was finishing a new album when I dropped into the Pye studios to see him. It was 7.00 pm and he had been at it all day but had finished early, with 3 hours left of his allocated session time, and not wishing to waste the remaining studio time, he suggested we have a go at *I Shall Not Be Moved.*

With Joe on the drums, his band The Bruvvers providing the backing and his lovely wife Vicki Brown adding amazing backing vocals, we got started. Three hours later we had produced the best of all my singles. It was typical of Joe's enthusiasm and genius that this came to be.

The recording received the best reviews by far of any of my singles with Don Nichols of Disc magazine headlining his review with: 'Eager guaranteed Number 1 with this one.'

It didn't make 'Number 1', but on one very foggy evening it acted as an ironical musical backdrop when, due to dense fog I found myself in a ditch. As I sat pondering the situation, unable to go anywhere as my car was stuck, the car radio was tuned into Radio Luxemburg when DJ Kent Walton announced. 'And now, one that's heading for the charts, it's Vince Eager and *I Shall Not Be Moved.*'

And I wasn't moved until the AA arrived 2 hours later!

Jack Good Could Clean Up!

Jack Good's 'Oh Boy' show was the ultimate show when it came to show-casing artistes' talents. Both managers and agents would offer all manner of things to persuade Jack to feature their artistes, as an 'Oh Boy' appearance could add a zero to an artiste's fee overnight.

As powerful as he was, Hymie Zahl was no exception. In spite of being the agent for some of the biggest names making records and treading the boards, he knew an appearance on Jack's show was priceless. It was for that reason he was desperate to get Jack to use Terry Dene.

Terry was going through a bad time. He was thrown out of the army, arrested for being drunk and smashing a shop window in Wigmore Street and then his marriage to Edna Savage failed. What Terry needed was positive press and under Jack's guidance he could get it.

Before being approached by Hymie, Jack had already decided he would use Terry on the show. Not knowing this, Hymie contacted Jack and put a proposal to him. Hymie's proposal was, if Jack was to feature Terry on 'Oh Boy', Hymie would buy him a vacuum cleaner. Jack thought this was hilarious but didn't have the heart to tell Hymie he'd already decided to use Terry.

Terry did appear on 'Oh Boy', but Jack didn't get his vacuum cleaner.

As I write this I'm delighted to hear that Terry is to work solo on the circuit again. He has been limited in his ability to work in recent years due to certain restrictions, alleged to have been imposed on him by his management. Welcome back Terry. If you get the opportunity go and see him. He's singing as well as ever.

Not, My Coo Ca Choo

'It's Hal Carter for you Vince,' yelled Jean our landlady. Like most pro digs landladies, Jean knew many of the show business agents and managers and wasn't fazed by who she had to talk to.

Hal was Billy Fury's manager and a pal of mine from the late 1950s. He was also one of the most popular and trusted guys in the business. He told me to get to a TV, watch the clown on the children's show 5 o'clock Club, and then phone him back.

My Group, The Clockwork Toys, and I were about to have dinner, when Hal phoned, so Jean gave me a tray and I watched the show as I had dinner.

The clown turned out to be a singer called Alvin Stardust dressed as a pierrot clown singing a very catchy song entitled Coo Ca Choo. I thought the song was great but the performance was nothing special.

When I returned Hal's call he asked me what I thought of the song. I told him I thought it was very catchy but that I wasn't impressed with the clown.

Hal then stopped me in my tracks by asking me if I fancied taking over the role of the singer, Alvin Stardust. He went on to explain that the present Alvin, Pete Shelley, was the song's composer but he didn't want to continue in the role of Alvin so they were looking for someone to take over immediately.

I told Hal that due to my diary being full for the coming months I couldn't do it if I wanted to, and also that I didn't like the clown image. He then went on to tell me they were going to change Alvin's image as Pete Shelley had used the pierrot clown only as a disguise.

A few weeks later I saw Shane Fenton on television in the re-invented guise of 'Alvin' with a glam-rock style based on our mutual friend, Gene Vincent's image. Shane was brilliant. He took the song to a new level and made it is own. His sultry presentation was perfect and he went from strength to strength as he deservedly conquered the UK and then Europe. It was a role I could never have pulled off.

I've had the good fortune to work with Alvin many times since and he is without doubt one of the nicest, and most talented, guys you could wish to work with.

£86 for Six Five Special, Drumbeat and Dig This?

In the mid 1970s I received a phone call from Frank Cvitanovich. Frank was a TV Director/Producer responsible for many television documentaries including, 'Beauty, Bonny, Daisy, Violet, Grace and Geoffrey Moreton', an acclaimed feature about a remarkable farmer and his shire horses that won a BAFTA award and the Prix Italia for documentaries.

Frank had moved from Canada to

England in 1957. He told me that I was the British pop performer who impressed him most and he wanted to produce a fly-on-the-wall documentary about me.

A few weeks after the phone call, Frank came to visit me in Swansea where I was appearing. He was very enthusiastic about the project, stating that it would necessitate him and a member of his crew travelling with me, and on occasion moving in with my family and me.

Also, much would depend on a visit he was due to make to the BBC Archives HQ in Windmill Road, London, which would reveal what footage was available.

Six weeks later a very despondent Frank phoned me. He told me that as storage space at Windmill Road was at a premium, the BBC were starting to destroy archive footage which meant shows such as Six Five Special, Drumbeat and Dig This were under threat.

Frank also told me that in order to prevent the BBC from carrying out such drastic actions he had offered to store the footage on their behalf and given them first, and free access. Surprisingly the BBC declined and thousands of feet of tele cine were subsequently destroyed.

A few years later I discovered that the scrapping operation yielded a total of £86 in scrap value, which was in the form of the melted-down silver oxide strip that ran down the edge of the film which the sound track was on.

In recent years there have been many projects that didn't come to fruition due to the BBC's short sightedness in destroying the archive footage. Along with Frank's Paul Pierrot wanted to feature me in 'Juke' Box Heroes', as did BBC's 'Arena' and 'Never Mind The Buzzcocks'.

I wonder if the BBC would have sold them for £87. Possibly not.

Mayhem in Montreal

A mixture of delight and trepidation greeted the news that 'Elvis the Musical' was heading to Canada for four months. The delight was because my mother was Canadian born and my brother and his family lived in Toronto. The trepidation, because Canada was the only country, other than America that Elvis had performed in.

Our season at the Royal Alex Theatre in Toronto received excellent reviews and played to capacity audiences. We also had coaches from Elvis fan clubs in America travelling up to see the show. Thankfully they seemed to love it and the many letters I received indicated that we were doing justice to the great man's memory.

During the Toronto season I flew up to

Montreal to appear on a couple of radio and TV chat shows to plug our forthcoming visit to the city's Theatre Saint Denis the following month.

As one of the radio shows was in French, my comments were translated, but during the show I got the feeling they were having a good laugh at my expense. With not understanding the language I found it difficult to defend myself when questions such as; 'Why should we go to see you when we have our own Elvis impersonators here in Montreal?'

I explained that I was not an Elvis impersonator and that it was an award winning London production that had received rave reviews in Toronto. Unfortunately my mentioning Toronto only seemed to fuel their determination to belittle me even more.

During the flight back to Toronto for the evening show, the publicist accompanying me told me that Montreal had the largest Elvis fan base per capita in the world and had more fans in Memphis at Elvis's funeral than any other city. This news only made me more apprehensive than I already was at the thought of entertaining the French Canadians.

On arriving back in Montreal four weeks later I had a busy media day with my first appearance being on a French-speaking breakfast TV show.

Great consternation greeted me on my arrival at the studio, when the TV show's producers discovered I wasn't wearing my 'Elvis Las Vegas' suit. 'You do not look like Elvis, you look like a golfer' was one of the comments that greeted me. We would, on occasions, take a jump suit to interviews but only if requested. It wasn't a given.

The TV show was a Richard and Judy type format with both presenters asking questions and it didn't take me long to realize that it was yet another Franco hijack as I became the butt of their jokes.

The crunch came when three guys dressed in Elvis Vegas style jumpsuits were produced, and I was informed there was to be a sing off, including me, to determine the best Elvis.

Thankfully my publicist was French-Canadian and she came into the studio during a commercial break screaming her head off and telling me we were leaving. My concern was the effect it would have on the show that evening if the news got out that I had walked out of the French speaking TV show. The media could have a field day and kill our Montreal season.

At that evening's Montreal premier of the show, I had never felt as nervous as I did when I made my first entrance singing *That's Alright Mama*. The audience didn't show their usual enthusiasm, and the general backstage feeling was that the story of the TV studio walk out had broken and a tough night was on the cards. As the show progressed however, the reception improved with every scene, with the first half finale, *How Great Thou Art,* receiving one of the best responses we had ever had.

The second half picked up where the first half left off. Never had we experienced an audience so up for the show. So much so that at the end of *Suspicious Minds* the audience stood up screaming for more and wouldn't stop. I couldn't deliver the dialogue that followed and looked to the wings for help.

The company manager, Tony, stood watching and mouthed to me, 'Do it again!' I mouthed back, with my finger pointing upwards. 'What about the lights?' They were programmed into a computer and couldn't repeat the previous numbers settings. 'No problem!' Tony shouted back. With that we launched into *Suspicious Minds* for a second, then a third time. It was a very physical number and after singing it three times I was wet through and standing in a pool of sweat.

When the local and national papers came with my breakfast the following morning, I digested those reviews that were in English, and waited to be told what the French editions had to say.

'Magnifique Elvis' was the headline in one,

which gave me an idea as to what they thought, and the English-speaking press reviews were equally enthusiastic. They turned out to be the best reviews we had ever received. In spite of the studio confrontation, Montreal and the French Canadians did us proud!

Mozzer Made Me Number 1!

Whenever I performed a ballad on BBC TV's Drumbeat show, there would be a lot of enquiries in record shops asking if I had recorded, it Paul Anka's *Lonely Boy*, Conway Twitty's *It's Only Make Believe* and Robin Luke's *Susie Darling* being the most popular.

My manager Larry Parnes seemed oblivious to the opportunity it presented us with and continued to bemoan, 'There are no good ballads available. When I hear one, you can record it.'

The following year I was with Jerry Lordon, composer of The Shadows *Apache*, and hits by Cliff Richard, Petula Clark, and Cleo Laine. I told Jerry of my search for an original big ballad and he said he had an idea. Fetching his ukulele from his car, he proceeded to sing and play me a great song he had written entitled *The World's Loneliest Man*.

At a meeting with Ron Richards of Top

Rank, he agreed it was a great song, suitable for me, and that I should record it.

My suggestion to Ron and Bill Shepherd the musical director, the man given the task of writing the musical arrangement, was to have a guitar introduction, similar to Paul Anka's *Lonely Boy*, and build it up by introducing strings, French horns, timpani drums and a vocal group. It was a big-ask for someone who was searching for his first big hit, yet one that Bill Shepherd agreed with. My only other request was to have Big Jim Sullivan on guitar. Not having played with Jim since his defection from my band to Marty Wilde's Wildcats two years earlier was a personal, as much as a professional, request.

Ron Richards was in charge of the recording session and we were both thrilled with the outcome and left the studio feeling that this could be the big one.

My optimism was short lived, however, when a few days later I heard the demo in Larry's office. It was a disaster. The master mix was terrible. The timpani, being way too forward in the mix drowned out much of the vocals and the strings. It sounded bloody awful.

I immediately phoned Top Rank to try and get a remix. Unfortunately it was already being pressed and there was no possibility of re-mixing it.

The record received varied reviews and

faded into insignificance, until 1989, when, according to a friend, it was mentioned in the New Musical Express as the number one on, 'the songs to be cremated with' list of Morrissey.

I wasn't aware of Morrissey, or Mozzer as he had become affectionately known, but I knew of his band The Smiths as they were popular in the ship's discos. When I discovered who he was, the only conclusion I could come to was that they were the records he liked least, and perhaps they should be cremated with him.

That proved not to be the case as, by courtesy of the Internet, I discovered they were indeed his favourites.

Morrissey's 'Singles To Be Cremated With'

1. The World's Loneliest Man
    – Vince Eager
2. Don't Take The Lovers From The World
    – Shirley Bassey
3. What A Nice Way To Turn 17
    – The Crystals
4. There, I've Said It Again – Sam Cooke
5. Loneliness Remembers What Happiness Forgets – Dionne Warwick
6. Strange, I Know – The Marvelettes
7. Third Finger, Left Hand
    – Martha Reeves And The Vandellas

8. I Take it Back – Sandy Posey

9. Heart – Rita Pavone

10. Shoes – Reparata

11. Terry – Twinkle

12. Attack – The Toys

13. I've Been A Bad, Bad Boy – Paul Jones

14. Insult To Injury – Timi Yuro

So my thanks go to Mozzer for my first number one. Even if it will be in the hereafter!

Yea! Yea! It Was Worth the Wait

While living in Florida, I received a phone call from John Beecher of Rollercoaster Records. John was interested in putting together a vinyl EP of my early Skiffle recordings with The Vagabonds Skiffle Group.

With being at sea on cruise ships for most of the time, it was difficult to arrange anything so I told John that I would be in touch.

On my return to the UK I contacted John and he put out a retro EP of *Money Honey, Cotton Fields, My Dixie Darling, Be Bop A Lu La,* I enjoyed working on the project with John as he told it like it was and produced a nice package.

A couple of years later John told me he would like to put out a CD using some of my old recordings along with some new.

The CD consisted of 24 tracks and I was

very happy with the end result. But where John excelled himself was in the packaging. It was brilliant and I was amazed that at that stage of my career someone should care sufficiently to produce a product of that quality.

It's been a very popular CD and I only wish John Beecher had been in my corner 45 years earlier. A nicer and more competent person you couldn't wish to meet.

The CD titled *'Yea! Yea! It's Vince Eager'* was well worth waiting for, and it is still available.

Elvis in the Loo?

The following is an extract from an interview in America between Gary James and Spencer Davis in 1999.

Gary: You're from Wales. What was the Rock 'n' roll scene like in Wales during the 50's and 60's when you were there.

Spencer: What was going on there was very much a reflection of what was happening here, and that was Buddy Holly, Fats Domino, Elvis Presley, The Big Bopper, Ritchie Valens, The Crickets, Eddie Cochran. I left Wales when I was 16 to work for Her Majesty's Civil Service. That only lasted 18 months in one department, 18 months in another department. 1957 to 1959 were very formative years in Rock 'n' roll. What tended to happen was our idols were modelling themselves after Elvis. We had Marty Wilde. We had Terry Dene. We had Tommy Steele. They were really copying Elvis. They really didn't have their own identity. We had one guy that never really did well but should have. His name is Vince Eager. What impressed me is he could sing Jailhouse Rock in the same key as Elvis. I was convinced that because he could do that he was God. That was it. He was marvellous.

I knew my vocal range was similar to Presley's and many people had remarked that I sounded like him, but I never set out to copy him.

That changed, when I was approached after a show in the early 1970s. The guy's name was Andy and he told me he produced budget cover albums of new releases for places such as supermarkets, elevator and background systems. He asked me if I would be interested in doing the Elvis cover sessions for his company, then went on to explain that the session fee was above the norm and nobody would know who the vocalist was. After upping the session fee from £50 to £70 plus expenses, which was very acceptable for a few hours in London,

I agreed.

My first session was to record *Polk Salad Annie,* followed by *Burning Love, Proud Mary, Way Down* and on it went.

The first releases were on the Hallmark label, then the Pickwick label, then unknown labels to complement the unknown vocalist. It all seemed very bizarre but I didn't encounter any problems, and always got paid following the sessions.

By the time I got used to hearing my dulcet tones belting out *Proud Mary* and other Elvis songs in lifts, supermarkets, and most embarrassingly of all, gents toilets in motorway services, I had been contracted by my good pal, and manager of Billy Fury, Hal Carter.

Hal told me that a company called Avenue Records were interested in bringing out a series of 12 albums entitled, 'A Tribute to Elvis', with ex Tornados guitarist Alan Caddy and Hal producing.

I was to be paid £200 per album, which would be recorded in one day, and my name would not be used.

The Wembley sound stage was used for the session and I thought Alan Caddy did an amazing job in replicating the original sound by using ambience microphones and other tricks. At the end of the 12 track session I was disappointed that my name wasn't going to be used on the project as, in those few hours, I had become really proud of it. Even my old Drumbeat pal Adam Faith popped in during a break from recording his TV drama 'Budgie' in an adjacent studio. 'You're singing brilliant Vince,' said Adam. 'Your voice just gets better.'

A week later Hal told me that Avenue Records now wanted to put the album out under my name, as would be the following 11 in the series. In order to do this they were prepared to pay me an extra £200 plus 5% of the sales and I could purchase them for 50 pence each to sell at my live appearances. It sounded good to me so I agreed. A few days later I received a cheque for £200.

The album supposedly sold over 80,000. I never did receive my 5%, but I did very well with after show sales.

Another company then used identical packaging and gave the record the title, 'Cliff Nelson Pays Tribute to Elvis'.

There are also 'Vince Eager Pays Tribute to Elvis' albums, all with different labels and packaging, available in Australia, Holland, Brazil, Mexico, Singapore, Canada and South Africa.

It would have been nice to have received more recognition for the album, but then again the music industry is not about being nice!

Pink n' Black records are including it in a double CD package, 'The Complete Vince

Eager' due out in October 2007.

Boy Meets 'Topless' Girl

For three days every week, the El Morocco Hotel in Didsbury, Manchester was home to the elite of rock n' roll, with Billy Fury, Marty Wilde, Joe Brown, Eddie Cochran, Gene Vincent, Johnny Cash and The Vernon Girls being just a few of the residents. The reason for them being there was Boy Meets Girl. The smash hit Jack Good TV show that followed on from Oh Boy!

The hotel boasted a Moroccan theme consisting of camel's heads, hookah pipes, giant brass plates, exotic carpets, and a mural painted on the dining room wall of topless belly dancers.

Now, I've been to Morocco on many occasions but I have never seen topless belly dancers. Scantily dressed, yes. Topless, no!

There were of course no complaints from the male residents. After all, they were rock n' rollers so what's wrong with having boobs with your bran for breakfast? Jack Good's secretary, Sheila Curtis, however expressed her concerns to the management that The Vernon Girls were not enjoying the breakfast backdrop as much as the guys, and some were finding it embarrassing.

Sheila's complaint was noted by the hotel

management and their reaction was prompt, yet somewhat disappointing to the male guests.

At breakfast the following morning the diners were greeted by the same dancing ladies, but with bikini tops. The mural painter had worked overnight to un-titillate the mural by painting bikini tops on the bare bosoms.

From Oh Boy to Oh Heck!

No More Pissin' In't Car Park!

The small South Yorkshire mining village of Greasborough boasted a miners welfare club, which was the centre of the community and recognised as being the Palladium of all social clubs.

The man responsible was the hard working miner and visionary concert secretary, Les Booth. Les had fast become known in Northern entertainment circles as the man who only booked the best.

My fondest recollection of Greasborough is that I was performing there for a week when my eldest son Simon was born on my last night, Saturday 28th August 1965. Instead of my usual opening, the band played me on with *Oh Mein Papa* and as the chairman introduced me he told the audience of Simon's birth earlier in the day.

It was for different reasons however that I went back to Greasborough a few months later. I was appearing at the Kon Tiki Club in nearby Wakefield, and as I didn't go onstage until 11.30 pm I could take in shows at social clubs in the area as they started earlier.

On this occasion I went to see Dusty Springfield at Greasborough. I had worked with Dusty on the BBC's 'Drumbeat' TV Show when she was with the Lana Sisters and I felt, and always will, that she was our greatest female vocalist.

Committees for miners clubs and social clubs were elected volunteers who did their best to run the clubs on a professional basis. Many however, assumed the roles of dictators when dealing with the artistes and the club members. They created regulations that were often impossible, or inhuman, to enforce and Dusty's introduction was a classic example of how they would endeavour to get their message across without consideration for the consequences.

As the chairman assumed his position in the Chairman's Box, he shouted for order as he had a special announcement to make. In a much more than usual sombre mood he made the following announcement in a wonderful broad South Yorkshire accent.

'Ladies and gentlemen, it has been brought to the attention of t' committee that lasses ave been pissing in't car park. If this practice does not cease forthwith, any lady members found pissin' in't car park will have their membership cancelled wi' immediate effect. And now Miss Dusty Springfield.'

With a girlie smile on her face, Dusty walked onto the stage and carried on as if nothing had happened.

That's the way the professionals do it.

Yet Can't Bring That Bloody Elephant In Eere!

The Stage was a weekly publication with a status of biblical proportions in the entertainment industry. There was a time when the two inside back pages, and sometimes more displayed all the clubs in the UK and which artistes were booked there for the following week.

Les Booth, the booker for Greasborough, would invariably show that he had the most daring, and members' money, to put together some of the most unlikely bills imaginable.

On one such week the top of the Greasborough bill was The Shadows, Cliff Richard's original backing group and one of the biggest crowd pulling acts in the business. The support act was also one who could pull a crowd but in more ways than usual. It was comedian Dickie Henderson's TV sidekick, Tanya the baby elephant.

As I was again working close to Greasborough, I went along to the late afternoon rehearsals to say hi to The Shadows who were pals from way back.

When I arrived at the club there was a Coal Board maintenance lorry backed up to the rear of the club. On entering the stage door area I noticed what appeared to be builders knocking down the rear wall of the club that backed onto the stage.

Approaching the main dressing room I could hear laughter coming from within. Knocking on the door I was greeted by a smiling Brian Bennett who invited me in and then went on to explain what the laughter was about.

Apparently, Tanya the elephant's size had not been taken into consideration and they couldn't get her onto the stage from the horsebox, her home for the week.

Watching the maintenance team make a way in for Tanya was only the first of two major structural problems she would present the builders with.

Once a sufficient sized opening had been constructed to get Tanya onto the stage, her first steps were greeted with howls of dismay and her handlers quickly got her back into her box. The stage had started to give way under her excessive weight and there were fears it would collapse.

This time, the maintenance men were asked to build support structures under the stage to take Tanya's weight. Fortunately pit props were ten-a-penny in Greasborough and Tanya was able to appear that night without the audience being any wiser as to her jumbo-sized stressed out afternoon.

Winging It!

One of the aspects of performing in cabaret I appreciated was that if necessary you could change your act to suit your audience.

I received a call from an agent I had never worked for, or even heard of, asking me if I had a tuxedo and could do a sophisticated act using just a pianist. I answered the affirmative to both counts and he then went on to explain the booking in more detail. It was a few months away at the reputable Railway Hotel in York and the function was to be held in the Ebor Suite. He told me the clients were the York Flying Club, a well-heeled classy group of people who were used to the best.

As the booking of the pianist was my responsibility, and all they required was 30 minutes of Sinatra swing style songs, I contacted Keith, a mate and a great pianist who could play anything. We had a quick rehearsal, got our tuxedos out of mothballs and set off for York.

We were allocated a nice hotel suite as a dressing room and told to go to the bar where we could have a drink and wait for the stage manager who would check any special requirements we had.

After a couple of drinks a young man

introduced himself as the stage manager and explained that he would control the sound system and give me echo if and when required. He also told us that we would go on following the presentations and he showed us where to stand and wait to be introduced. We went back to the bar to relax.

Keith and I noticed that we were the only people, other than staff, dressed in tuxedos, which was surprising considering the nature of the event. In fact many looked as if they wouldn't know what a tuxedo was.

Eventually we took our position side stage ready to be introduced. It was then that a gentleman, who looked more like a farmer than a pilot, asked me if I was Vince Eager and would I mind presenting the top prize.

I happily agreed and within minutes I was on stage looking at what was one of the most unusually turned out audiences imaginable.

The audience were wearing sweaters, jeans, cloth caps, boots and all manner of clothing other than anything we had expected. It was then that a gentleman came to the stage and introduced me as 'Television Star Vince who has offered to present the award for the bird of the year.'

What frigging bird? It was then I realised that the bloody flying club was for pigeon fanciers. We were going to perform sophisticated style material to bloody pigeon fanciers.

'I'll kill that friggin' agent,' I screamed at Keith, as I left the stage after the presentation.

'It's a fucking pigeon fanciers club,' Keith fell about laughing and within minutes we were both howling.

Thankfully my guitar and amp were in the car so a quick reappraisal of the situation saw us with bow ties off and ready to go. After starting with Mac the Knife, which received a lukewarm reception, we switched to Plan B and 30 minutes of rock 'n' roll on the piano and guitar. It finished up as a cracking night with many thanks from the organisers.

We never did work for the agent again. In fact we never heard of him again. Maybe he flew the nest.

A Chinese Takeaway

Artistes Theatrical Services in Leeds, or ATS, represented a majority of the top club artistes of the 1970's. The strength of the agency was that it was operated by the Joseph family, owners of the City Varieties Theatre in Leeds, the home of the BBC's top ranking television show The Good Old Days. With Stanley Joseph at the helm, ATS manoeuvred themselves into a position of strength by booking the world's premier overseas specialty acts for The Good Old Days and consequently having first call on them for their weekly variety shows at the City of Varieties.

The variety shows were tried and tested and a brilliant concept. A popular singer or comedian would usually headline before dashing off to perform at a nightclub, usually one booked by ATS, plus one of the top overseas speciality acts booked for the Good Old Days by ATS and a stripper, or exotic dancer as they were billed, the City Varieties being the only provincial theatre in the late 1960s to feature a stripper.

Being one who appeared at the City Varieties on a number of occasions, I often marvelled at the skills and dexterity of the speciality artistes, and none more so than Mr Ching the Chinese plate juggler. Tuesday afternoon was the dreaded matinée when the only act to gain any kind of audience response was the stripper, due in the main to the dirty-mac brigade sitting on the front row and the students, who were akin to a committee sitting behind them.

The students were there solely to check out the stripper and if she was OK they would recommend her to their fellow students who would turn up in droves to see her at the Friday performance.

For the finale of his plate juggling performance, Mr Ching stood on the right of the stage, directly in front of the footlights, and his assistant produced from the wings, a table with a pile of plates on it. Mr Ching then took the plates one by one and began to throw them towards the audience. As the audience gasped in amazement the plates would appear to take on a mind of their own as they returned to the stage where Mr Ching caught them and placed them on another table in a pile. They were boomerang plates! Who wants a stripper when you've got Mr Ching? He was awesome and I had never heard a matinée reception like it. The audience loved him.

Come Friday evening the house was full with a generous helping of students there to cheer on the stripper, or so we thought.

When Mr Ching was introduced the students greeted him with cheers of delight. The longer he was on stage, the more the audience cheered him. At the end there was expectation in the air as he stood next to his pile of plates in readiness for launching them over the audience.

After the first few plates were on their way, we discovered why the students were in such a receptive mood for Mr Ching, as half a dozen of them stood up and threw plates at him, forcing him to scurry off stage for his life.

The Tuesday matinées guys had coerced their fellow students into smuggling plates into the Friday performance to give Mr Ching a taste of his own medicine. Maybe they wished they'd had Mr Ching's timing as they were immediately escorted from the theatre. Missing the stripper!

Deep Fried Sword

A popular double date for artists on the cabaret circuit was an early show at the City Varieties Theatre in Leeds, followed by a midnight performance at the 59 Club in Huddersfield.

The club was owned and operated by Joe Marsden, a Yorkshire chicken farmer and entrepreneur who had Yorkshire right through his middle like a stick of rock. 'No mess Joe' was his nickname. If you messed with Joe you were history.

The success of his chicken farm on the outskirts of Huddersfield prompted Joe to take over a four storey terraced building in the centre of Huddersfield and turn the street level floor into a fried chicken and chips shop. With the chicken shop going from strength to strength it didn't take long for Joe to utilise the three upper floors by opening a nightclub. As the road address was number 59, Joe named it the 59 Club.

By turning the floor above the chicken shop into the cabaret lounge and the remaining floors into a casino, Joe soon found himself the owner of one of the north's most intimate and popular nightclubs. The cabaret artistes loved the atmosphere created by the Las Vegas style under lit glass cabaret floor and sultry lighting and they made it the 'must' place to visit either as a performer, or as a visiting guest if they were performing elsewhere in the area.

Tony Brutus was a speciality act with a Roman theme. Dressed as a Centurion, the hilarious Liverpool strongman would perform such feats of strength as, tearing a 'Roman telephone directory' in half, lifting two people off the floor while seated in a chariot, and lifting a 150lb sword above his head with one hand. A third of his act would be feats of strength and the remaining two-thirds were dedicated to typical Scouse humour that had the audience in stitches. I would watch Tony's act whenever possible as anything could happen – and it usually did.

It was a Sunday night and the start of another week's entertainment at the club. Tony had been on stage for about 30 minutes and was challenging a member of the audience to join him onstage in an attempt to lift the 150lb sword. 'It has to go above your head,' demanded Tony of the prospective volunteer in his lyrical Scouse accent, 'but you're allowed to use both hands.'

With time being called at the bar, and no doubt many members of the audience having knocked back a couple of quickies to keep them going for Tony's show, it came as no surprise when the member of the audience to take up the challenge walked onto the under lit glass cabaret floor with a bit of swagger.

Smiling and winking at the audience, the challenger took off his jacket, rolled up his sleeves and flexed his muscles as the broader, and obviously much fitter, yet considerably shorter Tony, explained the challenge to him. The ease with which Tony lifted the sword above his head with one hand brought cheers of appreciation from the audience.

The challenger however dismissed Tony's feat with a shrug of the shoulders, as he indicated once again by flexing his muscles, and posing like Mussolini, that he could lift the sword as high as he wanted.

With a certain amount of apprehension, and whispered advice, Tony gingerly placed the mighty sword on the cabaret floor and stood back. With an air of arrogance, and minimal humility, the challenger stepped forward, bent over, gripped the sword and raised it gingerly off the floor. With his effort in lifting the sword being equalled only by that of the audience's cheers, the distance between sword and cabaret floor slowly became greater.

It was as the sword reached waist level that it all went terribly wrong. With arms trembling and veins standing out on his neck, the challenger fought with his fading strength in an effort to avoid gravity's increasing dominance. Accompanied by a scream that could have been heard in Leeds, the challenger's trembling hand released the sword and it plunged towards the glass floor.

With all manner of shrieks and hollers coming from the audience, the sword shattered the glass floor and disappeared among a spray of sparks and flashes given off by the under floor lighting as it was smashed to pieces.

As the dust and smoke settled Tony stepped forward and gazed down into what was now a gaping hole where the stage used to be. For the first time in his life Tony's wonderful Scouse ad-libbing ability had deserted him, as the sword-lifting feat he had performed a thousand times before, finished up in a deep fat chicken fryer!

Clockwork Timing

My decision to invest more time and effort into the cabaret club circuit was due in the main to a band called The Clockwork Toys.

I initially hired the five-piece band for a seven-day tour of South Wales, but as the week progressed the band got tighter, the receptions got better and it soon became apparent that I should consider getting a permanent band again.

The boys normally worked with a great lead singer called Chuck but I wanted only the four musicians so Chuck remained in Nottingham. Towards the end of the week I explained to the boys that I might be in a position to take them on the road on a full-time basis if they were interested.

A few months later Vince Eager and The Clockwork Toys became an item but due to domestic commitments only three of the original musicians, Micky Finch, Johnny Grace and John Landon remained. All of them great musicians and fantastic harmony singers.

As well as being an accomplished bass player, Micky Finch bore a remarkable resemblance to Norman Wisdom. Before the show one evening, Micky produced a cap and small jacket similar to those worn by Norman. He put them on, and standing before me was Norman Wisdom. It was uncanny. I told Micky to leave the stage at a certain section in the show, put the outfit on and return to the stage, interrupting me as I chatted to the audience.

The most important part of humour is

timing. If your timing is right, and you have a reasonably quick wit, you should be a reasonable ad-libber. Thankfully I built up a reputation as being a good ad libber and it certainly got me out of many difficult situations.

As Micky made his entrance I was talking to the audience. The second he walked on I knew by the audience reaction that we were onto a winner. I didn't have to look if he had come on stage as the audience were in hysterics.

The 10 minutes we did together that night laid the foundations for what was to be a successful six-year partnership with the work coming in thick and fast as we became one of the hottest acts on the circuit.

He Didn't Make it!

Prior to going on stage, the Yorkshire Social Club Concert Chairman asked me if I was the Vince Eager who had appeared on 'Six Five Special', 'Oh Boy' and 'Drumbeat' with Tommy Steele, Marty Wilde, Cliff Richard and Adam Faith. I told him I was he simply replied, 'Ay, I thot thee wer!'

The chairman entered his little world of the Chairman's Box at the side of the stage and proceeded to ring his bell as he shouted in his broad Yorkshire accent, 'Order ladies and gentlemen please, order! Ladies and gentlemen it's show time!' Once he had the attention of the audience he continued, as The Clockwork Toys softly played the introduction to my first song, Frankie Laine's classic hit Jezebel.

'I'm sure you all remember such shows as the Six Five Special, Oh Boy and Drumbeat which made big starts of Tommy Steele, Marty Wilde, Cliff Richard and Adam Faith. Well now I'd like to introduce somebody that didn't make it.'

With that, The Clockwork Toys burst out laughing and I endeavoured to pull myself together in order to launch myself into Jezebel. Sadly the audience sat poker-faced. I don't think they do irony in Yorkshire.

BINGO!

Bingo, when played by visiting entertainers in Yorkshire social clubs, should have carried a health warning: 'You're welcome to play. But don't you dare bloody win!'

Arriving in a Yorkshire mining village social club at 6 pm. Setting up the equipment, doing a sound check then hanging around for three hours before you went on stage didn't exactly produce an adrenalin rush. A couple of pints of lager, accompanied by a 'mature' sandwich from the bar, while playing a couple of games of snooker, generally being the sum total of what you could do to kill time.

There was of course bingo, but that was subject to being allowed, or daring, to play. Bentley Social Club near Doncaster was a club that allowed artistes to play, so my road manager Neil and I did. Sitting at a table near the dressing room door was a pre-requisite for artistes playing bingo. If, in the unlikely event of winning and the natives becoming hostile, you could always nip into the safety of the dressing room and escape their wrath.

In wishing to attract members from the cradle to the grave, many clubs practised 'no bad language' policies, and anyone using expletives could find themselves, 'out the door,' never to return. Little did we realise that during our game of bingo we would witness the seriousness with which the policy could be enforced.

We diligently marked off the numbers as they were called and awaited the inevitable scream of 'house,' from an excited local.

'All the ones, legs eleven,' announced the bingo caller. Followed by, 'One and two, one dozen. Number twelve.'

With a wry smile on his face he then read out the next number. 'Unlucky for some, one and three, thirteen.'

Three consecutive numbers was not a

regular event, but not unheard of, but four?

The caller's demeanour then took on an air of surprise mixed with excitement as he followed 13 with, 'One and four, fourteen.'

Chuckles of surprise came from the audience as those playing realised they could be witness to bingo history being made. Four consecutive numbers. 'That's never happened before,' the caller told the audience. 'Four numbers on the bounce. That would be a first!' he went on to tell them.

He then turned the handle that rotated the cage containing the numbered balls and waited for the next ball to roll down the tube and into a bowl. The audience waited in silent anticipation as he picked the ball from out of the bowl. Could the impossible happen?

As he picked up the ball the look of amazement on his face told it all. 'Fuckin' hell! It's fifteen!' He screamed.

The club became a cauldron of pandemonium. There was laughter amidst looks of disbelief and general unrest as committee members attempted to separate the disbelievers of the number 15 being called, and those baying for the head of the bingo caller for using the 'F' word.

The game was abandoned with the caller being relieved of his duties and told to leave the club until the committee had held an enquiry into his behaviour.

Yes. Bingo really should carry a health warning.

A Dummy for the Chairman

On occasions, date sheets for appearances in the northeast could read like a death certificate and would put fear into the hearts of visiting entertainers. There were certain clubs which, given the choice, artistes would never work. They were the toughest and roughest imaginable, and some of them boasted Sunday lunchtime entertainment.

A blue comic or a sexy dancer was the usual fare set before the all male lunchtime audiences with every one of them looking like Andy Capp as they stared at you as if to say, 'Go on then. Bloody entertain me!'

One such club in South Shields had booked top ventriloquist John Bouchier to appear on a Sunday lunchtime show, and as I had worked with John a few months earlier I decided to visit the club and support him.

The all male audience greeted the first of John's two spots with the usual degree of apathy and he left the stage to the sound of his own feet interspersed with the occasional unconvincing clap. Most artistes looked upon Sunday lunchtime shows as a penance. If you weren't prepared to do them you wouldn't get booked for the rest of the week.

During the bingo session I went backstage to see John and he was his usual professional self and taking the situation in his stride. As we chatted, the concert chairman came in and John remarked to him that they were a tough crowd.

In a broad Geordie accent the concert chairman replied, 'No bonnie lad, they're a canny audience. The trouble is, they canna hear yuz dummy at the back o' the club. If yuz hold him closer to the microphone youz'll doo fine!'

Unfortunately, the biggest dummies were running the clubs!

The 'Joint' was Rocking!

A game of 'shoot' (a card game similar to brag), smoking a joint and/or reading, were the only pastimes available for whiling away the hours during coach travel on the Jerry Lee Lewis tour of 1962.

The first joint I saw was when folk comedian, and rock 'n' roll concert compere, Zom, rolled and then smoked one in the 2 i's Coffee Barr cellar a few years earlier. Zom's skeletal features and dour demeanour, would have been the perfect face for an anti drug campaign poster. The thought of looking like him due to taking drugs

298

would certainly have deterred those of us who were under the impression that our faces were our fortunes from partaking of the evil weed.

On one overnight journey on the Jerry Lee tour, the face of Zom became but a blur as I succumbed to the offer of a joint from Johnny Kidd's drummer, Frank Farley. With lips pursed I inhaled the first of many drags only to find that it had no effect on me whatsoever. I didn't know if I should be pleased at not succumbing, or dejected at not feeling as happy as everyone else smoking pot appeared to be.

During the coming years I took great delight in turning down the offer of joints that came my way, and at the same time pitied those who were partaking and acting out the effects.

Unfortunately a night club proprietor and good friend took the wind out of my sails when, to settle an argument, I agreed to sample the so called delights of a special brand of joint he rolled in coloured Sobranie cocktail cigarette paper.

The Beach Club, Redcar, was a popular six night date in my band's, The Clockwork Toys, and my diary and we would play there every nine months or so.

It was common knowledge that Gerry enjoyed a 'smoke' while wandering between the fishing boats pulled up on Redcar beach, and on many occasions he had invited me to join him to partake of one of his 'special smokes'. Always refusing, I usually related my Jerry Lee tour coach experience as to why I thought it was an overrated pastime.

Following a regular opening Monday night sound check, I went to the bar with my drummer Clive where we enjoyed a couple of drinks, mine being a Carlsberg Special Brew.

It was not a regular drink of mine but the draught lager had run out. As we still had plenty of time to kill before we were due on stage, and it being a nice spring evening, Clive and I decided to take a walk on the sea front.

Strolling along the pavement next to the beach we spotted Gerry meandering among the fishing boats and he beckoned us to join him. Following my couple of Carlsberg Special Brews, it didn't take long for Gerry to persuade me to prove my long standing argument with him once and for all by smoking one of his 'specials'.

Within minutes I was a different person in a different world. I vaguely remembered sitting in the entrance to the club where I supposedly told Gerry that my performance that night would be one of my greatest ever, or a load of old crap.

I felt invincible as I started my act with my usual opening number *Jezebel*. Never had a

I sounded so good, and it simply got better as the act progressed. The Clockwork Toys were also playing the best I had heard them play and everything felt perfect. But was it?

Arriving back in the dressing room, my drummer Clive and I threw our arms around each other and wallowed in mutual admiration at what we thought had been a brilliant performance. It wasn't until the other two members of the band, Mick and John arrived, followed by Gerry, who was in hysterics, that the reality as to what happened hit home.

We had somehow managed to condense an eighty-minute act into thirty minutes. Apparently I didn't speed up; I just left out most of the verses and choruses. Gerry continued to giggle and laugh as he reminded me that I did promise, 'either the best show ever, or the biggest load of crap.' Sadly it was the latter.

Anticipating problems, Gerry had warned the compere to be prepared and tell the audience I was unwell. Also, being a Monday it was a small crowd and as Gerry was on Christian name terms with most of the audience he wasn't unduly concerned.

At the following day's post mortem, Gerry was still wearing a big grin, and I was defending my corner by blaming it on the high alcoholic content of the Carlsberg Special Brew I drank earlier.

We continued our excellent relationship and returned to the Beach Club many times, but never again did a 'Sobranie Special', or a Carlsberg Special pass my lips.

Tommy's Good Samaritan

The Talk of the North Night Club in Eccles, Manchester was a top venue and run brilliantly by its owner Joe Pullen.

Joe had a bit of a reputation, and being a typical Lancastrian was a man of his word and insisted on professional behaviour. The club rules were stricter than those at most clubs and included men having to wear a collar and tie. This even included artistes following a performance.

During a tour of Scotland, a fellow artiste and comedian read an article to us from the Stage entertainment magazine reporting on a fire at the Talk of the North Club that had caused extensive damage.

Reading out the article he concluded by adding, 'The police stated that the extensive damage to the club was due to Joe Pullen stopping the firemen from entering as they weren't wearing collars and ties.'

Joe was the butt of many pro gags but they were always told with affection and reverence.

It was at a Sunday night show at the Talk

of the North, during a quick off-stage change, that our road manager Neil took a phone call in my dressing room from the compere. With 20 minutes remaining in my act the compere was insisting we got off after the next number. Maybe he was upset because I undid my bow tie?

When we returned to the dressing room after the show the compere told us we were to rush across Manchester to the Cat's Whiskers Club in Wythenshawe as Tommy Cooper had failed to turn up. Tommy was the biggest act in the business. He was always a sell out and couldn't be topped.

My imagination ran riot. 'Sorry ladies and gentlemen. Due to circumstances beyond our control Tommy Cooper is unable to appear this evening and in his place we have, Vince Eager and The Clockwork Toys!' 'Booooooo we only want Tommy,' was how my imagination envisaged our reception.

It didn't bear thinking about. Nobody could replace Tommy.

'No thanks,' I said firmly.

'It's worth £300,' replied the compere.

'OK, you're on.' I agreed.

It was three times our usual fee and I'd read about mercenary soldiers so why not be the first mercenary entertainer!

Packing instruments, clothes, etc into the van at a record breaking pace, we jumped in and our road manager Neil drove towards the car park exit where an arm waving compere stopped us. We wound down the window as he approached, and panted out, 'They've located Tommy. You don't have to go.'

Sod it! We'd already spent the money! A couple of us still went to watch Tommy's show and it was Kevin Kent, the Cat's Whiskers compere, who told us what had happened.

Tommy was travelling from London to Manchester and had to change trains at Crewe. While waiting for his connection he went into the refreshment bar and got talking to some railway workers who were having a pint after work. As only Tommy could, and would do, he started to do tricks and tell them jokes. It was only when one of the more sensible and sober of those present asked Tommy where he was going that it materialised Tommy had missed his connection and there were no more trains to Manchester that evening.

As it was now 10 pm, and Tommy was three hours late and much the worse for wear, the more sensible member and Samaritan of the party decided he should phone the Cat's Whiskers and ask them what to do with Tommy.

Kevin the compere told the Samaritan that Tommy was due on stage in 15 minutes and asked him to put him in a taxi and with a bit of luck he could be on stage in 40 minutes.

The Samaritan then became a taxi driver and drove Tommy to the club where he saw Tommy's show and received a handsome payment for delivering him safely.

Up on the Roof

No matter how big the star; from a young comedian learning his trade, to a star of the stature of Shirley Bassey, they'll all have a funny story to tell about something that happened in a northern club. The clubs have provided many classic comedy situations over the years, but none funnier then the one that happened to a good pal of mine from my hometown of Grantham, Terry Carey.

Terry had been a pro for many years as a vocalist/musician backing such artistes as Lena Martell, but decided to opt out of a pro career, settle down and start a full time roofing business while doing the occasional singing gig in the working men's clubs using pre recorded backing tracks.

It wasn't long before Terry's roofing business, TC Roofing, and his semi pro vocal act were going from strength to strength. The roofing business and the club act combined nicely. When it came to Terry transporting his equipment he would simply take his ladders and scaffolding out of the van and replace it with his sound system.

Terry felt the success his roofing business was enjoying was due in part to the advertising he had painted on the side of his van which simply read, 'TC ROOFING' and his contact details.

On his arrival at the Westdale Miners Welfare club near Chesterfield, Terry unloaded his equipment and parked his van outside a window.

Once the club chairman had given Terry his performance times, Terry got dressed and ready to perform. At the given time for his first spot, Terry turned on his backing track, which also had his spoken introduction on it, and waited for his cue to go on stage.

'Ladies and Gentlemen,' said the voice on the backing track, 'please welcome the fantastic Terry Carey!'

Terry did his 45 minutes and came off stage to a great reception from the enthusiastic audience. On reaching his dressing room he was greeted by the irate club chairman.

'Who the bloody heck did that introduction?' he screamed at Terry.

'It's only my backing track,' replied Terry apologetically.

'The only person that brings the turns on in this club is me! I'll bring thee on fer yer second spot when I'm good un bloody ready. Just wait 'til I introduce thee before thee guz on t'stage!'

Ready for his second spot, Terry waited apprehensively side stage for the chairman to introduce him. The chairman had a radio microphone and was standing at the bar.

'Order please ladies and gentlemen, order,' he commanded. 'Please welcome fer 'is second turn t'neet '… there was a pregnant pause. The chairman had forgotten Terry's name. Seeking inspiration his eyes wandered around the show room until they settled on Terry's van parked outside the window.

'The one and only,' he continued in a more confident tone, 'TC Roofing.' He had read the sign on the side of Terry's van!

Neither the chairman nor the audience had a clue as to what he had done. Terry of course, being the pro he is, continued as if nothing had happened.

From then on Terry's opening number has been *Up on the Roof.*

Baggage and Bullets

Ooh La La. What an Expensive Lay!

British promoter Jack Murray decided it was time to launch a rock 'n' roll invasion of Paris. Wee Willie Harris, Dave Sampson, Vince Taylor, Duffy Power, Nero and the Gladiators and yours truly were to be the heavy artillery in breaching the French resistance to Britrock. Jack had already had success cruising across the channel to Calais with rock 'n' roll and Skiffle weekenders onboard the SS Daffodil ferry.

Until now, the French singer Johnny Halliday was the only widely known French Rock 'n' Roller. The 18-year-old performer was laying the foundations of a career that would still be going strong 45 years later. Jack Murray, however, felt that once the Parisians saw the Brits they would drop Johnny and become anglophile rockers.

The year was 1962 and we were booked to appear for three nights at France's Palladium, The Paris Olympia. The four-day contract included economy travel, accommodation and breakfast.

Our mode of transport was the popular London Victoria to Paris Gare du Nord overnight train, and having left Victoria at

311

about 10 pm we settled in for what was to be a long night.

There was always tension in the air on the few occasions Vince Taylor and I worked together. My real name is Roy Taylor, which was changed to Vince Eager in 1958, and in the same year, Brian Maurice Holden changed his to Vince Taylor, so a certain amount of confusion developed. I also felt that Vince was riding on the back of Gene Vincent's leather clad image as developed by 'Oh Boy' producer Jack Good. Vince's group, 'The Playboys', was also made up on members of my ex backing band, which created a few problems as we were still mates.

Much of the journey was spent trying to grab some sleep as following our 6 am arrival in Paris it was to be a long day of rehearsals. A couple of the guys grabbed a few beers but generally speaking we were a very sober bunch. I had just started smoking and was yet to start drinking.

At 4.30 am, Jack Murray roused those of us who were sleeping, as he welcomed us to France. He then explained the day's itinerary and the dos and don'ts while in Paris.

He explained that our hotel was at the rear of the Olympia Theatre stage door on Rue San Marten and was very convenient for central Paris. With a sly grin he pointed out that Paris was known for its beautiful women and if we wanted a lady's company we should contact the receptionist at the hotel. Understandably this was greeted with cheers of delight, plus a few side remarks such as, 'What if we fancy the receptionist. Will she give us a shag?'

Jack then made an offer that would prove to be a life-changing event for one of us. He informed us that the press would be at the station at 6 am to meet the train.

The artist who was prepared to get dressed in his stage clothes and pose for photographs on the platform would feature on the front page of that day's Parisian newspaper and would close the show at the Olympia.

The only person to show any enthusiasm was Vince Taylor. He jumped out of his seat with excitement; so keen was he to do it. Wee Willie, Duffy, Dave and I were chuffed. Who in his right mind would want to get changed into his stage gear at that time of day and pose on a railway station platform? We were all delighted at being spared the embarrassment. 'He must be bleedin' nuts,' was the common mumbling from the rest of us.

As the train came to a halt at the Gare du Nord, Vince entered the carriage wearing his black leather suit and gloves and sporting a heavy silver medallion around his neck. This appeared even brighter than usual, set against Vince's heavily made up face, neck and chest. His four-piece group,

'The Playboys,' brought up the rear clutching their instruments and appearing very unenthusiastic.

It was only a few weeks earlier that 'The Playboys' had sacked Vince, but he begged them to do the Olympia with him, and they did. To say that it was a smart move is an understatement.

As Vince and The Playboys stepped off the train it was like bonfire night. The air was full of burning from the flash bulbs. The noise of the French press shouting posing instructions at Vince drowned out any other noise there may have been.

It was mayhem. Vince worked the press brilliantly, posing in every rock 'n' roll position imaginable whilst surrounded by The Playboys. The rest of us stood there like a bunch of idiots, totally ignored by the reception committee.

Eventually Jack ushered Vince into a waiting cab and he was whisked away with the press running after him in a manner well ahead of its time. We meanwhile endeavoured to find someone who was interested in us and who would show us to our hotel.

Dave Sampson and I shared a room. Dave was managed by Cliff Richard and like many of us, was still awaiting that elusive first hit record. He was a great guy and very keen to try his charm on the beautiful ladies of Paris as described by Jack. For the rest of our first

day, rehearsals and press interviews determined that we didn't spend much time in
the hotel. I went across in the late afternoon
for a shower and discovered Dave had spent
most of his day in the hotel entertaining one
of the beautiful Parisian ladies. They were
just about to leave as I arrived.

As Dave introduced her I was in awe. Beautiful, sexy, gorgeous, she had everything.
Dave then announced with his chest thrust
forward like a cock at dawn, that he was off
to the theatre and sexy would be going with
him. With that they left and I had a shower.
It was a colder shower than I had intended
but it needed to be after what I had just seen.

When I arrived at the theatre the buzz was
about 'Dave's bird.' 'Where's she from?'
Everyone wanted to know. They were looking into each other's eyes as if they were the
only people in Paris.

As we finished rehearsals Dave shouted
from the rear stalls, 'I'll see you at the Hotel
Vince.' With that, the lovebirds disappeared
into the darkness of the theatre foyer and
into the romance of the Parisian night.

I was in bed and it was approximately 3 am
when the bedroom light came on to reveal
the most Cheshire cat like grin I have ever
seen. A full set of pearly white teeth, courtesy of Mr David Sampson, made me squint.
'Isn't she gorgeous Vince?' shrieked Dave.

'I found her through reception,' Dave said

excitedly. 'She came up to the room this afternoon and we just clicked.'

'Dave, the receptionist is an agent for "fix-a-fuck". The girl's a bloody prostitute!' I said laughing. 'No, she was.' Dave stuttered, 'but she's not now. We're getting engaged and she's coming back to England with me.'

Eventually he managed to calm down sufficiently to tell me he was going to have to pay for his afternoon of pleasure. But she was packing it in as of now and would be with him as his fiancée.

'Have you got it in writing? I asked. 'I don't need to,' said Dave. 'She's promised me that's all I'll have to pay.' And so to sleep and sweet dreams.

Over the period of our stay in Paris, Dave was always accompanied by his 'fiancée.' He really did appear besotted with her, and she with him.

One afternoon we did manage to spend a couple of hours together and we went to a high-class strip club. It was 3 pm and we were seated very close to the dance floor. I didn't drink alcohol and ordered a Coke. Dave also only wanted a Coke, and so, as we hadn't had to pay an entrance fee, we felt we were in a for a cheap afternoon out of thrills. It wasn't until our bill came that we discovered we had been ripped off by having to pay the equivalent of £5 for a bottle of Coca Cola. In total shock we headed back to the hotel where Dave met up with his 'fiancée'.

Vince Taylor's decision to dress up for the photo shoot on our arrival in Paris had paid off handsomely. The day after our arrival his photo was all over the French press and he received an amazing reception when he closed the show. He was well on his way to becoming a big star in France.

The day of our departure was heralded with Dave at the reception desk contesting his bill. Yes, he had been charged for the three days he spent with his 'fiancée.' She had taken him for a ride. Not only was he a bachelor again, he was a very poor one. He couldn't pay his bill.

Poor Dave didn't know what to do. His hooker's bill was ten times more than he was being paid.

It was concluded that Dave would work in Paris for a month to pay off his 'fiancée.'

We left Dave in the hotel without a franc to his name, as promoter John Murray's representative had arranged for him to stay at the hotel until work was found for him to pay for the hooker.

A few hours later, all the artistes but Dave and Vince Taylor were at the station awaiting John Murray, who was due to pay us. As we started to get a little anxious, Dave showed up. He was out of breath as he told us that John Murray had done a runner and none of us would be paid.

It was a fun three days but the only beneficiaries were John Murray who pocketed the salaries and was never to be seen again, Vince Taylor who became a big star in France due to his early morning leather clad arrival, and Dave Sampson who enjoyed three wonderful days of shagging the most beautiful woman in Paris.

C'est la vie!

'Don't Shoot Him. He's Only a Rock 'n' Roll Singer!'

Shortly after marrying my first wife Sandra in 1966, I was booked to appear in a show entertaining the British Forces in Cyprus, Malta and Libya. The show was entitled 'No Strings', so called because of the rocking three piece band I was using at that time, 'The Puppets'.

It was a three-month assignment with a strong bill consisting of myself, my backing group The Puppets, comedian Wyn Calvin, vocal duo Kim and Erik Prince and magician Christine Martell.

Cyprus was our first destination and we arrived at a time when the Greeks and Turks were at each other's throats like never before. An area known as the Green Belt with a 6,000 strong United Nations peace-keeping force endeavouring to keep the two factions apart divided the island.

Due to the political problems the Cypriot tourist industry was at an all time low, but strangely enough the locals were quite happy with the situation as the international force was spending a lot of money on both sides of the divide, and more than making up for the lack of tourists.

It was the complexity of the peace keeping that provided me with plenty of opportunities to get myself into scrapes of one kind or another.

For the first week of our five-week stay on the island we stayed at the King George Hotel in Famagusta. It was during our stay her that we were invited by Derek Agutter, commander of ENSA, the armed forces entertainment section in the Middle East, and father of Jenny, of Railway Children fame, to attend the EOKA Celebrations in Nicosia, which were to be attended by General Grivas and Archbishop Makarios.

We watched most of the parade from Derek's apartment but at one stage went to the roadside as the cavalcade passed by. So close, and surprisingly unguarded was it that I managed to get my cine camera through the open window and into the limousine carrying General Grivas and Archbishop Makarios without being challenged by any form of security.

I also noticed, with a certain amount of humour, that when the young Greek National Guard members, mostly children and many no older than 14, were selling flags, they would pin the flag on you and then ask for the money.

It was this experience that was foremost in my mind when we were stopped a week later at a Greek National Guard check point on our way from Famagusta to Mount Troodos, where we were due to give a concert to one-hundred members of the Signals Regiment who were responsible for the communications system on the top of the mountain.

As I sat in the mini bus with my ever-faithful cine camera at the ready, a young Greek girl entered the bus with a tray full of Eoka badges around her neck. She then started to pin the badges on members of our party, before asking for the money. I decided it would make a cute piece of cine footage and began filming.

Before you could say Zorba, I felt something very hard and cold press against the side of my neck, accompanied by the broken English directive of 'you don' move'. My camera being taken from me, and a hand grabbing my arm and leading me off the bus followed. What had now become clear was that it was the end of a rifle barrel that was pressing into my neck. I was led to a tree where my face was pressed against the trunk and again told, 'you don' move'. The gun was still against my neck.

During our three-month sojourn in the Mediterranean, we were under the supervision of Charlie Matzola. Charlie was of mixed nationality, spoke eight of the region's languages fluently and was affection known as 'Charlie Come', as he was always saying, 'come on, now, come.'

Charlie and Derek Agutter had gone ahead of us and had become aware that the convoy, which should have been behind them, was no more. Their vehicle, our vehicle and the truck carrying our equipment were no longer as one. Thankfully their concern was sufficient for them to retrace their steps and come in search of us.

My face being pressed into a tree, and the remainder of our party trying to establish why I had been detained, was the scene that greeted Charlie and Derek as they arrived.

We soon discovered why Charlie was made responsible for our well-being. Within minutes he had the gun moved away from my neck, and had brought smiles to the faces of my capturers as he arranged for a line up of the Greek National Guard, with me in the middle, posing for photographs to be taken by the rest of our group.

I later learned that he had told them I was a big rock 'n' roll star in England and that I was taking cine film of the girls, as they were much prettier than the girls back home.

It was a ploy Charlie used again later in the tour when Turkish rebels in the infamous Kyrenia pass, north of Nicosia, decided we shouldn't go any further. Within minutes Charlie had their women folk standing in a line having their photographs taken with me as I sang *Love Me Tender* and *Jailhouse Rock* for them.

Stairway to Heaven

Entertaining the British and United Nations Forces in Cyprus, coincided with a visit by members of the United National Security Council who were there to review the Mandate and how many troops were required on the island.

Both the Turkish and Greek communities were as keen as each other to increase, or at least retain, the present compliment. A drop in the number of UN Forces on the island could be a financial disaster for all the residents.

Our tour manager Charlie came to my suite one morning to warn me that there was a possibility of gunfire in the coming days and we should keep our heads down. He then went on to tell me how the Greeks and Turks had a deal that whenever the UN Mandate Council was in the area they would fire in each other's direction but not at each other. The idea was to give the Council the impression that the situation remained precarious and that the UN forces should be retained.

Charlie then took me onto the stairway leading from my suite down to the pool and pointed out a building to the left with a Greek flag draped off the room, and a building on the right with the Turkish flag. They were the Greek and Turkish headquarters. The land, on which our hotel the Lidra Palace stood, was the neutral green zone.

Charlie then pointed out holes in the marble wall at the side of the staircase and holes in the paving surrounding the pool.

'These are all bullet holes,' said Charlie casually. 'Nobody was hurt. They just make out things are worse than they are.'

With that, he left my suite leaving me to ponder as to what the hell I had let myself in for.

Three days later I was swimming in the pool when I heard bullet fire close by. Floundering, and swallowing most of the pool, I managed to reach the edge where, on peeping over the side I could see both the Turkish and Green Headquarters.

As I tried to find the most protected area in the pool I could see the rifles, which were causing my consternation, poking over the edge of both roofs just above the flags. It was then that Charlie appeared from the bar area of the hotel with a big smile on his face. He walked over to the pool and asked if I was OK.

I told him I was fine, but what did he find so funny. He then went on to tell me that the shower of bullets had been solely for my benefit. He had seen me swimming in the pool and spoken to one of his Greek pals at their HQ.

'Good job I like your act,' chuckled Charlie. 'I could have had you shot!'

Cold Feet

Our visit to Libya during our 'No Strings' British Forces tour, was perhaps in some way to blame for the anti west propaganda Colonel Gaddafi was later to preach.

Our first infringement on the local hospitality was when The Puppets' guitarist Dave Millen and I decided to have a bit of what we thought was harmless fun at the entrance to a mosque in the city of Tobruk.

In those days I didn't know the difference between Protestant and Catholic, let alone anything to do with Muslims and their mosques.

We had noticed that as they entered the mosques for prayer they would take off their shoes and leave them in the covered courtyard at the entrance. Dave and I thought it would be a bit of a prank to mix up the shoes so when the owners came out their shoes were not where they had left them and hopefully a mêlée would ensure. We also thought it would be prudent to watch from a safe distance to take photographs, so we lay down underneath a horse drawn taxi known as a Gary.

As the worshippers came out, the anticipated mêlée developed and we began taking our photos of the confusion we had caused. It wasn't long however before the horse drawn Gary we were hiding under moved, to reveal Dave and I prostrate in the street for all to see.

With one quick glance at each other we were up and away with what seemed like half the male population of Tobruk in hot pursuit. The vehicle in which we had received a lift to Tobruk from our accommodation at the British Air Force base of El Adem, was thankfully parked close by and the driver got the hint of trouble and drove like the wind to get us back.

We heard no more of the incident but Dave and I felt it wiser to remain on base for the remainder of our stay in El Adem.

Pigeon Pie Anyone?

We were in the middle of a cold winter's tour of British army bases in Germany and two young soldiers were seconded to unload our equipment at the officers' club for the show later that evening, whilst we made ourselves at home in the guests' quarters. Holly Gold was a very attractive magician who always had the welfare of the four white doves she used in her act at heart. 'Please don't put the doves anywhere in the cold,' Holly pleaded to the obliging soldiers. 'And please make sure they're not in a draught.' 'OK miss,' replied the squaddies.

There were three acts in the show, comedian Andy Blackmore, magician Holly Gold, my band and myself. When we arrived at the club, all but Holly went to the cabaret floor area. She went to the dressing room to check her doves and as we started to set up our amplifiers we heard a scream.

Rushing to the dressing room we discovered a distraught Holy standing over the doves' cage sobbing her heart out. In the bottom of the cage lay her four doves, lifeless. The soldiers had put them in a warm place all right – on top of a gas heater.

We never did find out if they had been gassed or cooked.

Strange Customs in Zambia

Africa is my favourite continent and its magic never fails to capture my spirit and my soul. I can never get enough of it. Many of my highs and lows have occurred while visiting this wonderful place. They range from being escorted by a rifle carrying, and drunk, Zaire soldier when I went to the toilet at Kinshasa airport, to appearing at the Zambian Copperbelt Agriculture Show on the back of a low-loader in front of 12,000 Zambians who just wanted to rock 'n' roll.

Having visited Morocco, Algeria, Libya, Tunisia, Egypt, Senegal, Nigeria, Kenya, Angola, Djibouti, Tanzania, The Congo, Zambia, Namibia, Botswana, Zimbabwe, Mozambique, Swaziland, Malawi and South Africa, I can honestly say that the times when I have felt genuinely concerned were during the confrontations I had with white people.

Being 6 feet 5 inches tall, I have often found that people in authority, especially those who are vertically challenged, have created more problems than they have solved, such as the only white customs officer on duty when I arrived at Ndola airport in Zambia. I'd been travelling for 24 hours and was pretty tired. He asked me if I had anything to declare and I said no. He then insisted that I open every piece of luggage and take everything out.

My regular clothes, stage clothes, music and more were spread all over the table as he grinned at his black helpers, who I found out later had not seen him do this before. As I tried to keep my cool, not easy when you've just come from a temperature of freezing in the UK to 100F in Zambia, he picked up my guitar case. The case was new and held my beloved Gibson J160 safely inside. 'Open it,' he grunted. 'It only has my guitar in it,' was my reply.

With that, he grabbed the locked guitar case and tried in vain to undo the latch. His frustration then got the better of him as he pulled out a screwdriver, pushed it under the lock and broke it. 'You bloody idiot,' I shouted. 'I have the key here, why didn't you ask me for it?' 'I did,' he replied hastily. 'No you bloody didn't. That's a brand new case and you've broken it!' I shouted.

With that I became the centre of attention, and he became more determined to make my life as difficult as he possibly could. All eyes in the customs hall were now focused on the two Brits having a head to head.

His next action was to turn to his African colleagues and endeavour to get them to agree with him that I had refused to give him the key. Thankfully not one of them said they had heard me, collectively they all said that they were busy with other passengers. It was then that a healthy looking gentleman, with a very strange accent, approached me and enquired if he could be of assistance. I thanked him and said that I was fine but my guitar case wasn't. He then suggested in a very quiet tone that I should cut my losses and head for the airport exit.

Miles, the guy who had booked me for Zambia, was outside the customs hall waiting for me. 'Have problems with customs?' asked Miles, in a very broad Geordie accent.

'"Problems" is an understatement,' I replied. With that, we put my luggage on a trolley and headed for the car park. Once in the car Miles began to explain that I should be aware of 'ex-pats' such as the customs officer, who pick on their own kind to gain favour with the locals.

One of my first shows was at a club near N'dola Airport, close to where I had my customs fracas. It was a cabaret setting and a mostly ex-pat audience. I soon found the audience to be very responsive and in the mood for patter as well as the music, and I got into a friendly session of banter with some lads from London when I noticed a familiar figure stood at the bar. It was my customs officer friend.

I began to take the Mickey out of him and it soon became clear he was not on many Christmas card lists. The audience were on my side from the second I started on him, and every cutting comment I made about him was greeted with roars of laughter.

After the show I was at the bar enjoying adulation from all directions when the man from the airport with the funny accent appeared. 'Nice show Vince,' he seemed to say. 'Good to see you getting your own back.' I think that's what he said. It transpired that he was an Afrikaner and the head of Zambian Customs. It was very difficult to understand his dialect, but I soon got the gist that he was the boss of the guy I had problems with. He then went on to explain that the problem guy had been monitored for some time, and his behaviour, especially to whites, was proving to be an embarrassment to the Customs authority and he was being transferred to a distant outpost on the Zambia-Rhodesia border where he would be on his own and subject to a hard time if he picked on the Afrikaners.

A few years later I was working at the Royal Swazi Spa Resort in Swaziland. After I had checked in, who should turn out to be the front lobby porter, and the person who was to carry my bags to my suite, but my nasty Zambian Customs officer.

I must have been grinning like a Cheshire cat when he was told to carry Mr Eager's bags, including my guitar, by the President of the resort.

And no, I didn't tip him. But I did find out that he was married to a Swazi lady and had moved there following his dismissal from the Zambian Customs.

An Own Goal for Max

When Max Prien picked me up at Blantyre airport in Malawi, I had no idea of the rocky road that lay ahead. The Tropicana Club in Blantyre, a hotel, a restaurant, an outside catering business and a beautiful home were the assets this ex-German Bundesliga soccer player would have on the line within three weeks of my arrival in Malawi.

Six months before the Independence celebrations Max had been the Malawi national football team coach. Under his guidance the team had played the best football in their history and Max was a national hero. Consequently his business interests blossomed, and he gave up the coaching job as he no longer had enough time. It was certainly a busy period for Max. His outside catering company was supplying the parties being given by the local tribal chiefs to celebrate six years of independence. The Swaziland football team were staying at his hotel, and his restaurant was hosting the banquet for the Malawi and Swaziland football teams after their match at the National Stadium. The match against Swaziland was to be the first game under the new coach. In addition,

I was performing at his nightclub so it was a busy schedule by anyone's standards.

My accommodation during my six-week stay in Malawi was the guest bungalow in the grounds of Max's house. I didn't see him for three days before the football match, as he was so busy, especially with the catering for the tribal celebrations. On the morning of the match, he arrived home looking absolutely shattered. He had apparently been up for two nights preparing food. 'I take you to the match this afternoon Wince,' he shouted at me. 'I pick you and Andrew, (his son) up at 1.30 pm.' With that he was gone.

When we arrived at the ground, we were ushered into the President's Box. Other than a few colonial types, Max, Andrew and I appeared to be the only whites there. Max was greeted with great reverence, his success as the previous national football coach standing him in good stead.

'Let's see if they remember what you taught them Max.'

'Think you might have to put your kit on Max?' were a few of the many football related friendly jibes directed at Max by fellow guests in the Presidents Box.

Malawi's football success under Max was expected to extend into the Independence weekend celebrations with a win over close neighbours Swaziland.

Within twenty minutes however Malawi were trailing 1-0, and looking likely to concede more, when Max decided to coach the team from the President's Box.

'C'mon Malawi, the Swazis are fucking useless and you're playing like a pile of shit,' was an example of the colourful instructions Max began imparting to the team.

Drinking in the stadium was forbidden, but you could smoke, and many of the locals did, using a brand of tobacco not normally found in the corner tobacconists.

Though the smoking in the stadium created a party atmosphere that was second to none, the ban on booze was a rule Max didn't agree with. His argument was that he'd worked hard to set up the catering for the celebrations and he wanted to celebrate personally with his favourite tipple, vodka and Coke.

Not wanting to appear blatant, Max filled a 2-litre Coca Cola bottle with a 70/30 mix of vodka and Coke, but it was obvious what he was up to. I don't think anyone would have minded had he not already had a few, and as he got through the bottle at a rate of knots, his behaviour and his sideline coaching language got more and more unacceptable. Fellow guests turned on him, basically telling him to shut up and not to be such a bloody fool.

When half time arrived, I decided to have

a walk around the stadium and take some cine film with my camera. There was a fantastic atmosphere and everyone was very friendly, but this didn't lessen my apprehension at appearing to be the only white among the crowd of 40,000. When I returned to the box I felt a distinct air of uneasiness, and the few remaining guests were deep in conversation. As I took my seat, a very tweedy looking gentleman sporting a fine set of whiskers leaned over my shoulder from behind and whispered in the Queen's finest English:

'You're the rock 'n' roll friend of Prien's aren't you? Well, he's been arrested and taken into custody. Serves him bloody well right, carrying on like that in front of the President.'

'Where have they taken him?' I enquired.

'Local police station, I would think,' was his smug reply, as he slouched back into a cushioned VIP armchair, more suited to a gentleman's club in Mayfair than a third world nation's football stadium. I pretended I was engrossed in the football match, but the 45 minutes that followed felt like days, and the attitude towards me made me feel I shared Max's shame.

Nevertheless, I stuck it out until I was asked by my tweedy companion, 'Are you singing rock 'n' roll at Priens club tonight?' When I replied that I was, he appeared to take great pleasure in telling me that I had better get going as it was about a four-mile walk and there would be no taxi available.

As I stood up to leave I was tempted to give him a mouthful, but instead I turned to the President, thanked him for his hospitality and apologised on behalf of Max, saying that he was very tired having worked so hard for the past few days. I then excused myself and the President thanked me graciously, and I left.

As I approached the stadium exit, I heard the final whistle blow and a sea of supporters suddenly swept me up as they headed out of the ground and down the long highway from the stadium, where once again I was a solitary figure.

Despite differences in my skin colour and height, I seemed to be looking down on 40,000 people who appeared completely oblivious of me.

An hour after leaving the football ground I was at the club, where the news of Max's misdemeanours had preceded my arrival. The general opinion in the club was that he would be released with a slap on the wrist when he'd sobered up.

My act that evening included songs that I didn't always perform such as *If I Had A Hammer*, *Jailer Bring Me Water* and of course, *Jailhouse Rock*. All were introduced with an appropriate incarceration gag and everyone had a great night confident that Max would be with us sooner than later. However, when I went for breakfast with Max's family the following day the mood was much less jovial. He was still in custody, and his wife had spoken to their lawyer who had voiced his concern that the authorities might endeavour to make an example of Max.

Later that day Max appeared, bearing the news that he had been charged with using insulting behaviour in front of the President. If he was found guilty he could face prison or, since he was a non-national, deportation. During the next few days Max spent more time with his legal team than he did either at work or with his family, and it emerged that I might be the chief witness for the defence as I had been living, working and socializing with Max.

With only one week of my contract remaining, all the stops were pulled out for the case to come to court. I could stay on for a few days but that was all, as I was due to travel onward for an appearance in Salisbury, Rhodesia.

Eventually the trial was fixed for the following week, two days after my contract at the club finished, so I agreed to stay as the case would only last a few hours. When I was told the time of the hearing, I gasped.

I was told it would be 5am because, 'It's so much cooler and they can finish by 11 am,' explained Max's lawyer. The night before the trial was early to bed, but a sleepless night followed. I was worried sick as to how it would pan out, and I felt as if I was the one on trial.

Outside the courtroom, which judging by its derelict appearance was possibly the first building to be erected in Malawi, was a corridor with two benches that ran the length of the building. It was the waiting room, and it was enough to make you want to be a good guy for the rest of time.

The dark, dank, depressing atmosphere wasn't helped by the fearful expressions on the faces of those sitting opposite, who were so close our feet touched. Those being tried and those trying to help them were as one. Some were in handcuffs without shoes, others were wearing gold charm bracelets with Gucci sandals, but for now, all appeared equal. Peeking through the partially open door leading to the courtroom, could be seen the only people in the building with any semblance of comfort and they were the legal teams and the court officials who had the luxury of a ceiling fan and jugs of iced water.

I was tipped off that the cases of the privileged were heard first in order to avoid the advancing heat. The privileged, of course, were those in a position to employ the elite legal eagles who called the shots and were really the benefactors.

Thankfully we were the first to be heard, and being the prime defence witness it wasn't long before I was called. I was instructed to state my name, nationality and profession. Stating my real name rather than my stage name drew questions from the prosecuting council as he had seen my show at the club and was curious as to why I had two names. My nationality presented no problems, whereas my profession, which I gave as entertainer, was picked upon by the prosecutor who said he was under the impression I was a famous English rock 'n' roll singer. I tried to explain that though I did perform rock 'n' roll, all my legal documents stated that I was an entertainer. The judge then advised me that the questions would be asked slowly, and that I should answer them slowly, as the court recorder would be taking them down in long hand.

I'd entered the witness box at 5.40 am. The clock now showed 11.20 am, and we'd only had a 15-minute recess, so I was ready to drop. Max's hard work to the benefit of the tribal chiefs was the angle the defence was using, but I had got to a point where I felt like turning state's evidence, getting the hell out of there and heading for the nearest swimming pool with a bar.

Once my cross examination was complete, the judge closed the day's proceedings and we headed to Max's home, where later that day I was informed I wouldn't be needed any more and could leave the country. Leaving Malawi the following day was an anti-climax. I still didn't know the outcome of the trial and the judge wasn't due to give his decision for a few days, so maybe I never would.

Two weeks later in Salisbury, Rhodesia, I discovered Max had been found guilty of using insulting behaviour in front of the President, and that he and his family had been deported. Their hotel, house, club, restaurant and all their belongings had all been confiscated.

After losing everything, Max travelled to South Africa where he awaited the outcome of an appeal. I discovered a few weeks later that he lost his appeal and was beginning a new life in South Africa as a football coach. I hope he made his players aware that too much booze on the touchline could result in an own goal.

Nothing in the Boot

After Rhodesia's Unilateral Declaration of Independence in 1965, it went through a tough period when its Prime Minister, Ian Smith, and his illegal all-white government found their country facing economic and diplomatic sanctions.

The British ex-pats missed, and yearned for, everything that was British ranging from Kellogg's Corn Flakes to Land Rovers.

As in most romantic scenarios absence does make the heart grow fonder and the ex-pats were missing their 'Made in Britain' Union Jack stamped goods like no others. Loads were even smuggled in via the South African border to the south, a black market with highly inflated prices being the outcome.

After my one-month appearance at Brett's in Salisbury, I was to appear for a week at the Elizabethan Hotel in Kitwe, the capital of the Zambian copper belt. I was then to return to Salisbury for another month at Brett's.

It was during my week in Kitwe that an Afrikaner approached me at the Elizabethan Hotel with an offer to drive the 700 miles return trip to Salisbury in a truck laden with, among other items, HP Sauce, Kit Kat chocolate bars, Corn Flakes, Weetabix and Bassett's 'Licorice' Allsorts. I was to take a bush route, which he would show me, and he would supply me with a weapon for self-defence. The fee offered was US$3,000, to be paid on delivery.

As much as the money appealed to me, there was no way I was going to risk life and limb delivering comfort foods to frustrated ex-pats in Rhodesia.

My return journey to Rhodesia was by

road with a guy named Peter driving me. Other than a very intense bag search, my previous entry into Rhodesia had been without incident and I didn't expect this one to be any different.

Shortly before arriving at the Rhodesian border Peter enquired if I had experienced any problems with the Rhodesian Army during my previous visit. I told him I hadn't, and he went on to explain to me how they didn't trust the Brits.

Their opinion was that the imposed sanctions, and the manner in which the British Government was treating Rhodesia, meant that we were fair game in their eyes.

It was shortly after our entry into Rhodesia that I discovered the truth of this observation. A soldier taking an ostrich egg from one of my bags brought about our initial confrontation.

First he held it up to the light to check if it was empty. The person who gave me the egg had warned me that it must be blown otherwise the border police would suspect it has something suspicious inside. I told the soldier it had been blown and that it was for my son in England.

With that he dropped it onto the road and smashed it to pieces with his rifle butt. Laughing his head off, he shouted to his colleague in a broad Rhodesian accent, 'Nothing in there!' and continued to laugh.

Peter mouthed to me not to say anything and then said calmly to the soldier, 'Is there anything else sir?'

'Get in your bloody car man!' the soldier shouted at Peter. As Peter went to close the boot lid the soldier screamed. 'Get in the bloody car man and do as you're told. We'll close the fucking lid!'

Viewing what was going on behind through his wing mirror, Peter mumbled to me not to say a word. 'These guys are the worst type imaginable. If we were black they probably would have shot us by now,' he mumbled. With that the boot lid was slammed shut and the soldier shouted, 'Now fuck off you limey bastards!'

Many of the roads in Africa are straight and run for miles before disappearing over the horizon and we were on one such road. Peter was concentrating on his driving, but also looking anxiously into his rear view mirror. He muttered to me, 'Got to find a safe pull-in.'

Within minutes he appeared satisfied with what, or wasn't behind us, and what was happening ahead, and pulled off the road near some bushes. 'Quick, c'mon Vince,' he mumbled as he opened the car door, jumped out and ran to the rear of the car. I followed and found him lifting the boot lid where, laying across our suitcases, were two rifles. 'Shit! Where have they come from?' I asked. 'Those bastards planted them. When we get over that next hump in the road we'll be searched.' With that, Peter grabbed the rifles, ran into the bushes, from where he emerged a matter of seconds later without them.

With my heart racing faster than it ever had, I closed the door and slumped into my seat as Peter sped towards the horizon. 'They've been radioed by the bastards back there to expect us and they've told them what they have planted in the boot, so let me do the talking,' said Peter. As we cleared the brow of the hill we discovered an army truck at the side of the road and a soldier flagging us down.

We stopped, and without a word being spoken, the soldier went immediately to the rear of the car and opened the boot. Obviously not finding what he had been told was in the boot he came to Peter's window. 'Anything to declare?' 'No. Nothing sir,' replied Peter calmly with a wry smile.

'Where are you heading?' asked the soldier. 'Salisbury,' replied Peter. 'You have a tsetse control wash two miles ahead so off you go,' the soldier told us with a somewhat confused look on his face.

The tsetse fly can kill both man and beast and tsetse disinfectant control areas were set up along the borders to control its spread. What a pity they couldn't have had something similar to get rid of corrupt Rhodesian soldiers.

Mugabe's Cronies

My second visit to Rhodesia was two years after it had been granted independence as Zimbabwe and I was booked to appear in cabaret at the Monomatapa Hotel in Harare.

As I was the first UK artist to appear in Zimbabwe since its ascension from Rhodesia, the producers and hotel management had gone to great lengths to ensure that all eventualities had been covered.

Robert Mugabe and his cronies were already gaining a reputation for not being trustworthy so, in view of the strict money exchange restrictions my fee had been deposited in advance as a bond with a solicitor in England. I also visited the Zimbabwe Embassy in London to have my passport stamped with a work visa, plus a letter of authorisation to enable me to work while I was there.

Following four days of rehearsals we opened to a full house, including the usual smattering of VIPs and media guests who were invited in the hope that they would write and talk about the show. We received a great reception, with a couple of encores, and following the show the management threw a thank you party for the 12 piece orchestra, the three backing singers and myself.

During the party the hotel manager Perry told me he was delighted the show had been received so well and was confident we would get great reviews and business would be good.

The following day, Friday, I was awakened at 10 am by a call from Perry. He told me that he was coming up to see me as there was a problem we needed to discuss.

Four themed suites occupied the top floor of the hotel with fantastic views of a city centre park below which was covered by a carpet of flowering jacoranda trees, and adjacent to President Robert Mugabe's garden.

My suite was themed as a jungle scene with tropical fish tanks and a waterfall, a couple of palm trees and a 'sunset over the savannah' mural that ran the length of the wall opposite the floor to ceiling picture windows.

When I opened the suite door for Perry I was surprised to see him flanked by two soldiers sporting rifles. 'Can I come in?' he asked gingerly, and in he came, with the two soldiers taking up positions either side of the doorway in the corridor.

As he poured the coffee Perry began explaining that the department of immigration had phoned to say that there was a problem with my work permit and that I would not be able to perform again until the matter was resolved.

He then went on to tell me that basically they would have read the great reviews in the morning paper, which I had yet to read, and be aware that business for the coming weeks would be fantastic, but only the whites would benefit.

He told me we were to report to the immigration office in Harare at 3 pm, and that the two soldiers outside my door would ensure I didn't leave any earlier.

On the way to the immigration office Perry told me that they had made the appointment for 3pm. As they closed at 4pm for the weekend this would give the situation more edge, hence more bargaining power to them, in the knowledge that the shows for Friday, Saturday and Sunday were sold out.

'US$500 should do the trick,' Perry said ruefully. 'They'll keep us waiting for 20 minutes or so and then they'll say it's too late to do anything but they will allow us to put up a security bond which will clear us to do the weekend shows,' he continued.

Sure enough, at 3.20 pm we were duly invited into the immigration office where an officer explained that the Minister for Immigration, that's the person who had all my case details, was at the Lake Kariba Resort for the weekend and they were endeavouring to contact him but were not having much luck.

With 4 pm, and closing time fast approaching, the young officer asked tentatively, 'Would you be prepared to put up a bond?'

After enquiring again as to what the problem with my work permit was, and the young officer again passing the buck to the vacationing minister, Perry asked, 'How much?'

'One thousand US dollars will be fine,' he replied with an air of uncertainty.

'I only have $US500 on me,' replied Perry confidently.

'That will be fine then,' replied the young officer who was becoming more and more nervous.

With that, Perry asked him for a receipt for the $US500 and a letter confirming that I was allowed to work at the Monomatapa Hotel. Fortunately the letter gave no times or dates, which was in our favour for the future.

Bob Mugabe and the Wailers

During the six-week season of my show at the Monomatapa Hotel in Harare, Zimbabwe, a sound that became very familiar was the warning sirens from President Robert Mugabe's motor-cycle out riders as they escorted him to and from his residence at the rear of the hotel.

The sirens would start before he left his palace warning people to vacate the route as he drove past. From the minute he gained his dictatorial power he put fear into anyone who came too close.

Including innocent shoppers and tourists.

On hearing the sirens the public were told to clear the streets and people would hide in doorways in order not to be seen by his armed and heavy-handed guards.

One person who didn't heed the warning of the oncoming Mugabe was a young man aged sixteen who continued to walk down the street. As the entourage passed him, one bullet from a Mugabe henchman stopped him in his tracks. The following day the media reported his death as being, 'an attempted attack of the President'.

Mugabe killings were apparently commonplace, made worse for me by their immediate locality and being able to hear the sirens, and the shots.

Nervous banter would often accompany the sirens, none more so than when, in the middle of my show, the sirens could be heard and I joked to the packed audience, 'Here comes Bob Mugabe and the Wailers!'

The audience reaction was roars of laughter and I got the feeling that they were enjoying laughing at Mugabe without fear of reprisal. How wrong I was.

Reprisal the next morning when the boys with rifles turned up at my penthouse suite to arrest me for using slanderous behaviour towards the President. A stern looking man, who introduced himself as the head of security for President Mugabe, accompanied them.

He told me there were allegations that I had made a slanderous remark to the audience the previous evening about the President by saying, 'Here comes Bob Mugabe and the Wailers!'

I had no idea who could have reported me. I thought it must be a waiter as the audience was all white and very unlikely to have taken offence to any remark made against Mugabe. The waiters however were great to work with and really looked after me during my stay, but at the end of the day they had to look after themselves and their families.

Just when I thought I was on my way to the slammer, my saviour arrived; it was Perry, the hotel manager. When working overseas I would always try to use my 'celebrity' status to get me into places that were usually no go areas for regular tourists.

On one such occasion I was visiting the Kariba Dam hydro plant when I met up with a senior game warden who had seen my show a few days earlier. Over a beer in the hotel bar he told me of the problems they had experienced relocating the animals following the flooding of the dam in 1959. He also brought to my attention the immediate threat to the sable antelope, a majestic animal close to extinction and the national emblem of Rhodesia before becoming Zimbabwe.

As usual, a beer became a couple, which became a few, which became too many. It was during the 'too many' stage that I committed myself to performing a charity show to raise money and awareness of the sable's plight.

The venue was to be the park at the rear of the hotel in Harare. As it backed onto Mugabe's residence I made a comment during the press conference to launch the event that I hoped we wouldn't be too loud for the President, but if he did hear us and he liked our music he would be very welcome to join us.

'UK Rock 'n' Roll Star Invites President to Party,' was the quote which made the press, and it was this headline that Perry thrust in the face of Mugabe's head of security as he fumbled for his handcuffs.

'He likes the President! He's invited him to the party in the park! If you take him into custody what will happen to the biggest charity event this city has organised in years!' was Perry's accompanying rhetoric.

Standing up the security chief said sarcastically. 'Maybe you should sing a Bob Marley song for the president at your party.' Mugabe didn't take me up on my offer. But we included a few bars of *One Love*, just in case.

I Made the Maltese Cross

The friendliness of the Maltese people, the history of the island and its rugged beauty always made a visit to Malta an enjoyable experience.

I made regular visits to Malta as a cabaret performer, I was appearing at the Sky Night Club on the top floor of the Astra Hotel in Sliema. It was a classy venue that attracted a sophisticated clientele. Being invited to join guests at their tables after the show was a regular occurrence and usually an enjoyable one.

An invitation to join John and Frances Evans one evening was no exception. It transpired that John was the chief of the St Andrews Radio Station, an important link in the communications relay system between the Far East and the UK.

John and Frances were nearing the end of a three-year tour of duty and had grown very familiar with Malta, the Maltese, and their customs. As John's work entailed long hours, Frances had immersed herself in the local community and social work to pass the time away.

Malta was a bastion of Catholicism with the island boasting many fine churches and traditions and practices centred on the Catholic faith. It was Frances, a good practising Catholic, who introduced me to some of these practices as she showed me a side to Malta I was unaware of. Most of the journeys she took me on were made using the local bus service where the colour of the bus was the indication of its route.

We were returning on the yellow bus to the capital city of Valetta from the silent city of Mdina when my first encounter with the eccentricities of Maltese Catholicism bit me in the backside. As we approached Valetta all seats were taken and the bus became standing room only.

A few stops before our destination I discovered that good manners were no replacement for a humble Catholic indoctrination. As the bus door opened the first passenger to appear at the top of the steps was a young priest.

Walking down the crowded bus the priest was greeted by many of the seated passengers as they stood up, as if to offer him a seat. Among those offering was a young, very pregnant lady sitting directly in front of me.

I was amazed that so many people were prepared to give up their seat to a young priest, and secondly I was astounded when he walked past them to take up the offer of the pregnant lady.

Standing up, I tapped the priest on the shoulder and offered him my seat. Suddenly Frances was pulling my arm and telling me to sit down and be quiet.

Too late. If looks could kill I would be in a hearse, not a pretty yellow bus. Throughout the howls of derision and the ensuing mélée, Frances decided to err on the side of caution and, grabbing my arm, she ushered me off the bus. What a good job it was Frances and not my mother; otherwise the priest would have got a clip behind the ear.

As the bus disappeared, Frances suggested that we should calm our nerves with a drink in a nearby bar. Over a pint of their finest Amstell I was read the riot act. 'Children of Christ, or nuns and priests to you,' Frances told me firmly, 'are never questioned in Malta. They're God's representatives. They can do no wrong in the eyes of the islanders. You must respect that.'

Next day, as Frances and I walked through the streets of Sliema she pointed out an umbrella leaning against steps to the front door of a house. 'The umbrella will possibly belong to a priest,' Frances told me. 'If a couple have been married for more than 18 months and have not produced a child then the local priest is at liberty to assist. He leaves his umbrella next to the front door so that if the husband comes home he won't go into the house until the priest removes the umbrella. If the wife has a baby in the following months it becomes a child of the church. If it's a boy – a priest. If it's a girl – a nun.'

If anyone else had told me I would have thought they were pulling a practical joke, but not Frances. She was a God-fearing Catholic who loved the island and she would never compromise her loyalty to the locals or her religion.

The following week was Easter, a time when the Maltese people really nailed their religious colours to the mast. These were penance marches, where those seeking forgiveness carried huge statues or crosses through the streets, and entertainment was not allowed on Good Friday.

As we had the night off, Marco, the drummer in the Skylight band, suggested we should visit The Gut, one of the most infamous stretches of walkways in the world that stretched from the centre of Valetta down to the harbour and was a must visit for horny mariners calling at the island. Flanked by seedy low-lit bars, it was home to the ladies of the night. Walking past the bars was akin to running a gauntlet of flesh as they endeavoured to entice prospective customers inside for a good time.

Being Good Friday very few of the seediest bars were open. The only light came from table lamps sporting tacky red shades in various states of disrepair. As we made our way through the smoke and haze we heard giggling and mumbling noises coming from a corner. In the corner was a television showing the Pope's Good Friday blessing and beneath it we could see a lady bent over a table with her skirt over her head, and a guy in an American sailor's top, with his bell-bottoms around his ankles doing an impression of a Maltese Terrier.

My Uncle Tony the Prime Minister

Michelle Eden was a true blonde. Sweet and talented, but a benchmark blonde. As a dancer in the Australian production of 'Elvis the Musical', in which I had the lead role, she was one of the first Aussies I met and became a very dear friend.

In the early weeks of our Sydney season, our director Kevin Robinson, who was sharing the house I had in Paddington, Sydney and was soon to return to the UK, decided to cook a farewell dinner for 'Young Elvis' JJ McLean, Michelle and myself.

During the course of dinner Michelle told us of her aspirations to visit England with a view to getting work.

It was relatively easy for Aussies to get a work visa in England compared to the difficulties the Poms experienced going the other way. English grandparents were all that was required of the Aussies, and Michelle was keen to mention that she thought she could get help from her Great Uncle Tony's family as he had been 'something to do with politics'.

'What did your Uncle Tony do?' enquired Kevin.

'I really don't know. I just know he was pretty high up in politics.' Michelle replied.

'Do you know his name?' asked Kevin.

'Well, he had the same name as my father,' said Michelle in her broad cute Australian accent.

'So his name was Tony Eden?' Kevin asked enquiringly.

'Yea, Tony Eden, that was his name,' was Michelle's innocent sounding reply.

'Could he have been Anthony Eden?' Kevin asked excitedly.

'Yea! I think...' Before Michelle could finish the sentence...

Kevin screeched at the top of his voice, 'Michelle, your great uncle Tony was the Prime Minister of Great Britain. He could buy you the friggin' Palladium!'

A Different Kind of Rockin'

Bournemouth, Tenerife?

In the 1970's I made regular appearances on cruise ships as a cabaret style entertainer. The Fred Olsen Cruise Lines' 13-day cruise to the Canaries from Tilbury was a favourite itinerary of mine and had a two-fold purpose. One was to give participating passengers a wonderful cruise experience, and the other was to collect some of the tastiest tomatoes available from Gran Canaria. It was a quality product that attracted quality passengers.

An illegally overheard radiotelephone conversation on one cruise however proved that two of our passengers were far from being quality. We were four days into the cruise and four hours out of Lisbon and heading for Madeira when the fun started.

As I stood at the lounge bar talking to passengers, Peter Glen, the Cruise Director, walked in wearing a worried look. He told me of a lady passenger believed to be in an advanced stage of appendicitis and in need of immediate hospitalisation.

In the event of medical emergencies and the need to increase speed to arrive at a port earlier, the ship's insurers would be contacted, as they would be responsible for the excess fuel consumed by the increase in speed.

Our intended arrival time in Funchal Madeira was 7 am, but with the increased speed, at a cost of £2,000 to the insurers, we arrived at 10 pm the previous evening.

On our arrival in Funchal the priority was to get the patient into the waiting ambulance and off to hospital. Once the patient was safely off, the crew disembarked to enjoy a rare overnight stay in port. There were no scheduled overnight stays on any of our Canary Island itineraries so the crew in particular were keen to take advantage of this one.

Being a regular to Madeira, the Captain suggested a visit to the exclusive nightclub at Reid's Hotel and he loaned his VIP guest card to two others and myself.

Shortly after arriving at the club we were joined by two of our passengers. Roger and Jayne were a couple who had been enjoying the cruise, so much so that they often sent drinks over to the entertainment team. We all stayed in the club until 3 am, with Roger and Jayne picking up the drinks tab.

The next day we were in port and I didn't see the pair of them until the evening, after our departure for Gran Canaria. Post dinner they normally went to the lounge where they would stay for the rest of the evening. On this occasion they went to their cabin instead. It was here, as I discovered later, that the Cruise Director, Peter Glen, had visited them about a complaint they had made.

Peter arrived at the bar shortly before midnight and told the Assistant Cruise Director, Michael and me, that Roger and Jayne were not enjoying the cruise because of the poor quality of almost everything. They insisted on being flown home from Tenerife. We were astounded, as they had repeatedly told us of their delight at the entertainment and the cruise in general.

Fred Olsen Cruises had a policy that any passenger who was not satisfied at the halfway stage, Tenerife, would be offered complimentary air fares to return to the UK. It was, however, a policy that was not advertised and not commonly known, to avoid passengers taking advantage.

Michael was given the unenviable task of taking Roger and Jayne to lunch in Gran Canaria the next day to try and get them to rethink their decision. He returned appearing much the worse for wear, and not the bearer of good tidings. Roger and Jayne had not been swayed by his charm, or the endless supply of wine, into changing their minds and they were adamant in their demands to be flown back to the UK.

I had sailed many times with Chief Radio Officer Bjorn and spent many a happy hour in his company propping up the late night bar. He was always good for a yarn or two and between Gran Canaria and Tenerife he revealed the contents of a late night radiotelephone call made by Roger.

When an on board phone call was made the only person who could eavesdrop, but shouldn't, was the Radio Officer. They were sworn to secrecy and in no circumstances allowed to divulge the contents of any conversation they may overhear. On this occasion however, a couple of large brandies helped loosen Bjorn's tongue and he spilt the beans.

Roger had made a radiotelephone call to a lady in Bournemouth, England. It transpired that the lady was Roger's wife and she said she was having problems looking after their pub as the head barmaid Jayne, had disappeared. We already knew Jayne wasn't Roger's wife because of her passport.

During the call Roger continually made reference to the poor telephone reception, explaining to his wife that it could be due to the thunderstorms in Scarborough, from where he said he was phoning her. He told his wife that he would contact Jayne and fire her. He then went on to tell her that he had spent most of his time on 'one of those great new sun beds that give you a brilliant tan. When you see my colour you'll think I've been abroad. I'm really dark.' He ended the call by telling his wife he would leave Scarborough late the next morning in order to get home in the early evening.

The next morning Roger and Jayne disembarked in Tenerife.

We never did find out if Jayne got the sack or what Roger's wife thought of his Scarborough tan.

They didn't want 'Elvis' the Cruise Director

After my five years in the lead as the mature Elvis in 'Elvis the Musical,' which included my four years as a born again bachelor, I married my beautiful Canadian girlfriend Anette in 1985.

My good friend and agent Roger Kendrick, whom I had worked on cruise ships for in the 1970's, suggested Anette and I had an interview for the position of Cruise Director and Social Directress.

The successful interview took place in London and the following week Anette and I flew out to Piraeus in Greece to see the ship, The MV Aquarius. Our reason for going to the ship was because the owners were concerned I might be too tall and catch my head on the sprinklers. Following my walk down every corridor on the ship without having to stoop, I was given the all clear and the job was ours. I was a Cruise Director.

Our first season was eventful to say the least. 1986 was the summer the PLO decided to attack American passenger carrying cruise ships. Once the cruise ship Akili Laro had been hi-jacked, and a New York invalid passenger was shot and pushed over the side, all Americans who had booked Mediterranean cruises cancelled. The Aquarius lost 98% of its bookings and had to lay up for 10 weeks while the company re-marketed in Europe.

The season was eventually re-launched with European passengers but the company decided not to pursue their cruise policy the following season and sold the Aquarius.

It appeared our cruise careers were doomed when Roger contacted us and asked us if we would be interested in similar positions on The Ocean Islander. She was the smaller of two ships operated by Ocean Cruise Lines, or OCL as they were more commonly known, a company catering mainly for American passengers but who did book quite a few English.

The owner was Gerry Herrod, a man who once fired a ship's Doctor because he had a big nose. 'How would you like to be treated by someone with a nose that big hovering over you?' he asked the operations manager who had hired him. Our interview took place in London with the company's Entertainment Director. He thought we would be ideal for the job, but he was concerned as to my rock 'n' roll background. He felt the appointment of a rock 'n' roller being responsible for the entertainment on a luxury cruise ship wouldn't sit well with the owner.

The literature we had seen of the Ocean Islander indicated that she was a beautiful ship and made us want the job more. I suggested to Alf that I would be happy to take the position in my real name, Roy Taylor, and he thought that was an excellent idea. The only other proviso was that I would never sing rock 'n' roll on the ship and if I did then our contract could be terminated. The contract was duly signed without the name Vince Eager being mentioned.

Our first season on the Ocean Islander was to be the Mediterranean but due to the ongoing political tensions in the region we were switched to the Norwegian Fjords and the Baltic.

Shortly after the revised itinerary was announced we received a package from OCL containing information on the new itinerary and literature about the region and the ports of call. There was also an OCL brochure entitled CRUISE NEWS, a quarterly publication for Cruise Club members, who were in essence repeat passengers who received special offers and inside information on what was happening within the company.

On the front page of the brochure was the

headline, 'Vince … Eager to Join the Ocean Islander.' Followed by a full colour portrait photo of me and an article explaining how delighted the company were to have acquired my services.

So much for Roy Taylor the Cruise Director! I phoned Alf to enquire as to the implications re Gerry Herrod the owner and he told me, 'As long as you don't sing rock 'n' roll you'll be OK.'

A part of my job description was to give port and excursion lectures so I had to do a crash course to familiarise myself with the area and learn how to pronounce the names of places correctly and convince the passengers I knew the area like the back of my hand.

We fell in love with the Ocean Islander the minute we set eyes on her, little knowing that she would be our home for the next five plus years.

The crew made us very welcome and it only took a couple of months, though somewhat stressful months, before we felt at home.

The short Northern European summer nights proved a big rival to the indoors shows we offered. Walking around the deck and taking in the beauty of the Fjords in almost 24 hours continual daylight was a given. Consequently shows such as the passenger talent and the masquerade were, on occasions, cancelled. It was on one such evening when I broke my 'no rock 'n' roll' vow.

Against my wife Anette's better judgment I had taken two of my favourite Elvis Vegas style suits and matching footwear onboard. During my five years in Elvis the Musical, the producers had more than 20 Vegas style suits made for me and allowed me to keep many of them, so I thought they might come in useful for the ship's masquerade and passenger talent show.

As there was a sign up period for the passenger's talent show, and at the closure of the sign up time we had no participants, I went to plan B where I would get a couple of the crew to perform. The crew, especially those in public areas such as the bars and dining rooms, enjoyed performing for the passengers as it raised their profile and helped with their tips. Plus they would get US$20 for their effort.

I decided to close the show with two Elvis songs, *Suspicious Minds* and *American Trilogy*, wearing a white Elvis Vegas suit. The audience reaction was fantastic. They stood and cheered for more and continued in their praises after I had changed and gone to the bar.

Onboard was the Vice President of Hotel Operations, Hans Haan. Hans was a jovial character and always good company for a nightcap.

As I arrived at the bar he took my hand, nearly shaking it off as he raved about my performance. 'That's what this bloody company wants! Exciting entertainment not these bloody poofters,' alluding to a couple of male dancers we had onboard.

Thanking Hans, I then related the 'no rock 'n' roll' scenario and asked him not to mention anything back at head office. His reply was, 'You'll be fine. They'll love it. Don't worry!' With that we retired to the Peppermint Cocktail Lounge balcony where we soaked up more than just the beauty of the Fjords well into the early hours.

Hans disembarked the ship the following day and returned to London.

Bergen is a beautiful port and one where Anette and I would always try to grab a couple of hours' relaxation ashore visiting the scenic flower and fish market.

On the day following the departure of Hans from the ship, we returned from our walk in Bergen to find a note under my cabin door telling me to contact Dimitri, the Hotel Director, immediately.

As I sat before Dimitri he wore a very worried frown and informed me that he had received a fax from head office re the entertainment programme and myself. As well as being my immediate boss, he was becoming a good friend, and the manner in which he appeared to be addressing the contents of the fax really worried me.

Handing me the fax he asked me to read it. It was addressed to him.

It has been reported that Vince Eager, the Cruise Director on the Ocean Islander, has been presenting rock 'n' roll as part of the onboard entertainments programme. An agreement was made between Mr Eager and Mr Alf Radcliffe that he should not perform rock 'n' roll onboard and if he did the contracts of he and his wife could be terminated.

As Mr Radcliffe is no longer the Entertainments Director at OCL we are hereby instructing Mr Eager to include his rock 'n' roll act in the entertainments programme at least once per cruise. If Mr Eager does not comply with this directive both he and Mrs Eager's positions within the company will require reassessing.

Please congratulate Mr Eager as we have received excellent reports of his performance of Elvis Presley songs.

Signed,

Natasha Tutt

Entertainments Director OCL

Even in the Fjords, Rock 'n' Roll ruled!

The Orinoco Vikings

On the night of the Passenger Talent show, the Masquerade parade and then the Caribbean midnight deck buffet, passengers would often enter into the spirit by making themselves a costume or just opt for putting on one of the many party hats we made available, leaving the rest to the imagination.

It was during a stock take that we noted a certain Viking helmet we put out for passengers was proving more popular than the others and stocks were close to running out. In my next monthly requisition I ordered a further 2,000 flat-pack Viking helmets, giving the item number from a previous order. Six weeks later, in our winter homeport of Barbados, Tony, the chief housekeeper, informed me that there was a big delivery for me.

My assistant duly checked and signed the delivery as OK. It was mid-afternoon when Tony came back to me, concerned at my not having stored the boxes. I went to the dockside to investigate and discovered two hundred boxes; each containing ten fully formed Viking helmets complete with plastic horns.

As we were in the middle of embarkation I decided to place all but five boxes into our storage warehouse on the Barbados dockside. The remaining five were stored in my limited storeroom onboard. Following a fax to Operations in London it was determined that the company we ordered from had run out of flat-pack Viking helmets and head office had accepted without consulting the ship. We were lumbered with the moulded ones, and during the next four years of cruising Europe in the summer and the Caribbean in the winter, we slowly used up more and more of the Viking helmets.

In 1991 we were told to empty the warehouse in Barbados, which still held over 600 Viking helmets, as we were not going back to the Caribbean. I had to come up with an idea to get rid of them.

Every Tuesday afternoon at 2 pm, as we entered the Orinoco River, we received a welcome from over 150 Indians from a local riverside village who paddled their dugout canoes alongside the ship to greet us.

The Indian greeting was set up by our Venezuelan port agent who rewarded the villages with US$100 worth of provisions for their efforts. The cue for the Indians to paddle out to meet us was given by a couple of blasts on the ship's horn 15 minutes before our arrival off their village.

As the Indians surrounded the ship I would give a commentary from the bridge explaining their history, while encouraging the passengers to take apples and oranges, not available in the Orinoco Delta, from the buffet, put them in a plastic laundry bag from their cabin and throw them to the Indians, who would be thrilled to receive them.

During our penultimate cruise up the Orinoco River my staff prepared about 125 laundry bags with apples, oranges and plastic Viking hats inside, and we gave them to the passengers to throw to the Indians.

As the Indians paddled back to shore some Indians put the Viking hats on, presenting a very funny picture both to themselves and to us. When we arrived in Ciudad Guyana, 180 miles up the mighty Orinoco River, a few hours later for our overnight stay, I hatched a plot with our port agent for our final visit to the mighty Orinoco the following week.

When I'd told him that we had thrown Viking helmets along with the apples and oranges he replied, 'They'll be selling them in the market by now.' That gave me an idea. I gave him all the boxes of Viking Helmets I had on board and he agreed to give them to the Indians, on one condition; they had to wear them when they rowed out to welcome us for the last time the following week.

Sure enough, and right on cue, the ship's horn sounded and over 150 Indians wearing Viking helmets paddled towards us. This enthralled the American passengers, and there was much speculation about whether the Indians were a distant relative of the Vikings!

Archbishop Eager

'Where are we?' enquired the passenger.

'What day is it?' I asked.

'Tuesday,' he said.

'Then it's Aruba,' I answered.

Cruising was like that. On a seven-day cruise programme season, routines soon became established and the day of the week determined which country you were inn. On this particular itinerary, Aruba on a Tuesday was my telephone check-in day with head office in Miami and my land-locked boss. A disgruntled passenger from a previous cruise may come back to haunt you with a letter of complaint, eg., 'Why didn't the Cruise Director put in the daily programme that the Northern Lights, (Aurora Borealis) would be visible on the Wednesday night of our cruise?' 'Why didn't the Cruise Director point out the equator to us when we crossed it as we didn't get to see it'. And so on.

On this occasion my boss, Paul, at Regency Cruises in Miami, answered the phone with, 'Get your dog collar dry-cleaned, Archbishop Eager. The Christmas Priest can't make it! No available flights from Miami to Jamaica. You'll have to do it.'

Christmas on a cruise ship is the most de-pressing cruise of the year. The only people who have a good time are the crew. Many passengers are sent on a Christmas cruise as a gift from their families who don't want to spend that time of year with them. Other passengers can be made up of those of religious faiths who don't recognise Christmas and went to get away from it. The one thing you can guarantee that won't apply to Christmas at sea is peace and goodwill towards the Cruise Director, especially if he hasn't got a priest to conduct midnight mass on Christmas Eve. Thanks to Paul, this would be the situation on the upcoming Christmas cruise out of Jamaica. He couldn't get the priest a flight because he'd left it too late.

Our regular itinerary of Montego Bay, Port Antonio, Curacao, Bonaire, Aruba and back to Montego Bay, had little to offer at the best of times. Leaving Montego Bay on a Saturday evening got us into Port Antonio, Jamaica early on the Sunday morning. This enabled us to have a church service onboard at 8 am. It was Father George from a local parish in Port Antonio who took the service. He was fantastic; his multi-denominational service appeared to satisfy all religions. He was such a nice guy and a wonderful character.

Four weeks before Christmas I approached Father George for his guidance. Over a cup of coffee and a croissant, I explained my plight of the forthcoming priestless Christmas. What could I do? The passengers would lynch me. If I do have a service they'll complain that we're ramming Christmas down their throats, and if I don't, they'll sue, because it states in the brochure that you'll have a priest on board for Christmas. It's the biggest no-win imaginable!

'I will put together a multi-denominational Christmas Mass for you, Vince, then you can conduct the service yourself,' George said calmly. 'Me, George?' I screeched, 'they'll have me over the side. I'm not a priest.' However, George possessed an amazingly tranquil persona, and within minutes he had me believing I could do it.

One week before the Christmas cruise, George informed me he had finished the service and that he'd go through it with me. Within minutes I was feeling more nervous than ever before. How could I pull it off? The one saving grace was that Christmas Mass was on the second day of the cruise. This meant that the passengers hadn't got to know me and may not notice that I was the Cruise Director as well as the Priest.

As the Cruise Director's role is one of the highest profile positions on board a ship, I decided to avoid a few of the first day duties. This included the Captain's Welcome Aboard Party, where, alongside the Captain and Hotel Manager, I would normally shake hands and greet the guests.

Christmas Eve and the Welcome Party

helped take my mind off the daunting task that lay ahead. Port lectures, introducing shows, overseeing the lifeboat drill and commentaries from the bridge on places of interest are all part of the Cruise Director's duties. Why should reading a Church Christmas Mass be any different?

The cruise staff and entertainers were to be the choir and I begged them to look the smartest they had ever looked. I arranged to meet all my staff in the bar before mass as I felt we could all do with a touch of liquid confidence. They looked immaculate and certainly put me in a much more relaxed frame of mind.

With the choir looking resplendent and in good voice, we started. Once the first carol was done and dusted I felt as if I had been a priest all my life. At last, my years as a chorister were beginning to pay off. Watching all those vicars preach their sermons every week must have crept into my subconscious. Before you could say 'BAH HUMBUG!' 40 minutes had gone and it was over.

The seasonal Bible references with wonderful stories and the great selection of carols George put together for me had worked a treat and I had loved every shaky moment. As I thanked the congregation and wished everyone a Merry Christmas, I so wanted to do it all again. In wanting to cherish the moment even more, I rushed to the lounge door in order to wish my flock goodnight and hopefully gauge a favourable reaction to the service.

Being dressed in a similar uniform to my staff, and having my name badge and position on my breast pocket, didn't appear to give many of the passengers a clue to who I really was, as many of them said, 'Goodnight Vicar, or Father, and thank you for a lovely service.'

Maybe 'Songs of Praise' next? Amen!

Brandy and Cornflakes

A phone call between the hours of 1 am and 5.30 am was always bad news. Engine faults, bad weather, port visits cancelled or a passenger dying being the favourites. The call I received at 5 am between Istanbul and Mykonos didn't come as a surprise, as I had been informed by the ship's doctor the previous evening that a passenger, Mr Flowers, had experienced a heart attack and was in a serious condition.

The voice on the phone belonged to Captain Efthimiou, the Staff Captain on my first ship as a Cruise Director, the MV Aquarius. His voice was sombre as he instructed me to meet him in the Captain's office. Negotiating the five decks of stairs between my cabin and the Captain's office was a challenge at the best of times, but if you had been drinking in the bar until 2.30 am as I had, it was a nightmare.

Due to the anticipated serious nature of the call, and wanting to appear respectable, I had a cold shower to try and clear my head and then climbed into a clean uniform. As I knocked on his door the Captain summoned me in. He was sitting with the ship's doctor, the Staff Captain and Mrs Flowers. He then informed me of the passing of Mr Flowers an hour earlier and asked me, along with my staff, to take care of Mrs Flowers and ensure that she had everything she wanted.

Following formalities from the Staff Captain, such as explaining the arrangements for having a casket delivered to the ship at our next port of call, Mykonos, and then arranging for the body to be disembarked to the island, Mrs Flowers was free to return to her cabin. I asked her if I could get anything for her to eat or drink, which she declined. She then went on to voice her concerns as to the photographs taken of her and Mr Flowers during the cruise by the ship's photographer, Alex. The photographs were displayed daily, and Mr and Mrs Flowers had intended to buy theirs on the final day of the cruise.

My efforts to console her, and at the same time assure her that I would get the photos for her, were unsuccessful. She was becoming more and more distraught until I told her that I would go and get them immediately and bring them to her. She calmed down and I went to my office to phone the photographer. Alex sounded as bad as I felt, and even worse when I told him to bring all the cruise photos to my office. 'What! Now?' he mumbled.

'Yes, now Alex!' I begged. Twenty minutes later Alex staggered into my office looking more like the corpse and carrying two boxes full of photos. 'What the bleedin' hell's going on?' he asked. Once I'd explained Mrs Flowers' plight, Alex mellowed and placed the boxes in front of me on my desk.

'Holy shit!' I screamed. 'Look at this Alex!'

On top of the pile in the first box was a photograph of Mr Flowers taken in Kusadasi. The ship's photographer would take photos of the guests as they left Turkey underneath a sign on Kusadasi pier that read 'Goodbye' and 'Gule Gule,' Turkish for goodbye. We went through the contents of that box 1, holding about 300 photos, but there were no more of Mr Flowers. My nerves having settled a little, I lifted box 1 to reveal box 2.

'Jesus Christ Alex, did you know?' 'Know what boss?' he asked. 'He's on top of box 2 as well!' I said in shaky tones. There again was Mr Flowers, peering at me from the top of the pile of photos in box 2 in a photo taken at the Captain's Welcome Party. With that, I rang the night steward and told him to bring me a bottle of brandy and two glasses.

The look of fear on Alex's face confirmed he had no idea of Mr Flowers' passing and he couldn't explain why his photographs were the first we came across in both boxes.

Without uttering a further word, Alex and I sat down and I poured us the largest brandies imaginable.

Mr Ravel's Bolero

In 1994 my wife Anette and I were hired by a Greek lady name Mrs Keuseoglou, a tough uncompromising lady who was the head of Sun Line Cruises, she had inherited the company from her husband, and was known, but not always affectionately, as 'Mrs K'.

The Sun Lines product had been successful for many years, being aimed at the American market for cruises in Europe, the Caribbean and South America. General operations for Sun Lines were operated out of Piraeus in Greece, whereas reservations and entertainment were operated from New York. The head of entertainment was Tina Jones whom I first met when I visited the MV Stella Solaris in Fort Lauderdale, having agreed to take over as Cruise Director. In discussing various aspects of the onboard entertainment Tina appeared very naïve and not of the quality I was used to dealing with.

When I joined the ship in Piraeus, Greece, I discovered I was also inheriting as members of cruise staff, four Spanish dancers, three girls and a boy known as Ballet Espanol. They explained they were busy rehearsing Ravel's Bolero in the hope they could perform it as part of the ship's entertainment programme. The following day I watched the rehearsal of the Bolero and my prayers were answered. Their dancing was brilliant and I knew the American passengers would love it.

With the date set for their first performance, I put the word around the senior officers to come and support them – not that I thought they needed it, but officers can be good PR when chatting up passengers. Staff such as dining room waiters, bar staff and cabin stewards could also suggest which shows passengers should or should not see, making a big difference to the turnout, and, consequently, to the reception a show would receive. As it was fourteen minutes long I took a gamble and programmed the Bolero to close the show. They would follow nineteen-year-old world-class juggler Romano Frediani, son of the world's fastest juggler Nino Frediani. Romano's act never failed to please as he was an awesome juggler and a natural-born entertainer.

The booker of the Moss Empires Theatre circuit in the 1950s, Cissie Williams, once told me to always be happy to follow a great act. They lay the positive foundations for you to build on, and this gamble paid off. The reception the Bolero received was fantastic with a standing ovation and cheers for an encore. As the weeks passed, the reputation of Ballet Espanol grew from strength to strength. Their popularity knew no bounds.

Two-months into the season Entertainment Director Tina decided to pay us a visit. Joining the ship in Piraeus she was due to stay for the first four days of a 7-day cruise. I usually programmed Ballet Espanole and Romano's show towards the end of the cruise, when passengers would complete a comment form using a rating system, marking out of 10 for all aspects of their cruise. Since placing the Bolero and Romano show towards the end of the cruise, and using Cissie's best til last theory, our entertainment ratings had shown a big improvement. Armed with this I felt confident in putting the Bolero and Romano's show earlier in the cruise so Tina could see it.

Following the usual standing ovation for the show, I retired to the bar where Tina was enjoying a drink with her onboard mole, Carol. Carol was a tall, blonde, pearly white toothed leggy American, whose position was meant to be that of hostess, but she spent more time shagging the Maître d' and belittling the entertainers. Tina called me over. 'She's going to buy me a drink', I thought. 'Can you join me for a breakfast meeting tomorrow morning, Vince? Say seven-thirty?' asked Tina abruptly as I approached her. 'I'll be there,' I replied.

'The entertainment is quite good, Vince,' said Tina whilst filling her face with a breakfast croissant. 'I understand Mrs K has become a big fan of your singing, so well done. I am, however a little concerned about the Spanish dancers. I feel their dance is too long and I would like you to shorten it.'

I was astounded. My worst fears had been realised. She knew nothing whatsoever about entertainment. 'What would you suggest we do Tina?' I asked. 'We need to cut about five minutes of the Bolero,' she replied.

I was curious whether she knew anything about Mr Ravel, who'd lived until about 1950 and whose Bolero was one of the most famous pieces of its genre. 'Would you like me to ask Mr Ravel if he could knock five minutes off his Bolero Tina?' I asked sarcastically. 'That would be wonderful darling; do you think he would mind?' she enquired.

I never saw Tina again. I remained with the company for the remaining four months of my contract during which time the Bolero, in its original form, continued to wow the audiences and Carol returned to America, after I'd fired her.

Super Bowl Cruise

In 1993 we had just left Montego Bay on the M/V Regent Spirit to sail to Aruba, when an all-American guy asked me where on the ship he could watch the Super Bowl later that evening. As it wasn't until the mid 1990s that television signals via satellite could be picked up by cruise ships, I told him he was out of luck but I would try and get the result from the radio room.

Not being too happy with that, he told me he would be at the bar and that I was to keep him informed of the score – his demeanour indicating that he had already spent a fair amount of time at the bar.

The Regent Spirit was a recent acquisition to the Regency Cruises fleet, and, though a nice little ship, she was in need of major renovations. Unfortunately, the company were financially in deeper water than their ships, and the chances of any decent investment in her were out of the question. Sadly the ship's Greek officers reflected the company's predicament by the manner in which they treated the guests.

My request to the Radio Officer to keep me updated with news on the Super Bowl as it became available was met with a huff and 'we see.'

Show time started at 10 pm and ran for an hour. Shortly before the end of the show, I asked my assistant to go to the radio room and get the 2nd Radio Officer to write down any score he may have on the Super Bowl.

As I was about to go on stage to pass on news about the following day's programme, my assistant pushed a piece of paper in my hand with the Super Bowl final score written on it.

I read out the result, Dallas Cowboys 17, Buffalo Bills 52, it was greeted with howls of delight and approval by most of the audience, and especially by those sat at the bar. Their reaction as I passed through the bar later was as if I had actually won the game. Champagne and cigars were in abundance and I was expected to join in and ensure their depletion.

With the excuse that I still had work to do, I bid my goodnights and retired.

MarSat, Marine Satellite, offered a service whereby ships could receive news via satellite in the early morning in a newspaper format that could then be printed and delivered to the cabins. As the morning following the Super bowl was a day at sea, many of the passengers enjoyed a room service breakfast while reading the MarSat Daily News, which had been delivered to their cabin.

It was one particular article in the MarSat Daily News which so nearly resulted in a mutinous situation when read by our Super Bowl fan from the bar.

The Daily News article gave a totally different football score to that given to me by our beloved 2nd Radio officer. The team he had put down as winning had actually lost.

The Hotel Director called me to his office to tell me the news. 'This guy is livid and he'll sue the arse of us … and you personally.' He then went on to tell me that the guy had a big bet on the game and instead of winning, he had lost, plus he had run up a considerable tab at the bar, which he was refusing to pay.

The root of the problem was of course, the Radio Officer. He thought it was a huge joke and there was speculation that it was deliberate. Even fellow Greek officers were sceptical.

As the cruise progressed, a major 'butter up the passenger' offensive was put in place in the hope of dissuading him from taking any form of legal action.

He did pursue the matter when he returned home with his lawyer sending a threatening letter but he apparently settled for 50% off a future cruise.

All Stuck Up!

With Cruise Directors having one of the highest profiles on a cruise ship, you are there to be shot at when things go wrong ... or right. Bad weather, poor excursions, unfunny comedian, bad flights, lost luggage and on it goes ... you take the rap for it all. Most passenger's opinions would be reflected in their marking on the ship's comments forms they are asked to fill out at the end of a cruise. Some, however, appear to be hell bent on upsetting anyone, or everyone.

One such couple were Mr and Mrs Black who reported that their luggage was lost and made the familiar complaint that this would ruin their holiday. Lost luggage passengers usually received perks such as drinks, party invitations, complimentary excursions and vouchers for the gift shop to buy replacement items, so it wasn't all-bad.

Mr and Mrs Black were at the information office every day. The more they complained the more perks they received, until, at a Captain's meeting one morning, Tony the Chief Housekeeper revealed that he had found their lost luggage under their bed. They hadn't lost it, they were hiding it. We agreed that it was perhaps something they did on a regular basis in order to get perks. Maybe it was even empty.

We checked that the luggage under the

bed had the same tag code as the reported supposedly missing items, then removed it. The Blacks looked bemused when they were told their luggage had been found and would be on the ship later that day. They knew they had been tumbled but couldn't say a word.

They received their 'missing' luggage and, no doubt thought that was the end of it. But we had ways of paying back guests who abused the hospitality and courtesies of the staff. It was an act of sweet revenge I used about five times in fourteen years of being a Cruise Director.

Passengers were requested to place their luggage outside their cabins the night before disembarkation, and, if they were staying at a hotel after the cruise, they wouldn't see it again until they were in their hotel room.

After the midnight buffet on the final night of the cruise I would sometimes walk the corridors, under the pretence that I was checking luggage outside the cabins to ensure they had the correct disembarkation tags. When I arrived at a victim's luggage I would pretend to check the tag and at the same time squeeze a touch of super glue into the keyhole or on the combination lock.

At least Mr and Mrs Black would have a genuine reason to complain next time.

Mike Stoller

Silversea Cruises are the premier luxury cruise line with four of the most beautiful cruise ships imaginable. With prices starting at around US$500 per passenger per day, fully inclusive, passenger expectations were understandably high.

Towards the end of a cruise the heads of department would have a meeting to discuss the next cruise. From food and beverage special requirements to VIP passengers, we would cover everything. At the start of the meeting the hotel manager would hand me a list of the expected VIPs, and then give a quick run-down of the list to check if I had any queries about who they were, or if there were any VVIPs (very, very important passengers) amongst them.

On this particular occasion the Silver Cloud Hotel Director, Klaus, asked me if I knew the Stoller party from Los Angeles who were on the list. It stated in the VIP manifest that Mr M Stoller was a respected songwriter from L.A. who was travelling with his wife Corky and two friends. I told Klaus I didn't know of him but I would check.

On embarkation day in Singapore I received an envelope from head office via the port agent with a VIP update. Included would be additional information about the VIPs such as their likes, dislikes, or subjects to avoid in conversation. VIPs were usually very happy if they were left to their own devices but on occasions they could prove to be divas.

One such VIP was Californian business-man, and regular cruiser, Bill Evans, who had just sold a part of his business for $250million. His beautiful wife Linda was a milliner who would bring 14 hats on the cruise with her, one for every day of the cruise, to be worn at dinner every evening.

The hats were transported in what looked like a 6-foot high drum case and Bill would book a two-bedroom suite so Linda could lay her hats out on the spare bed. That was an extra $500 a day to prevent the hats from being crushed.

With the Stoller party due onboard in Singapore later that day I opened the VIP update envelope. Along with the VIP list with additional notes was a brochure. On the front was a black and white retro photo of two men and underneath the photo it read … Leiber & Stoller. Shit! The M Stoller VIP is Mike Stoller, Elvis's songwriter, who, along with his partner Jerry Leiber, is one of the leading songwriters of all time. And I had told the Hotel Director that I didn't know of him but I would check who he was! I couldn't believe it. What a prat I was!

When it came to organising the guests who were to be invited to the officers' tables at the Captain's welcome dinner the following evening, I informed the social hostess that Mike and his party were top of the list for my table. Just after lunch the Social Directress informed me that the Stoller party had accepted. I was over the moon.

Table placings' protocol decreed that the male officer hosting the table should have a lady on either side. On this occasion, to hell with protocol! I placed Mike on my left and his lovely wife Corky on my right.

Guests were invited by the officer hosting their table to pre-dinner cocktails in the bar. All of my guests, other than Mike, showed for cocktails with Corky tending Mike's apologies for being late. When the time came for me to escort my party to the table Mike still hadn't arrived, so Corky told me he would join us at the table. We had just been served with the second course when Mike arrived. It was the first time I had seen him and he looked everything I expected of him, dapper, grey-haired and sporting a great pair of sideburns.

He seemed a very shy and humble man as he continued to apologise for being late saying he had a problem with his shirt and that it had taken him longer to fix than he anticipated. During the meal I told Mike that I had toured in Elvis the Musical for five years and his chuckling reply was, 'It took Jerry and I ages to get any money for that show.'

Mike went on to tell me that he and Jerry had seen the show when PJ Proby was in it and they thought it was fabulous.

The norm following a show was for the officers to take their chosen guests to their theatre table where they would hopefully enjoy the Captain's Welcome Show. As I sang a song at the end of the show and was unable to sit with my guests, I asked Mike and Corky to join me for a drink afterwards.

We met later on in the cocktail bar for what was to become a nightly liaison. The first thing Mike said was, 'You have an amazing set of pipes man. I bet you were great as Elvis.' I felt much more confident with him in the knowledge that he enjoyed my singing at the end of the show. Mike then asked me which night I was doing my own show as he would definitely be coming and he then went on to ask if I was doing any of his songs. I wasn't, but suggested that if he would like to accompany me on the piano I would love to. He then explained that he had never played his own songs on stage without Jerry. I suggested that he thought about it and let me know later in the cruise.

Three days later we were due in Java and most of the passengers would visit the ancient Buddhist site of Borobudur. Mike asked me if it was worth visiting so I invited him to be the guest of my wife Anette and I as we had a car laid on and he could then judge for himself.

It was a rainy day but it didn't dampen our spirits. Mike's wife Corky stayed onboard as she is a jazz pianist and took the advantage of a quiet ship to rehearse for an upcoming tour. Mike appeared to love every minute of our trip to Borobudur and managed to get some great photos.

On our way back, Mike asked me what numbers I would like him to accompany me on in my act. I told him I would like to put a medley together so perhaps we could work out a routine in the theatre the following day. At 5 pm rehearsal was agreed on. Five hours before the show.

The ship's bandleader's name was George. A very talented Hungarian musician, who, like most musicians, was never happy at having to do extra rehearsals. George was also smart and had worked cruise ships long enough to realize that the Cruise Director could make or break his onboard stay. From hours played to accommodation, the Cruise Director held all the cards.

George wasn't especially impressed when I told him who Mike was, but then again I had once asked George and his band to play *Y.M.C.A.* for a passenger, and he told me he didn't know it or have the music. A few days later they did play it. When I approached him saying, 'So you found *Y.M.C.A.* then George?' He replied in his staccato Hungarian accent, 'This song called Yimca, not one you ask.'

Before the rehearsal I read the brochure on Mike and Jerry, part of the VIP update envelope, as it gave a list of many of the songs they had written.

I showed George and his band the brochure and there was a sudden change in attitude as they realised that they were to perform with a song-writing legend.

Mike and I soon had a ten-song medley put together with Mike agreeing to sing *Is That All There Is My Friend*, a more recent composition of his, which had reignited the recording career of Peggy Lee.

Jailhouse Rock, Treat Me Nice, Hound Dog, Stand By Me, On Broadway, Kansas City, Is That All There Is My Friend, Spanish Harlem, Yakety Yak and *Loving You* made up the medley and the audience loved it. As they showed their appreciation with a standing ovation I gave Mike a big hug and presented him with a crystal decanter. It really was very, very special.

Silence of the Lamb's Chop

We first met Karen and Irwin Schwartz and their family when they boarded our cruise ship, the Ocean Islander, in Caracas, Venezuela in 1988. It proved to be the first of many cruises they would take with us, and the beginning of a very close friendship.

Karen and Irwin turned out to be the nicest people you could wish to meet, and Karen being the craziest woman in the world was a bonus. They would often plan their holidays based on our cruise itineraries and on one occasion joined us on an eastern Mediterranean cruise with Haifa in Israel being one of our ports of call. Karen and Irwin had visited many places in the world with us but never Jerusalem, so Irwin booked a mini bus and guide to take us from Haifa to Jerusalem.

Along with their two travelling companions Cal and Lesley, plus Mortikay, the guide and driver, we set off for Jerusalem. With the Wailing Wall, the Arab Bazaar and Bethlehem under our belts, lunch called and our guide Mortikay took us to a kosher restaurant in the centre of Jerusalem where initially we were the only customers.

Shortly after our meal had been served, a group of about forty Dutch Christian pilgrims, as I found out later, entered the restaurant and occupied the remaining tables.

For lunch I had ordered kosher lamb chop and it didn't take me long to discover what 'kosher' really meant. In this case. Dry, tough and cremated! It was like a piece of burnt leather and distinguishing the meat from the bone was impossible.

So involved was I with my battle of the lamb chop that I hadn't noticed what was, or wasn't, going on around us. As I hacked intensely at my burnt offering, a silence descended on the restaurant, and without looking up, as I'm assured by my wife, and in a volume that was more suited to overcoming a rock 'n' roll band, I said, 'It's gone bloody quiet in here hasn't it!' With which I felt an almighty kick on the shin from Anette that indicated all was not well.

Looking up I saw the Dutch group standing as one and staring at me in disgust as I had interrupted their pre lunch thanksgiving prayer.

Red faced, I apologised while bowing my head slowly and returning to my ongoing battle with the lamb chop.

Burial at Sea

It was said that Australians who died at sea, and were subsequently buried at sea, received substantial tax benefits on their estates for being out of the country when they died. There were apparently many elderly Australians who spent much of their final years cruising while awaiting the Grim Reaper.

It was during a cruise in the South Pacific with Australian passengers that my pal, big band trumpeter Jack Smith, experienced his most embarrassing moment. A death at sea would be followed by a burial at sea. The Ship's Chaplain, Captain, Staff Captain, relatives, friends, a couple of sailors and Jack would make up those present.

As lead trumpeter with the big band in the ship's main ballroom, Jack would leave his position with the band at 11.30 pm and head for the deck area, usually via the bar where a large Hennessy would help keep the chilly night air at bay, then up to the rope deck, which was out of bounds to passengers and where the committal to the depths would take place. Jack's responsibility was to play the *Last Post* as the body in the weighted body bag slipped gently off the flag-covered plank and into the deep. Punctuality was an essential part of Jack's responsibility so he would arrive 10 minutes early to ensure he was ready when required.

Burials at sea could never be classed as a pleasant experience and would be even less so if the weather conditions were unfavourable. On one such occasion during choppy seas and with the ship listing heavily, Jack arrived only to see the body bag slip from beneath the covering flag and into the sea before the mourners arrived. The Staff captain immediately summoned two sailors to rush to the galley, get two sacks of potatoes, stop at the morgue on the way back and pick up another body bag. They were then told to put the two sacks of potatoes into the body bag and place them on the plank, covered by the flag.

As the sailors were putting the final touches to draping the flag over the body-bag, the mourners arrived. Completely oblivious to what had happened, the mourners took up their positions and the Chaplain began the service.

Jack described the ensuing moments as total embarrassment as he blew every wrong note imaginable, while trying not to laugh as he played the *Last Post* to 2 cwt of King Edward potatoes!

The publishers hope that this book has given you enjoyable reading. Large Print Books are especially designed to be as easy to see and hold as possible. If you wish a complete list of our books please ask at your local library or write directly to:

Magna Large Print Books
Magna House, Long Preston,
Skipton, North Yorkshire.
BD23 4ND

This Large Print Book, for people
who cannot read normal print,
is published under the auspices of

THE ULVERSCROFT FOUNDATION

... we hope you have enjoyed this book.
Please think for a moment about those
who have worse eyesight than you ...
and are unable to even read or enjoy
Large Print without great difficulty.

You can help them by sending a
donation, large or small, to:

**The Ulverscroft Foundation,
1, The Green, Bradgate Road,
Anstey, Leicestershire, LE7 7FU,
England.**
or request a copy of our brochure for
more details.

The Foundation will use all donations
to assist those people who are visually
impaired and need special attention
with medical research, diagnosis
and treatment.

Thank you very much for your help.

JP 27/4/10